Praise for *From Every End of This Earth*

"An homage to the sacrifice generation and the children for which they make that sacrifice. . . . Roberts offers not only diversity of geography, but also diversity of experiences. . . . Roberts focuses on each family and tells its tale in a compassionate, engaging way."

—*Washington Post*

"For his entire writing life, Steve Roberts has been inspired by the extraordinary heroism and exceptional wisdom of supposedly ordinary people, especially new arrivals to our shores. For Roberts, there are no 'ordinary' people, and *From Every End of This Earth* is testimony to his passion and his empathy and also to his admiration for those with the courage to journey to a new land. The phrase 'immigration debate' is deadening. Roberts brings to life the real immigration story through the lives of those who are its authors."

—E. J. Dionne, syndicated columnist and
author of *Why Americans Hate Politics*

"If you want to feel optimistic about the future of America, give Steve Roberts's new book a read. He chronicles our national miracle of drawing together and assimilating diverse people who are drawn, as the title says, 'from every end of this earth.' Far from posing a threat, the new immigrants—with their hustle and drive and their yearning for success—are America's secret weapon in the global economic competition"

—David Ignatius, syndicated columnist for the *Washington Post*

"Gripping, well-told human stories are the best antidote to policy debates muddled by prejudice and partisan politics. In these pages, Steve Roberts artfully tells the fascinating stories of thirteen immigrant families and leaves us far better equipped to understand the choices facing the United States as it debates how to reform its broken immigration system. This book should be obligatory reading for anyone who wants to have an objective and well-informed opinion about immigrants in America. Or for anyone who simply wants to read a good book about real and inspiring human experiences."

—Moisés Naím, editor in chief of *Foreign Policy* magazine

"I kept finding favorites, and then new favorites, as I read about these people. I love the daily details—their food, the marriages, the jobs, where the kids will go to school. I was fascinated by their relationships with their children and how they grapple with the possibility that their kids may leap as high and as far as they did."

—Linda Wertheimer, senior national correspondent for National Public Radio

Praise for *My Fathers' Houses*

"A warm and welcoming memoir."   —*Library Journal*

"Calls to mind a kinder, gentler time. . . . Brings back a time when children were able to entertain themselves, when imagination rather than television ruled, a time of rare and wonderful innocence. . . . With much the same sweet, self-deprecating tone of fellow journalist Tim Russert's *Big Russ and Me*, Robert recalls growing up Jewish in New Jersey, in a community where everyone looked out for one another. . . . In this endearing book, treasured family stories are passed along from generation to generation, along with a strong sense of the American dream and all its attendant possibilities. . . . The greatest tribute a son can offer."

—*New Orleans Times-Picayune*

"A good story. . . . A sweet book."   —*New York Times Book Review*

"When a memoir is penned by a familiar figure, it's all the more interesting to walk through the door that's been opened into childhood. . . . This is a warm and thoughtful book about family values and a valued family."   —*Hartford Courant*

"Warm. . . . Roberts charges ahead, writing the story of three generations—from Rogowsky to Rogow to Roberts."   —*The Forward*

"Roberts's *My Fathers' Houses* is deeply personal and redolent of a larger American story—the immigrant experience."

—*Harrisburg Patriot-News*

"Roberts's book is a classic American success story, a warm memoir of U.S. immigration when it was in its heyday, and a loving reminiscence about a neighborhood." —*Providence Journal-Bulletin*

"Striking." —*Washington Jewish Week*

"Taking the boy out of Bayonne may be possible, but taking Bayonne out of the boy is not—at least, according to this warm and welcoming memoir by journalist Roberts, who hails from the New Jersey city. . . . As he makes clear in this memoir, his Bayonne beginnings greatly informed the man he is today. Recommended." —*Library Journal*

"A picture of immigrants arriving in this country and how they became Americans." —*Fort Wayne News-Sentinel*

"Set against Bayonne's population, made up of Eastern European Catholics and Jews, Roberts's affecting recollections of sports, girls, and family seldom omit an ethnic component, and fairly burst with his feelings about his family's lore. A singular saga of assimilation." —*Booklist*

"[*My Fathers' Houses*] is at once a deeply personal family history and an archetype of the Jewish-American immigrant success story. . . . What makes it stand out are its chatty, down-to-earth tone and frequent flashes of humor." —*New Jersey Jewish News*

From Every End of This Earth

FROM EVERY END
OF THIS EARTH

13 Families and the New Lives
They Made in America

Steven V. Roberts

HARPER ● PERENNIAL

NEW YORK ● LONDON ● TORONTO ● SYDNEY ● NEW DELHI ● AUCKLAND

HARPER ● PERENNIAL

FIRST HARPER PERENNIAL EDITION PUBLISHED 2010.

Designed by Eric Butler

The Library of Congress has catalogued the hardcover edition as follows:
Roberts, Steven V.
  From every end of this earth : 13 families and the new lives they made in America / Steven V. Roberts. — 1st ed.
    xxiv, 323 p. ; 24 cm.
  ISBN 978-0-06-124561-9
    1. Immigrants—United States—Biography. 2. Immigrants—United States—Attitudes. 3. Immigrants—United States—Social conditions. 4. United States—Emigration and immigration—Biography. I. Title.

                                                                2010277179

ISBN 978-0-06-124562-6 (pbk.)

12 13 14   OV/RRD   10 9 8 7 6 5 4 3 2

To my students at George Washington University,
who inspire me with their stories and their spirit

Contents

Introduction

As I listened to Barack Obama's inaugural address, I heard him say, "We are a nation of Christians and Muslims, Jews and Hindus, and nonbelievers. We are shaped by every language and culture, drawn from every end of this earth." I knew then that I had a title for this book. I liked the lilt of his language, but more than that, I shared his sense of what makes America great. This country's genius flows from its diversity. "We know," said the new president, "that our patchwork heritage is a strength, not a weakness." Or as Eddie Kamara Stanley of Sierra Leone puts it, "It's the nation of nations, you can see every nation in America." But diversity only describes color, not character; ethnicity, not ingenuity. Over many generations, the immigrants who chose to come here, and were strong enough to complete the journey, were among the most ambitious, the most determined, the most resilient adventurers the Old World had to offer. "The greatness of our nation . . . must be earned," said the new president, and building that greatness has never been "for the fainthearted." Rather, he added, "it has been the risk-takers, the doers, the makers of things" who have led the way. "For us they packed up their few worldly possessions and traveled across oceans in search of a new life." The "fainthearted" stayed behind.

This book is about the doers, the risk-takers, the makers of things that Obama describes. The president knows them well because his own father was an immigrant from Kenya, and his stepfather was from Indonesia. I know them well, too. All four of my grandparents came from the "Pale of Settlement," areas on the western edge of the Russian empire where Jews were allowed to live in the nineteenth century. They were born between 1881 and 1892, and while they all described themselves as Russian, borders have shifted so often since then that their hometowns today are in three different countries: Poland, Belarus, and Lithuania. Both of my grandfathers were carpenters, "makers of things," who settled in Bayonne, New Jersey. One lived with us, in a house he had built himself, while my other grandparents were three blocks away. I thought that everybody grew up that way, and indeed, most of my friends did. Our grandparents all had accents and our babysitters all were related. If our families weren't Russian or Polish, they were Irish or Italian, with an occasional Czech or Ukrainian or Slovak thrown in. I grew up thinking WASPs were a tiny minority group.

Most of our relatives had fled a life of poverty or persecution in the Old Country and would not talk about the past; they wanted to leave all that behind and become American. But I was lucky. My Grandpa Abe used to tell me tales of his youth in Bialystok, a town that achieved a fleeting notoriety when Mel Brooks used the name "Max Bialystok" for the main character in his play *The Producers*. In fact Abe, like many immigrants, moved more than once, and spent his teenage years as a Zionist pioneer in Palestine, working on the first roads ever built in what is now Tel Aviv. He arrived in America on April 7, 1914, aboard a ship called the *George Washington*, which sailed from Bremen, a port on the North Sea. The manifest spells both of his names wrong ("Awram Rogowski" instead of "Avram Rogowsky") and persistent mistakes like that have hampered the search for my family's records. On her birth certificate, my mother is listed as "Dora Schaenbein," while in fact her name was Dorothy

Schanbam. At her ninetieth birthday party I took note of that discrepancy and joked that perhaps we were celebrating the wrong woman.

This background left me with a lifelong interest in ethnicity and immigration. My previous book, *My Fathers' Houses*, chronicled my family's arrival in the New World and the lives we made here. This book is really an update, the stories of thirteen families who are living the journey today that Grandpa Abe and my other ancestors made almost one hundred years ago. In a sense I have been working on this volume for my entire writing life. As a teenager, I had an after-school job on the *Bayonne Times*, the local daily, and one of my first assignments was to write about an émigré artist who was decorating the walls of the Police Athletic League building, a dilapidated old place where I played basketball. When I eventually became a reporter on the city staff of the *New York Times* in 1965, I convinced the editors to let me do a series about the ethnic neighborhoods of New York. One favorite was Arthur Avenue, an old Italian section near the Bronx Zoo, and I remember coming back from that assignment with some great anecdotes, and a box of delicious cannolis from a local bakery. On weekends my wife and I occasionally roamed the Lower East Side, the district where many Eastern European Jews first settled in America. One favorite destination was Katz's deli on Houston Street, started by Russian immigrants in 1888 and famous for its slogan, "Send a salami to your boy in the army!"

My next assignment for the *Times* took us to Los Angeles in 1969, and while most reporters from eastern news outlets focused on the glamorous side of California, I was always more interested in the Armenians of Glendale than in the actresses of Hollywood. I wrote about farm towns like Kerman, where the Portuguese-American home was the center of social life. Or villages like Solvang, which still celebrates its Danish heritage. And I profiled old mining camps—including one actually named Chinese Camp—where you could still sense the spirit of the immigrant laborers who built those historic settlements. I spent a lot of time in the Central Valley writing about Cesar Chavez and the United Farm Workers union, and I remember him describing how the grape growers were still defined by powerful ethnic loyalties. In fact, Chavez (a Mexican-American himself) told me he had to conduct three separate negotiations with the Armenian, Italian, and Yugoslav farmers. One man who could occasionally bridge those rivalries was Tony Coelho, a Portuguese-American congressman who once invited me to a lunch he held regularly at a Basque restaurant in his hometown of Fresno. For one meal, at least, the warring tribes of the valley would sit side by side at long family-style tables, but Coelho's peacemaking had limits. When he tried to join the Hispanic caucus on Capitol Hill by invoking his Iberian heritage he was flatly rejected.

When I moved to Europe for the *Times* in 1974 and settled in Athens, I got to write about immigration from a different perspective. Many Greeks were deeply anti-American, because they thought Washington had sided with Turkey in their endless dispute over Cyprus. But their animosity was tempered by the fact that they all had cousins in Queens or Chicago. I often said that if you waded into a protest demonstration in front of the American embassy and announced that you were awarding six scholarships to Michigan State, the protesters would immediately drop their signs and sign their names. On one reporting trip to southern Greece I interviewed Stavroula and Paraskevas Kourtsounis, whose three children had all moved to Long Island. Their home village of Skoura was dying; all the young people had left. But like many immigrants, they still regularly sent back cash from America. One villager described the place as "an old-age home with green dollars," and the stores in Sparta, the biggest town near Skoura, took dollars as readily as drachmas. Remittances were a sturdy pillar of the Greek economy and in every village it was common to see a black-clad *yaya*, or grandmother, return from the post office, furtively open an envelope, and slip a wad of greenbacks into her clothing. The American embassy told me that nineteen thousand recipients of Social Security payments had retired to Greece, which was a whole lot cheaper than Greenwich or Greenpoint. So many transplants had settled around Sparta that when their monthly checks arrived in the mail, the banks sent mobile vans to the surrounding villages to cash them. When I tracked down the Kourtsounis sons, Pete and Sam, to include them in this book, they graciously told me they had displayed my article about their parents on the wall of their diner for many years. Then Pete said a bit uncomfortably, "I'm surprised to hear from you. I thought you'd be . . . gone by now." I assured him that I'd been a *very* young man when I interviewed his parents.

I returned to America in 1977, just in time to cover the decision of many ethnic voters to abandon the Democrats and join the Republicans. These were my people. In Bayonne, hardly anybody had a last name with fewer than three syllables or that ended in a consonant (okay, so a few Ryans and Robertses were the exception). I had bowled at the Knights of Columbus hall and played on teams sponsored by the Elks Club and the VFW. And since many of my *Times* colleagues didn't know a kielbasa from a cauliflower, I became the paper's expert on these "Reagan Democrats." My assignment took me to Pittsburgh, where private delivery services, run out of storefronts on Butler Avenue, sent packages directly to relatives back in Poland; and to Charlestown, an Irish neighborhood of Boston once represented in Congress by Jack Kennedy, where voters told me that his brother Ted was too liberal to be president. And I was in Milwaukee's Serb Hall (which still has a Friday-night fish fry) in the fall of 1980 when an overflow crowd went nuts for Ronald Reagan—and convinced me he would be the next president.

After Reagan won I covered Congress for the next six years and learned how new ethnic groups were starting to rival the old Italian and Irish political machines. My brother Glenn worked for Norm Mineta, the son of Japanese immigrants and the first Asian-American to sit in Congress. (The adjoining district was represented by Leon

Panetta, an Italian, and a lot of people got them confused. Mineta was frequently invited to address Italian organizations and was even named, as I recall, to at least one Italian hall of fame.) Norm had two constituencies: his voters back in San Jose, California, and Asians from all over the country who saw him as their hero and advocate. He worked this vein well, mining the Asian groups for campaign cash, but there was a problem. All of them—Chinese, Filipinos, Vietnamese, Koreans—were fiercely proud of their national cuisine and insisted on providing the food for the fund raisers. I realized that many ethnic congressmen served two constituencies, and to illustrate the point, I wrote a story about lawmakers of Lebanese ancestry. The list included both senators from South Dakota, Jim Abdnor and James Abourezk, and Representative Mary Rose Oakar of Ohio, the first Arab-American woman to serve in Congress. But the most interesting case was George Mitchell, a senator from Maine. Orphaned at a young age, he was adopted by a Lebanese Christian family and learned some basic Arabic serving Mass in the town of Waterville. That linguistic ability should serve him well as President Obama's peace envoy to the Middle East.

In 1997 I started teaching a course in feature writing at George Washington University, and I encouraged my students to write about their families. I wanted them engaged and energized by their material, and as I still tell them, your grandmother never says "no comment." What I didn't expect were the powerful and poignant stories they produced. They taught me that the immigrant experience is as vibrant today as it was when Avram Rogowsky set sail from Bremen in the spring of 1914. No one example, or even a half dozen, can capture the entirety of that experience, but I hope this book resembles the mosaics I used to see in the ruins of ancient Greece. Separately, these thirteen families reflect fragments of line and color; fitted together, they complete a whole picture. In a few cases I've changed their names to protect their privacy, but in every other way these stories are as true as I can tell them.

Over the last hundred years, one dimension of the immigrant experience has never changed: it is still one of the most challenging journeys any human being ever makes. The words of the Indian poet Rabindranath Tagore remain wise: "You can't cross the sea merely by standing and staring at the water." Bao and Tuyen Pham tried many times to escape from Vietnam, and once, drifting aimlessly on the open ocean, Tuyen thought she would have to slit her wrists and feed her blood to her children to keep them alive. When the Phams finally washed up on the shore of Thailand, Tuyen was pregnant with a daughter, who was then born in a refugee camp in the Philippines. They named her Thai Phi in honor of the two countries that gave them sanctuary before they moved to Pennsylvania. Eddie Stanley fled the African nation of Sierra Leone one step ahead of a rebel army that decapitated his father and seized his sister as a sex slave. His wife and two children spent more than two years in primitive refugee camps before he was able to bring them to America. Jose and Beti Reyes both entered this country illegally by sneaking across the border with Mexico. Both were arrested, thrown in jail, and deported to their native El Salvador. Both returned, evaded capture for years, and eventually became citizens. Immigration is not for the "faint-hearted."

Some journeys, of course, were not so dramatic or dangerous. Asis Banerjie got on a plane in New Delhi and flew to Cleveland for graduate study at Case Western Reserve University. Pablo Romero traveled by bus from Mexico to California, where he picked lettuce under a program that legally imported farmworkers. But every immigrant faces the pain of dislocation, of missing home, of living in two worlds and never feeling completely comfortable in either one. Marie Aziz, a political refugee from Afghanistan, quotes these lines

by the thirteenth-century poet Rumi, to describe her feelings toward
her homeland:

> *Listen to the song of the reed,*
> *How it wails with the pain of separation:*
> *"Ever since I was taken from my reed bed*
> *My woeful song has caused men and women to weep.*
> *I seek out those whose hearts are torn by separation*
> *For only they understand the pain of this longing."*

Rumi's words are as true today as they were eight hundred years
ago. Every immigrant is like a reed plucked from its bed. "That's why
they say East and West never meet," says Tuyen Pham. "We stand in
the middle. Sometimes, when I stay here, I feel homesick, but when
I go back I don't feel I can stand to live there. I think Bao and I are
the sacrifice generation. We don't belong to Vietnam, we belong to
America, but inside there is something that is not really American."
Ulla Kirschbaum Morris Carter says simply, "I have no roots" in
America. "Here, I don't have anybody with whom I share a past.
There's nobody who knows anything about me." Those who do share
her past are back in Germany, where she was born, or in Cairo or
Beirut or Athens, the cities where she lived most of her adult life. But
they're not in the hills of northern California where she lives now.
Malak Kemal came from Burma twenty-five years ago but still warns
her three daughters to be careful. "My mother has this immigrant
mentality—always be nice, don't say anything bad, because they can
always send us back," says her youngest child, Deeba, who resides in
Minnesota. "And I always say, 'You know, Mom, there's freedom of
speech in America.' But she would say, 'No, no, we're immigrants.'"

For the "sacrifice generation," one goal keeps them going: making
a better life for their children. And in many cases they have. Sarah
and Nicholas Stern left Ukraine with $120 apiece; now they own an

apartment overlooking Central Park and a condo in Florida. One son runs the family investment company; the other just graduated from law school. Haaroon Kemal never learned much English or made much money after he arrived from Burma, but his three daughters all finished college and two are now earning graduate degrees. Jose Reyes was an illiterate farm boy from El Salvador who opened a successful restaurant in Washington; his daughter, Ana, earned a degree in marketing and took over as the manager. Pablo Romero dropped out of school in rural Mexico at age eleven; his daughter Kaija-Leena went to Harvard.

But being a child of immigrants can be a complicated way to grow up. Generation Next is often pulled between the past and the future, between celebrating their own tradition and creating their own identity. For years, Haaroon Kemal dreamed of escaping the tyranny of Burma and enjoying the freedom he would find in America. But once he got here, that very freedom became a threat—to the purity of his religion, the virtue of his daughters, the authority he commanded in the family. As a result he swaddled his girls in "bubble wrap" and banned them from talking to "anything that looked like a man." Indira Banerjie, who came to America as a teenager, dropped out of school and ended her hopes of becoming a doctor to enter an arranged marriage with her husband, Asis, a fellow Brahmin from the Indian state of West Bengal. Today she sends her two daughters mixed signals: Don't do what I did, get your degrees, become independent women. And by the way, marry a Brahmin from West Bengal. The bad news for Indira: her daughter Piyali has four tattoos. The good news: one depicts the sacred Hindu symbol Om. This constant search for a new identity is so common in the Indian community that there's a label for it: "ABCD," or "American-Born Confused *Desi*." (*Desi* is slang for a South Asian immigrant.)

Sometimes children from the same family take very different paths. Ana Reyes manages the family restaurant but her two brothers want to be rock stars. Tom and Maggie Chan's son Herbert went to college in northern California and joined the family business, importing fireworks from China; he lives downstairs from his parents and within walking distance of his grandmother in San Francisco's Chinatown. Arthur, Herb's younger brother, came east for college and redefined his "Chineseness" by identifying with all people of color and joining a Hispanic dance troupe. "That was all new to my parents, being Asian as part of a general minority, empathizing with the experience of black Americans or Latinos or other marginalized populations," he says. "It wasn't just about being Chinese." Today Arthur lives in New York and wants to be a filmmaker. These paths are not straight and these lives are not predictable. Haaroon Kemal did not want his daughters to live in the dorms at the University of California at Irvine because they would be tempted by too many outside influences. He was right in a way, but the influences they encountered in college made them more Eastern, not Western, more conservative, not liberal. All three became devout Muslims and adopted headscarves, a garment their own mother seldom wears.

All immigrants, of any era, are part of the "sacrifice generation." All understand Rumi's description of them as "those whose hearts are torn by separation." And all have children who must make their own way in the New World. It happened in my family and our name tells the tale. Grandpa Abe dropped the "sky" from Rogowsky at some point and I was born "Rogow," the same name my cousins on that side still have. As a young man my father had occasionally used the name Atlas to obscure his Jewish origins, and he changed our name to Roberts when I was two. My father always worried about his place in America, but I never have. That gave me the freedom to embrace my heritage, not evade it. The first time my parents ever attended a seder, a Jewish ritual celebrating Passover, it was at my house (and my Catholic wife cooked the dinner). In my heart I'm a Rogow, even a Rogowsky, not a Roberts. But I understand my father's impulse to blend into American culture. If Odysseus had landed in Troy, New York, instead of Troy, Turkey, he might have changed his name to Oates or O'Dwyer. Or perhaps Dr. Sseus.

In other ways, however, the modern immigrant experience is very different from Grandpa Abe's day, starting with the countries that send people to America. Growing up I never met families like the ones in this book—from Rwanda and Burma, El Salvador and Sierra Leone. But my hometown has changed dramatically. Bayonne's roster of churches now includes the Arabic Assembly of God and El Ultimo Llamado, First Filipino Baptist and True Light Korean United Methodist. Our Lady of Assumption, once the center of the Italian community, now offers masses and pastoral counseling in Spanish. Arabic signs have sprouted in some neighborhoods. The recent winner of an essay contest about the Holocaust, sponsored by local Jewish organizations, is a Muslim from Pakistan who wears a headscarf. Many of the stores on Broadway once owned by Jews are now run by Indians. Today the people of Bayonne, like the rest of America, truly come "from every end of this earth," not just Krakow or Calabria or Killarney.

After Abe left Russia he was out of touch with his sister for fifty years. Mail was blocked, travel was impossible, phone calls were a fantasy. In the mid-1960s he learned from a distant relative that he had a sister alive in Moscow, and they met once before he died. Today most immigrants are in constant contact with relatives back home. Asis Banerjie's mother still lives in the remote Bengali village where he grew up without electricity or indoor plumbing, but he talks to her frequently by cell phone. Eddie Stanley's mother, back in Sierra Leone, doesn't always recognize his voice on the phone, but when he sings her a song from his childhood, she knows who it is. Pablo Romero's daughters have spent summer vacations with his family in Mexico. Alice Ingabire-Schaut returned to Rwanda and videotaped the whole visit. I know of a Brazilian woman, in this country illegally, who got married in New Jersey. Since her family could not obtain visas to attend the wedding, her sister-in-law took digital photos and sent them during the ceremony to the bride's relatives, clustered around a laptop in Brazil. Kushi Gavrieli celebrated his son's bar mitzvah in his home village in Israel's Negev Desert (complete with musicians in Kurdish dress; most of the villagers originally immigrated to Israel from the Kurdish region of Iran). Pete Kourtsounis actually built a house in his home village in Greece and vacations there every summer, but he's too Americanized now to lapse back into his old life. So he imported most of the building materials from Home Depot, and he can no longer tolerate the Greek custom of late nights, heavy dinners, and skimpy breakfasts. When he's back, he hangs out with other *xeni*, or foreigners, not the locals. And a bunch of them have convinced a café owner to put omelets on the menu, so the *xeni* can enjoy a proper American breakfast.

The flow of information across borders is matched by a flow of capital. In Bayonne there might have been an Italian family that imported cheese or olive oil from the Old Country, but today many immigrants have established strong business and professional ties with their homelands. Marie Aziz returned to Afghanistan for the first time in twenty-four years, as head of an agricultural aid program financed by the American government. Asis and Indira Banerjie actually moved back to India for fourteen years after he got his doctorate in America. Today they live in Ohio, but Asis owns factories making high-tech plastics in both countries and does business throughout Asia. Tom Chan's family fled China in terror after the communist revolution, but now he practically commutes from San Francisco to Liuyang, the center of China's fireworks industry. He's there so often the staff of the Grand Sun City Resort hotel saves him the same room, number 1211.

Many immigrants regularly send money to relatives back home and private remittances are by far the most important aid program in the world. Eddie Stanley can only afford a hundred dollars every few months, but to his mother in Sierra Leone, even that sum is "a very big thing." Alice Ingabire-Schaut works two jobs, selling shoes and cleaning churches, to support her mother and two sisters back in Rwanda. But many others expect her help as well and sometimes the demands can be overwhelming. "Most people, from any third world country, believe that once you reach America, it's a safe heaven. An answer to everything," she says. "Some of those, who know I'm married to a white American, think I have all the potential to help them. They think I am rich and I have it all. They don't know that I have to work twice as hard to maintain my life and my marriage and also care for my family needs in Africa." This reaction back home—"They think I am rich"—is a common problem that can create enormous frustrations. Haaroon Kemal's daughter Ameera says her father suffered from a "pavement-of-gold imagination" back in Burma. "There was a gap between his expectations and what life became," adds her sister Deeba, and he was never able to help the rest of his family immigrate to America. "He still holds on to a lot of feelings of anger," says his daughter Khalida. But for those who have prospered in their new country, directing donations to charities back home can be a source of great pride and satisfaction. Jose Reyes eagerly displayed a blown-up copy of a check for $1,860, the amount he helped raise for a library back in El Salvador. Munr Kazmir, a wealthy doctor in New Jersey, has financed a school in Pakistan, based on a Western model, that is designed to counteract the influence of fundamentalist Islam.

This is a book of stories. It's not about policies or politics. But it comes out at a time when immigration is a hot topic and many dimensions of the problem are being debated in Washington and across the globe. For example:

* President George W. Bush tried and failed to enact legislation that would provide a path to citizenship for the 12 million undocumented workers now living in America. Republicans de-

cided that fanning anti-immigrant feelings would energize their base and drive them to the polls, and many GOP candidates in 2008 ran strongly against "amnesty" for illegals. But Obama, the son of an immigrant, believes strongly in reform and in March 2009 he told a town hall meeting in California that "the American people . . . appreciate and believe in immigration." These newcomers, he said, "have become our neighbors. They've been our friends. They may have children who have become U.S. citizens." But he also warned that undocumented workers who have "broken the law" would not get a "free ride." They would have to pay fines, learn English, and "go to the back of the line" behind other applicants who have played by the rules. But "over a period of time," he said, illegal immigrants should have the chance to "earn [their] citizenship."

✳ Obama did deal with legal immigrants on a critical issue just days after taking office. He signed legislation reversing a policy of the Bush administration that forced newcomers to wait five years before receiving benefits under a program called S-CHIP, which provides health insurance for poor children. Access by immigrants—legal and illegal—to social services and aid programs will continue to be a major source of controversy.

✳ Early in 2009, the U.S. military began a new recruitment program: skilled immigrants living here under temporary visas could join the army and attain citizenship in as little as six months. Both sides will gain something. The military desperately needs recruits with medical and language skills, and that is what these immigrants possess. Nurses who speak Pashto. Doctors fluent in Farsi. To say nothing of translators and intelligence officers who know Arabic—and look Arabic. Uncle Sam needs you! As Lieutenant General Benjamin C. Freakley, the army's top recruitment officer, told the *New York Times*, "The American Army finds itself in a lot of different countries where cultural awareness is crucial. There will be some very talented folks in this group." Talented folks who want to become American citizens but find their way blocked under current rules. Many who are here under work or student visas face years of delay before they can stabilize their status—if ever. Joining the army now enables them to cut through that red tape. Once the model is established it could be extended to other forms of public service. Perhaps a nurse from the Philippines could trade three years of service in a rural area for a quicker path to citizenship. Or a Spanish-speaking math teacher from Honduras could make a similar deal by working in the South Bronx.

Under a program called H-1B visas, highly skilled and educated immigrants can get work permits if employers prove that comparable Americans are not available. The program has been very popular, but only 65,000 visas are available every year and they are swiftly snapped up by high-tech companies eager to tap this pool of innovation and entrepreneurship. Efforts to raise the cap to 150,000 visas have failed in recent years, blocked by pressure groups claiming that American workers are being displaced by foreigners. In the large stimulus bill signed by Obama in February 2009, financial companies receiving federal funds were actually restricted in their ability to hire holders of H-1B visas. *New York Times* columnist Tom Friedman called this amendment "S-T-U-P-I-D." Every study shows that immigrants make enormous contributions to economic growth and job creation. In a report for the Small Business Administration, University of California economist Robert W. Fairlie found that immigrants were 30 percent "more likely to start a business than are nonimmigrants." Analyzing statistics from the 2000 census, Fairlie found that newcomers represented 16.7 percent of all business owners and generated $67 billion in yearly income. Economists from Harvard and the University of Michigan reported a fascinating trend: when the number of H-1B visas goes up, applications for patents follow the same curve; when visas dwindle, so do patents. Vivek Wadhwa, an executive in residence at Duke University, argues that "more than half of Silicon Valley startups were founded by immigrants over the last decade." Shrinking the number of H-1B visas or restricting their use would be extremely damaging to the U.S. economy, he wrote in *BusinessWeek*: "We will scare away the world's best and brightest who have always flocked to our shores. But the next Silicon Valley won't be located in the U.S. It will likely be in Hyderabad or Shanghai." Not every newcomer will create Google or Intel. But without immigrant men, lawns would not get trimmed and buildings would not get built. And without the women, every hospital and nursing home in this country would collapse overnight. I know this firsthand. My mother's caretakers are all from the same Caribbean island and we refer to them as "Team Jamaica." My mother-in-law's aides are "Team Philippines."

These vital debates will continue. But they are background music for the great human drama of immigration. Every day, families "pack up their few worldly possessions and travel across oceans in search of a new life." Every day, parents join the "sacrifice generation" and place their hopes in their children. Every night, they nurse the "pain of separation," the feelings of longing and loneliness that come from leaving home. These immigrants are like the sun and the rain to America; they replenish our soil and our spirit. We are a better, brighter nation because they come and join us, every day, from every end of this earth.

Part I

THE
SURVIVORS

Immigrants come to America for many reasons: to enjoy freedom, expand opportunity, escape tradition. But for some their goal is simply survival. Every day, across the globe, the forces of tribal conflict, ethnic hatred, and political repression destroy some victims and drive others into exile. The living and the dead are often separated by the thinnest of lines. A gunshot barely misses. A warning comes just in time. A hiding place remains undiscovered. A neighbor of mine in suburban Washington is a Tamil, part of a persecuted minority in the island nation of Sri Lanka. She and fifteen relatives were trapped in a house surrounded by a howling mob. They crowded into one small Japanese car and tried to escape. The engine stalled. Then it started, and the overloaded vehicle rocketed to safety. Another misfire and many could have died.

These survivors leave behind unmarked graves of family and friends, and unshakable memories of danger and death. Their dreams are filled with the faces of loved ones who could not run or hide or duck in time. Often they became rootless refugees, clinging to life in makeshift camps, deprived of a home for months or even years at a time. In his book *Outcasts United*, Warren St. John quotes Paula Balegamire, who fled the Democratic Republic of the Congo with her five children and moved to Georgia after her husband was imprisoned for political dissent: "There's no point in thinking about where to go back to. Because there's nowhere to go back to."

Bao and Tuyen Pham represent the refugees who escaped the political turmoil of Southeast Asia during the 1970s. They are Vietnamese, part of the largest and most successful group (in 2008 Anh "Joseph" Cao became the first Vietnamese immigrant to be elected to Congress), but sizable communities of Laotians, Cambodians, and Hmong have also settled here. Bao was a naval officer under Vietnam's old government, and on the day Saigon fell to the communists in 1975, he pleaded with Tuyen to flee the country. She refused; they were not married or even engaged yet. It was the kind of choice, made hastily in a moment of chaos, that proved fatal to many others. But for six years the Phams survived, six years of failed plots and frequent prison terms. When they finally sailed free of Vietnam, and saw land in the distance, that line between destiny and disaster narrowed one last time. If their small boat was drifting toward Cambodia they would probably die; if they washed ashore in Thailand they would be safe. It was Thailand.

Eddie and Marie Stanley could have died many times. He was traveling with a group of journalists, covering the civil war in his homeland of Sierra Leone, when they ran into an ambush. A bullet nicked his finger and killed the man behind him. Marie was in her living room when stray shots slammed into the wall above her head. Eddie's father and brother were decapitated by rebels. His sister was so disgraced by repeated rapes that the family held a funeral for her. Marie managed to avoid a similar fate by telling rebels soldiers she had AIDS. She spent more than two years in a series of refugee camps before Eddie tracked her down and brought her to America. But still, on some nights, the memories make their way across time and space and their house in suburban Philadelphia fills with her screams.

Alice Ingabire inherited a legacy of exile. A member of the Tutsi tribe in the central African country of Rwanda, she was raised in a refugee camp in Uganda after her parents and grandparents were driven from their homeland by rival Hutu tribesmen in 1959. As a teenager, she was recruited by Tutsi fighters to join a guerrilla campaign against the Hutu overlords, and was about to ship out for advanced training when her uncle arrived at the camp with news that Alice had passed her secondary school exams. The rebel commander decided she would be more valuable reading books than shooting rifles, so she was safely attending school in Uganda when the Hutus slaughtered hundreds of thousands of her fellow Tutsis in 1994. After the war, she returned to Rwanda and fate winked once more. She took an exam to study in Ethiopia, and the results crossed the desk of an official at the education ministry. He had just received a letter from an American college offering scholarships to students from war-ravaged countries, and he noticed that a girl named Alice had beaten all the boys in math. A week later she was on her way to Mount Mary College in Milwaukee, where she still lives.

1.

Bao, Tuyen, and Thai Phi Pham

VIETNAM

I don't want my kids to die. So I'm thinking of cutting my
wrist and feeding them with my blood to help them survive.

It was April 30, 1975. Saigon was falling to the communists and the
city was in chaos. As an officer in the South Vietnamese navy, Bao
Pham saw his future collapsing as well. "I know the communists," he
says. "I know they will not let me be free." So he left his ship in the
harbor, where it was undergoing repairs, and walked six miles to the
home of Tuyen, the woman he loved. "I had to avoid the big roads and
go on the small roads," he recalls. "No one controlled Saigon at all.
The people, they rob each other right in front of you. There was no
government, no nothing. If you strong enough you can do whatever
you want at that point." As he slipped through the city, Bao saw cars
burned, motorcycles stolen, vigilantes wearing red armbands killing
people with machetes. When he reached Tuyen's house, he pleaded
with her to leave with him. He knew the port area, he knew a lot of
foreign ships were preparing to depart, and he wanted to be on one:

"At that point we don't care where we go, but we have to go. We have to escape from the country." But Tuyen said no. The couple was not even engaged, let alone married. It was unthinkable for her to violate tradition, to be seen in public with a man not her husband. Asked why she wouldn't leave, Tuyen responded heatedly: "Because I'm not his yet, I'm not his yet. I still have my family here." At that moment, Bao had to make a choice—freedom or love. He chose love. "I cannot leave her here," he remembers thinking. "I cannot leave without her."

That moment of indecision cost Bao and Tuyen six years. Six years of fear and frustration, betrayal and danger. Six years of flawed plans and faulty engines, work details and prison cells. As Bao recalls his thoughts during that period: "Escape. Escape. Escape. That's all there ever was." Time and again those dreams were thwarted. Finally, in 1981, their leaky, overcrowded boat washed up on the shores of Thailand. Buddhist monks from a nearby temple took in the refugees, giving them food and shelter, and Tuyen remembers the next morning: "I get up and I look out and I see green things, all the trees around the temple. After thirteen days of sky and water I can stand on the soil, I can smell the fresh air. I feel like I've come back to life."

As children of wealth and privilege, Bao and Tuyen were not well prepared for life as resisters and refugees. Her family owned land; his family ran a prosperous seafood business. They were born a month apart in 1951, and raised in the same neighborhood. Their brothers were classmates and they actually met when they were fifteen, "but I not notice her," Bao recalls with a laugh. He did notice a few years later when his older brother, who was Tuyen's math tutor, had too much class work and passed the job down to him. She remembers him this way: "He was tall and white, his skin was real white, that's the first thing I see. He's different. When he taught me math he wrote on the chalkboard and I say, he has a very pretty hand. Not rough like it is now." (At five feet eight, Bao is taller and stockier than many of his countrymen. Tuyen, only three inches shorter, is also taller than most Vietnamese women.) Tuyen says Bao "fell in love with me" that night, and he agrees. On the way home he ran his motorcycle into a pothole: "That night I left her house and I have an accident on the road, because I keep thinking about my student." But she was not yet convinced. She still thought her ideal husband would be an "older man," not this boy with white hands.

During their teenage years, Bao and Tuyen were largely insulated from the war gathering all around them. "Saigon was very peaceful, a very safe place to live," he recalls, "but outside of Saigon there were guerrillas everywhere." The threat kept growing closer. Tuyen studied English and Japanese and wanted to be an airline stewardess, but she took a class trip to help war victims in the countryside, and she's never forgotten a scene she saw from the bus window: "I can see the bodies lying down in the field, because they got shot last night. I don't know if they are communists or farmers or whatever, but they got shot, and I saw them lie down in the fields." The war touched her in another way. Tuyen worked occasionally for her mother's boss, Clyde Bauer, an American businessman who ran a transport company called Air America. He seemed, on the surface, to be a civic-minded figure, starting chapters of the Lions Club and a branch of the U.S. Chamber of Commerce in Saigon. But it was all a cover. His company was a CIA front and Tuyen now admits that Bauer "was a spy, too."

"Most of the rich families," says Bao, "tried to avoid having their kids go into military service, and my family is one of the richest in Saigon." He studied hard, passed his exams, and stayed in school, but his friends who failed the tests and dropped out were sent into combat. Many did not return: "Half of my classmates, they are in the ground." By the time he finished college, Bao knew he could no longer avoid the military. The navy opened a training class for officers and he joined up, despite the fact that he hated the water and couldn't swim. "I picked the navy because I thought it was safer," he admits. "The communists don't have big ships like we do." But if the communists lacked ships, they didn't lack soldiers, or devotion to their ideals. In college, Bao had read many books about communism and he understood his enemy. That's why he came to Tuyen's door, pleading with her to leave; and that's why he knew, when she refused, that he was in for a very rough time: "I was part of the old regime; I knew they would try to do something about me." Before that could happen, Bao proposed marriage. "She's nothing to me yet, she's not my wife, so I can lose her," he remembers thinking. "That's why we decided to get married." Tuyen recalls his proposal with a laugh: "I say okay. I have free time." They were married two months after Saigon fell, and because of the turbulent times, the wedding was a small one. Tuyen was disappointed and "she's still talking about it," Bao says. Following tradition, the bride moved in with the groom's family. Less than three weeks later, they heard the news Bao had been dreading: officers from the South Vietnamese military were ordered to report to a local high school. They were told they would be gone for ten days.

"We know we have no choice," Bao recalls, because the communists controlled the city "and they have ears and eyes everywhere." But a lot of the men were also naïve in believing what they were told: "It was very stupid thinking by most people, including myself at that point. That's why we show up." After dark the men were loaded onto trucks. Half an hour later Bao sneaked a peak out the back and was alarmed at the changing landscape: "We don't see any light anywhere. Then I know we go far away from Saigon. I was in the navy so I don't know anything about the jungle at all. But I'm strong in math and I think logically and I know, at that point, there was no way we could return home in ten days."

Once the men were deposited in the jungle, the routine quickly became familiar and exhausting: up at five, a bowl of rice soup for breakfast, a half hour of exercises, and then a day of hard labor. The officers were put to work building their own prison. Each group of ten was given only one machete—to avoid the possibility of an armed uprising—but they were directed to cut down trees and haul the wood back to the central campsite for buildings and fences. Once patches of land had been cleared, the men planted rice. At about five or six in the evening they were allowed a brief shower (there was one well for every hundred prisoners) and fed a bowl of rice, with some salt for seasoning. By eight the men were in bed, but their sleep was seldom peaceful. After a few hours they were often rousted out and forced to march deep into the jungle. "Sometimes, you just stood for an hour," Bao recalls. "They didn't say anything at all. You'd just stand there, and then they'd allow you to walk back to the tent." A few hours later, "They'd wake you up again and swear at you, just yelling, not beating." A favorite line of their captors: "We don't want to kill you; if we kill you we waste a bullet."

The men were so hungry they'd eat anything they could find: leaves and berries, cockroaches and crickets. Many fell ill from the diet, while others contracted malaria. But the psychological stress was worse than the physical. A man who tried to escape was beaten to death in front of the other prisoners and "that scared everyone." Once they completed a building, the guards would laugh at them, tear it down, and force the inmates to start over. "Many people became crazy," Bao says. "Some people were screaming in the night. They can't survive."

So how did he survive? "I think about my wife a lot," he replied. "I think, I have to survive, I have to get out of here somehow. I believe that someday I will get out of here. I don't know how soon, but I think about her all the time." Tuyen interjects: "And you think about my being pregnant, too." Bao agrees: "Yeah, somehow my wife, I think that she's pregnant, I don't know why. I think my wife have a child. I have to stay alive. I cannot die."

Bao was clever, too. He volunteered for harsh duty: trekking to another camp and bringing back food for his unit. "They only select the strong people, because the load is very heavy and the distance is very far," he says. Bao always wore a loose jacket with a big inside pocket. "When I go, I always steal something to put in the pocket." A bit of salt fish, some dried shrimp. Most of it he gave to his uncle, who was in the camp with him: "I give it to him to eat; if not, he will not survive. He have a very weak body and very weak mind." Bao's body and mind were both strong, and he was armed with another weapon: a detailed knowledge of communist tactics. He had augmented his college reading by talking to local party members in the weeks following Saigon's collapse. So he knew that he would be asked, many times, to write a personal history for his captors. And he knew that if there were any discrepancies in his accounts, he would be accused of lying. When he wrote his story, he kept a copy, so he could repeat the exact same version the next time. "The only way to beat them, to beat the system, is to write the same story again and again," Bao recalls. "That saved me a lot."

Back in Saigon, Tuyen was totally in the dark: "We don't know where he is, we don't know if he still alive. We have no contact whatever, we hear nothing about him." She was living with Bao's family and they were practically strangers: "I was so lonely in his family, I had to live in his house with all these people I don't know." She was not just lonely, she was pregnant. Bao's instincts about his wife's condition were accurate. Pregnancy made her sick much of the time, but she still had to obey custom and serve her husband's family. They had fired their servants, because they didn't want to seem too rich to their new rulers, and Tuyen had to get up early every morning to prepare her father-in-law's tea. She was also responsible for the washing, which was done by hand, and since Bao had thirteen brothers and sisters, it was a mammoth job. With a bitterness that has not dissipated over all these years, she describes the scene: "I never have to wash for my parents but now I have to wash a stranger's clothing. Every day I see a bunch of clothing."

Months went by. Families that had heard nothing from their loved ones started to protest. To relieve the mounting pressure, the communists chose a few "good people" and set them free. Because Bao had outwitted his guards and written the same personal history on every occasion, he was in the first group selected. "One day," Tuyen recalls, "I got a letter from the communist government saying your husband would be released. Come over and pick him up." She had two reactions: "I was so happy. I knew he was alive, but I was also nervous and shy. Last time he saw me I was skinny, and now I had a big belly." He had been gone almost four months, not ten days, and when she met him at the train station, both had changed. "He was strong, real muscular, a he-man," she says with a laugh. "I tried to cover my belly, I tried to hide from him. I feel shy. He didn't know I was pregnant."

But the couple was still under suspicion. Bao: "They use the people, they know that in that house there's an officer, they have their spies." Tuyen: "They're watching." Bao: "They never trust you." Tuyen: "The communist people from the north, they don't know you. But your neighbors, they're really dangerous. They know how rich you are, they know your history. They come to your house, they talk like a neighbor, but they actually spy on you." So the Pham family made a decision: send the pair to the country, to an orchard they owned sixty miles away. There was a small shelter on the property, a one-room cabin. They had little money, and ate potatoes and watermelons provided by a neighbor; at night, with nothing else to do, they would sit on a rock, under the stars, and the navy officer would explain the constellations to his wife. "It was a good time, a happy time," recalls Tuyen. But it had to end. Tradition was strict on this point: when a baby was born, a woman moved home, so her mother could care for her and her child.

After their son Lanh was born, Bao was more determined than ever to battle the communists. During the day he worked as a street vendor, selling anything he could find to earn a bit of money: old clothing, fruit, cassette tape recorders. At night he would seek out old friends and comrades, trying to organize a resistance movement. "Most of the time we were just meeting and talking," he admits. "We try to make contact with groups outside the country, to get the weapons. But we not trust each other. That's why it was fruitless, very, very hard to organize."

Two years went by. Another son, Hien, was born, and Bao learned that local authorities in Saigon were open to bribery. Some rich Chinese families were still living in the area, and if they paid in gold, the officials would look the other way when these families tried to escape. Since he knew how to pilot a ship, Bao was often asked to join these attempts. But the organizers would not let him take his family along, so he rejected their offers: "I said no. If we go, we go together. If we die, we die together. I didn't want to be in America without my wife and children."

Resistance had failed. The Chinese option was out. So Bao made a new plan: finding a boat of his own. Friends introduced him to a fisherman in the far south of the country who promised to help. They had saved some money but it wasn't enough, so they sold Tuyen's jewelry—all her wedding presents—to raise more cash. They gave the man money for gas and supplies and made a date to meet in Saigon. "He never came back," says Bao. "We are afraid to go back to his area because we don't know about him for sure. If we go there we may get captured." He was so angry and disappointed, he spent hours throwing up blood: "Everything we had was gone; we had to start all over." Tuyen: "It was very, very hard. We were young. Till then we didn't realize people cheat you." Bao: "My family was mad at me, too. My mom, she gave me some gold so I could take my brother with me. How can you explain the money they gave you is gone? It hurt really badly."

But they did start over. Bao kept searching for a vessel and was arrested a dozen times. On one occasion, he was introduced to "Christian people from North Vietnam" who had settled in a coastal area.

He carried gold pieces in his pocket to pay for a boat, but local authorities got wind of their mission: "Somehow they find us and they chase us and they put us in jail." Just before he was carted off, Bao complained that he needed to urinate: "I turn sideways and slide my gold pieces into the bushes at the side of the road." Their makeshift cell was built on sand, so that night Bao and two friends dug their way out. They went back to the spot where they'd been captured, and the gold was still there, hidden in the bushes. They bought bus tickets and went home. "When he came back he looked like hell. He told me he had just escaped," remembers Tuyen.

Hell was just beginning. Bao was asked to pilot another boatload of escapees, and this time the organizers allowed him to bring his wife and children. The plan was for Bao to go on ahead, and take over a small riverboat that would ferry the families out to the ocean, where a larger craft would be waiting for the trip to Thailand. So Tuyen was on her own with the two small boys. She packed documents, a few photos, some medicine. Food was too heavy, since she had to walk through the jungle to reach their meeting point. Seven families, about forty people in all, boarded the craft and headed for the ocean. After a long day on the river, Lanh (then four) was tired and hungry and began to cry. Fear swept the boat. Patrols might hear him. So Tuyen doped him with medicine and he fell asleep. But she looked with envy at other mothers, whose husbands had been able to carry food for their kids: "I felt so bad. If you're hungry, it's okay, but when your children are hungry, it's terrible."

They finally reached the large boat and headed for the open sea. Success was at hand. "We so happy," recalls Bao. But the organizer of the escape had betrayed them. He had put only one engine on board, selling the spare one "to get extra money for himself." So when the engine burned out, the boat was set adrift. "We just pray at that point; we don't know what to do," recalls Bao. They tried to make a sail from spare clothing but there was no wind. They threw provisions overboard to make the ship lighter, including their heavy water jugs. At one point Tuyen dipped a towel into the sea so she could wipe her sons' faces, and the current pulled it out of her hand: "It was terrifying. I kept thinking, what if that happened to one of my kids? Neither of us could swim."

After two days they were almost out of food and water. Each passenger was limited to a few drops, no more than a capful, and Bao and Tuyen saved their rations for the boys. To stay alive she collected their urine and drank it: "It was so salty!" There was no land in sight and Tuyen felt like "a leaf blowing on the ocean." She knew the kids would soon die of thirst and she had only one way to save them, her own body: "I don't want my kids to die. So I'm thinking of cutting my wrist and feeding them with my blood to help them survive." On the third day the tides pushed them back to shore, a swampy, uninhabited area. Bao tried to go fishing but he stepped on a poisonous blowfish and within seconds, his whole leg swelled up. Tuyen: "Food we didn't have. Water we didn't have. Bao had a terrible infection and couldn't walk. Lanh and Hien were so little. I looked around and I thought there would be skeletons of us there." Spotting a fishing boat offshore, Tuyen took off Lanh's pants and waved them like a flag. It worked. The boat came over, and they thought they were saved. But they were wrong. The fishermen turned them in to the police. "I couldn't believe it," recalls Bao, still angry at the memory. "I don't know what they get for turning us in. A good citizens' paper? That's what the communists gave them."

At the police station, the couple faced a dire decision. They knew that boat captains and mechanics could be executed for trying to escape, as a warning to others. So they split up—Tuyen kept the older boy, Lanh; Bao took the baby, Hien—and pretended not to know each other. "They cannot think I'm the captain of the boat because I have a small child," he says. That left Tuyen to explain why she was traveling alone, and she proved to be as clever as her husband in outwitting their captors: "I make up a story, I had to. They ask why you leave your country, they think you betray your country, they hate us. So I said I was looking for my husband in America, because he left me." But Hien almost did them in. As the captives were being taken off to jail, he saw his mother and started crying for her: "I kept hearing Hien screaming, 'Mommy! Mommy!' But there was nothing I could do but keep walking. My heart broke."

Lanh was hungry and Tuyen decided to bribe a guard with her engagement ring in exchange for food. He took the ring and brought her nothing, but since women were not deemed fit for hard labor, she was released three days later. Again she begged the guard for help, and this time he gave her a small sum of money—just enough for milk, rice soup, and a bus ticket home. "I went back to my mother's house," says Tuyen. "I don't know when my husband and son will come back. I live with so much stress, so much worry. I know nothing about the future."

On the men's side of the prison, Hien was suffering badly from sunburn and mosquito bites. He coughed frequently and threw up dark green mucus. Bao stayed up through the night, fanning his child with a palm leaf. He had no medicine to relieve his son's suffering, and no family in the area to provide help. But a fellow inmate, a local man, did have contacts outside the prison. Disturbed at Hien's condition, the man urged his family to smuggle in some nose drops, and in a few days Hien was better. Jail food was rice and salt, just like at the reeducation camp. Local criminals had their families bring extra rations, but Bao and Hien were far from home and always hungry. The child asked the other inmates for their discarded shrimp heads to eat with his rice. Since Bao had to care for the boy, and couldn't go out to work, he was released after a month. He left jail with no money, a pair of slippers, and the clothes on his back. At a nearby town he begged enough to buy food, rice cakes, and mung beans, but he had no way to get home, one hundred and fifty miles away. Finally he hailed a bus and pleaded with the driver to let him and Hien sit on the roof, with the luggage. That's how they rode back to Saigon, with Bao using his shirt to shield the boy from the blistering sun. With no way to warn Tuyen he was coming, Bao just showed up. "I heard the knock and when I opened the door it was him!" she recalls. "I was so happy." But Hien hung back. After a month in jail he had grown wary and fearful. "I make a meal for him and he just hold tight to Bao," Tuyen remembers. "He just look at the food. I know he's so hungry but he won't let me touch him. My face was like a stranger to him."

Immediately Bao started planning another escape. He was a marked man now and had no choice: "We have an idiom in my country, if you hop on the tiger's back you cannot come off. You have to ride or the tiger will kill you." A year later there was another plot, another boat, another failure. This time they were trying to navigate the complex Mekong River delta on their way to the ocean. Another man was driving but he was distracted by his wife's seasickness. "I tried to tell him, I know the ocean more than him," Bao remembers. "I tried to tell him we head in to the land, not out to the ocean, but he didn't listen." Two days later a communist patrol boat stopped them. This time the parents decided that Tuyen would take both kids, that the time in jail had been too damaging to Hien, and after two days she was released. But again she had no money to get home. Her only marketable commodity was a pair of Bao's pants, bought new for the journey. Outside the jail she flagged down a bus, and when the driver asked for the fare, she offered him the pants. But the pants were too large and he didn't want them. "So I ask the passengers if they want to buy the pants from me," Tuyen says. Finally "a gentleman, an educated person," agreed to buy them. It was clear they wouldn't fit, he was much too small, but he took pity on her, and Tuyen and the boys made it home a day later.

Without his children, Bao was in for a long stay. The jail was in a swampy area, and the prisoners had to cross rivers and canals to get to the rice fields where they worked. He'd never learned to swim and more than once he almost drowned: "A friend cut a big palm leaf and let me hold on as he pulled me across the river." It was wild country, the paddies were filled with snakes and mice, and the prisoners would catch those creatures to supplement their meager diet: "When mice are the only meat you have, they're a delicacy." The mosquitoes were terrible and "I had rashes everywhere," but escape was impossible. A seventeen-year-old boy who tried it was captured and executed: "They pulled a gun out and shot him right in the head, right in front of me." Bao had been in enough jails by now to know the ropes. He worked hard and fast planting rice, trying to impress his guards. And while he staged a small protest, breaking the stems of the rice seedlings so they wouldn't grow, he did it underwater and out of sight. And he knew the drill: when asked to write a personal history, be sure to tell the same version every time. Six months later he was released. By now it was 1981 and the Phams were getting desperate. Rumors were flying that Thailand was closing its refugee camps and pushing boatloads of escapees back out to sea. They were still riding the tiger. They had to try again.

It was three years after their first attempt. Tuyen was pregnant again but there was no time to lose. Experience taught her what to pack: changes of clothes for the kids, medicine, a few pictures, small containers of milk. She wore a green outfit, a lucky color in Vietnam, and as before, the Phams boarded a small boat that was to take them to a larger ship waiting off the coast. But when they couldn't find the ship in the dark, they had to return to shore and hide for the night. Early the next morning most of the party reunited, but Bao's brother, who was carrying the family's provisions, was missing. So they set sail without him—and without any extra clothes, medicine, or food. (They later discovered he had been captured during the night by a police patrol.) This time they made it to the ocean, pretending to be a fishing party, but soon were intercepted by pirates. "They take everything," says Bao. "They have experience, they know what they're doing. Usually people put gold in the sole of their slippers or the cuffs of their pants, so they go through everything." Before the raiders reached him, Bao swallowed his twenty-four-karat gold wedding ring.

Just then another boat of escapees drifted by. The pirates seized one of the vessels and forced all the refugees into the other one. That made 120 people in a frail wooden craft, six feet wide and eighteen feet long, with no working engine. "That was when the nightmare started," recalls Bao. The overcrowded boat drifted for days. Fishermen and pirates stopped them frequently. Some were kind, offering a bit of food or water, but many were ruthless. When there was nothing left to steal they turned to rape. Tuyen tried to smear grease on her face and hide with her kids inside the boat, and most of the time, the raiders preferred young girls. One ten-year-old was assaulted so often she would leap into the sea when the lights of a boat approached. The attackers would shine candles in the faces of the women, selecting the ones they wanted, and despite her efforts to make herself ugly, Tuyen was targeted by one raider: "They hold my ponytail and I think, this is it, I'm going to die. I was holding Lanh and Hien on my lap, I was so scared." Bao was on deck, manning the steering wheel, and through a hole in the roof of the boat, he saw what was happening and was able to blow out the attacker's candle. Then another boat approached and the raiders fled, releasing Tuyen. At one point pirates dumped twenty additional refugees into the boat, bringing the total to 140. Their chances of survival were dwindling rapidly but a good omen emerged from an accident: a man was blown overboard and Bao insisted on trying to rescue him: "I got him, he was alive, I was so happy. I knew then we'd make it. I believed strongly that if he did not die in the sea, neither would we. We were going to America."

Not quite yet. After thirteen days on the water, Bao spotted land, but he didn't know what country he was seeing. If it was Thailand they would probably be safe; but if it was Cambodia, they might well be killed. As the boat drifted to shore, Bao called out to people gathering on the beach, asking where they were. The answer was Thailand. "I collapsed right away," he remembers. "All my energy was gone." They were taken to a nearby temple, where they were fed fruit and rice soup. The monks had cared for many boat people and knew that starving refugees could not eat very much right away. In fact, one seven-year-old gorged himself and died during the night. It was the next morning that Tuyen arose from a peaceful night's sleep and felt as if she had "come back to life." That day the family was trucked to a nearby refugee camp where Bao—with some food in his stomach— went to the bathroom and expelled the gold ring he had swallowed during the journey. They took it to a market and traded it for money. The Phams were truly "back to life." But the scars from their journey were slow to heal. In one camp the outhouse was on a platform at the edge of the sea. Hien was so petrified of the water, he had to be carried to the toilet and often screamed, "No! No! I don't want to go." To this day, ocean waves can trigger anxiety in both boys.

Over the next few months the Phams lived in three different camps in Thailand administered by the United Nations. They thought about moving to Australia, where Bao had an old navy buddy, or to France, where Tuyen had a brother. But Bao preferred America, mainly because Washington and Saigon had been allies during the war: "So they may help us more than the other countries. That's what I think." Tuyen had a half brother in California and they asked him to sponsor the family, but when the paperwork got lost, they had to find another option. Bao had a friend in Lancaster, Pennsylvania, a classmate from the naval academy, and his church was willing to sponsor the family. The United Nations sent the Phams to the Philippines for their final processing. There wasn't much to do, and as Tuyen recalls, "Every night I would come out and look at the stars. I have two boys now. I wanted a daughter. I heard that when you look at a star and the star starts to fall, and you wish right away, maybe your dreams will come true. Every night I come out and wish, I would like to have a girl." Early one morning, outside a market, she went into labor. Bao went racing around, looking for help, but the local clinic was closed. Tuyen delivered the baby right there, in the open air. It was a girl. When they finally got to a hospital, the staff asked for the child's name. The parents had discussed many options but at that moment the new mother blurted out "Thai Phi," the first syllables of the two countries that had given them sanctuary.

Two months later, the long journey that had started six years earlier, on the day Saigon fell, finally ended. The Phams had their love and their freedom. They flew to California, spent a few days with relatives, and moved on to Pennsylvania. It was winter when they arrived and they saw snow for the first time. Bao recalls: "I get a handful of snow to see how it feels. In Vietnam we eat ice with syrup, like a snow cone, so I go to eat the snow. But my sponsor says, 'Don't do that, it's dirty.'" Tuyen has her own memory: "The next day I sit by the window to see the snow and it's so beautiful. But when I went out I slipped down and I thought, 'My God, it's cold and it's dangerous.'" Their main sponsor was an older woman named Dorothy (the Pham kids called her "Grandma"), and she and other church members helped the family get settled: renting an apartment, cooking meals, driving them to doctors' appointments, negotiating the government bureaucracy, and signing them up for welfare. But the adjustment was very difficult. They kept slipping on the snow.

The main problem was that Bao couldn't find a job: "I walk around downtown Lancaster and no one will talk to you. I see 'help wanted' and knock on the door and ask for an application. But I can't speak English and they ask me some questions and I don't know how to answer them. At that point I had to translate everything before I can respond and they say, 'We don't need you, go away.'" Church people helped him get a job at a local market, preparing the produce before the store opened. But one night, as Bao was trying to wrestle a large cart full of ice, it broke loose and crashed into him, injuring his hand. The manager fired him, saying he wasn't strong enough to do the job.

After three frustrating months, Vietnamese friends suggested Bao get some advanced training. He joined a class to become a machinist, and while he still struggled with his English, his math skills were excellent, and he wound up helping the instructor teach some complex concepts. After completing the course he found a job at a local company making telecommunications equipment: "I was really happy, I was making good money, I could buy things for my kids." But after six months, a round of layoffs put him out on the street again. Now Bao's primary goal was security. He heard about R.R. Donnelley, a printing company in the area: "I talk to people and they say some people work there forty to fifty years and never get laid off. They always have a job for you, all the time, and a lot of overtime, too." When Bao applied to Donnelley the only opening was for a forklift operator—an unskilled job paying far less than a machinist's wages. But he took it: "I said yeah, anything, if I can provide for my kids, I don't care." Meanwhile Tuyen went looking for work as well. She considered taking the high school equivalency test, in order to qualify for better-paying jobs. But the test cost thirty-five dollars, and she couldn't afford it, so she took a manual job in an ice cream packaging plant: "We live paycheck to paycheck, it was a rat race, the cycle never ended."

In many ways, that cycle still hasn't ended for the Phams. Bao eventually got promoted, and today runs a bindery machine at the Donnelley plant. He is always the first to volunteer for overtime, often working twelve-hour shifts and sometimes sixteen hours at a stretch. He also works weekends and only takes time off when the company forces him to, after eighteen straight days on the job. "It's not a desk job. He's on his feet all the time," says his daughter, Thai Phi. "There's never been a time when he really gets to relax and have a good time."

One of his few diversions was playing the guitar, but after an accident at work sliced his finger to the bone, he had to give that up. Still, Bao has few regrets: "I always ask for extra hours. Many people don't like to work long hours, but to get some extra money for the family, I do it." And he's achieved his main goal, building a lovely new house for Tuyen in a rural area outside Lancaster. "I build the house for my wife; it's her wish," he says. "When the family gathers we have room for them. She likes that so I say okay, I work a little harder."

For years after they arrived in America, the Phams suffered from homesickness. They could only communicate with their families back in Vietnam through irregular mail service, and visits were impossible. Now phone service is cheap, two or three cents a minute. Relatives come to the United States periodically and Tuyen's mother actually moved here briefly and saw her grandchildren before she died. Bao's family has revived its seafood business in Saigon "and they make really good money there, too." But when the Phams returned for a visit, during the Vietnamese New Year, something was missing. They were Americans now.

"If my parents were still there, still alive, I would feel like I was coming home and celebrating with them," says Bao. "But my parents are not there. I came to my sister's house, and I feel like I'm going to a hotel. They've lived with the communists for thirty years. The language is changing. North and south they mix and match together; they've created a different language and I don't understand what they're saying. And I can't stand the weather there anymore. The food tastes different now; it doesn't taste good anymore. Everything over there is raw and my allergies came back." But his sense of strangeness, of not belonging, went beyond food and weather: "They change and we change, too. I learn a lot about this culture, the way Americans are thinking, more logical thinking, not like the Asian people. Americans think more logically and realistically."

Tuyen chimes in: "That's why they say East and West never meet.

We stand in the middle. Sometimes we never belong here, sometimes we never belong there. Sometimes, when I stay here, I feel homesick, but when I go back I don't feel I can stand to live there. When I speak English you understand only fifty percent of what I say. But when I went to Vietnam, I forgot the Vietnamese words. I think Bao and I are the sacrifice generation. We don't belong to Vietnam, we belong to America, but inside there is something that is not really American." For Tuyen, this feeling of living between two worlds is summed up by the holidays, especially Christmas. The Phams are Buddhists. They don't attend worship services often, but they do maintain a small shrine to their ancestors in a corner of their kitchen. "The kids would come home happy with the holiday, excited about Christmas, but deep down inside me, there's nothing, there's nothing, the holiday is nothing to me," she admits. "The New Year in Vietnam. That's something I grow up with, from when I was born. But when I went home I don't feel anything anymore, because my parents are not there." But if they are the "sacrifice generation," not feeling fully at home in either place, they know where their loyalties lie. In America. Bao: "This is my country." Tuyen: "I love this country very much. This is the country that accept my family."

I met Thai Phi when she was a student at George Washington University, taking a course I teach in feature writing. I encourage students to write about their families, and she accepted the challenge enthusiastically, interviewing her parents at great length, and she remembers the experience as "a distinct turning point in my relationship with my mother." During her teenage years, Thai Phi recalls, "we just never got along, I didn't understand her. We had a lot of tension between us, especially when she would nag me about my weight. But after hearing her story I realized I had to take a step back and appreciate the things she had done for me." Thai Phi is now a mother herself and says, "I love my son, but she was pregnant, she had two kids, and she just picked up and left, risking her life. I've always wondered if I would have the same strength she had. I live in a town house outside of Washington. My biggest problem is not wanting to drive on the Beltway, so I have a deeper, deeper respect for her. Definitely."

As parents, there were tensions between the Phams. Tuyen was "extremely traditional" raising the children, according to her daughter, while Bao would say, "We brought them here so they could have their own life, their own choices. They didn't have choices in Vietnam when the communists took over." But even in America the past remained. The daughter of a mother who was almost raped by marauding pirates was never allowed to sleep over at a friend's house. "My parents just didn't trust anyone, at all," says Thai Phi. "They were afraid I was going to be raped."

Tuyen was protective of her daughter in other ways. When she first met Adam, the man Thai Phi later married, she said to him, "This car is too nice for you. You have to start saving up for a house for my daughter." Thai Phi cringes at the memory: "It was two weeks into the relationship. I buried my head in my hands and I said to myself, I really liked this guy, there he goes . . ." But he stuck it out, and Thai Phi and Adam now laugh at the story of Tuyen, in fractured English, asking Thai Phi about their sexual relationship: "Do you still have your virgin?" After the wedding, adds Thai Phi, Tuyen "actually said to Adam, 'She belongs to you now,' and I started laughing. 'Oh no, he belongs to me now.'" After all, when Tuyen got married, she moved into her husband's house and spent the day washing his relatives' clothes. "The way she felt, I can't imagine that, because here women have rights and they're independent," says Thai Phi. "I'm used to being an independent woman. To even think about belonging to a man is beyond me."

Tuyen's traditional ways emerged again when Thai Phi's son Ethan was born. The Vietnamese custom was for the daughter to move home with her mother, and do nothing for weeks, but when Thai Phi refused to return to Lancaster, Tuyen came to Washington. "It was rough; we had a really hard time," says the new mother. "I was taking the baby outside, and doing things around the house she just didn't think a mother should be doing yet. Two neighbors came by to say hi and I stepped outside to talk to them and my mother just about flipped out, because she thought I was going to get sick." The main symbol of their clash was the baby's blanket. Whenever he cried Tuyen said he was cold. Thai Phi had a different view: "To this day, she still puts blankets on him whenever she sees him. Now I just quietly take them away."

If Thai Phi does not agree with her mother's traditional views of child rearing, she does embrace her Vietnamese heritage in other ways. When she was a teenager, she wanted to be called "Emily Michelle," after a character in the story book series The Babysitters Club, but now she says, "I'm so glad my parents never caved in to that. I have this name that I'm so proud of." Her mother-in-law is a high school guidance counselor and recently put Thai Phi in touch with an Asian girl who wanted to change her name from Ying to Katie. Thai Phi told her, "I love your name; Ying is such a beautiful name," and today the girl has reverted to Ying. "She should be proud of where she comes from," says Thai Phi, and she is determined to live that way, vowing to take Ethan to Vietnamese language classes when he's older and to brush up her own skills. "I don't want him to lose that part of him," she says. "He's growing up American, but I hope he'll be Vietnamese American. My parents went through so much for me, and for me not to know their language would feel disrespectful." Lanh and Hien are both living near their parents in Pennsylvania, but neither has children yet, so Ethan is their first and only grandchild. When Bao takes a rare day off, the Phams often drive to Washington to see the baby, and Thai Phi fears that her parents will get lost finding her house. But Adam scoffs at her, saying: "Your parents made it from Vietnam to America. They can make it from Pennsylvania to D.C."

2.

Alice Ingabire-Schaut

RWANDA

Mom, I'm going to America on Saturday. Good-bye.

Alice Ingabire belongs to the Tutsi tribe in the central African nation of Rwanda, but she spent most of her childhood as a political refugee in neighboring Uganda. In 1994, the Hutu government ruling her homeland slaughtered thousands of Tutsis and then collapsed in the face of rebel attacks. Alice, who was just finishing her high school exams, joined a wave of Tutsis pouring back into their old country. "It was a joy," she recalls. "People fainted and cried; we had been in exile for so many years. People were just so happy being in Rwanda again." But their joy did not last. The stench of death was everywhere. The economy was in ruins. Alice enrolled in an advanced secondary school, dodging unexploded land mines on her way to class. But when she graduated, there were five thousand students competing for three hundred places in the country's only public university, and she failed to get one. By 1998 her future seemed hopeless: "I was lost, I didn't know what to do. Education was so competitive, it was really tough. Everybody was wondering, what is next?"

Alice uses one word to describe what did happen next. *Miracle.* Her friend Jackie told her about a scholarship program, for a one-year marketing course in Ethiopia: "She came to where I was working and said, 'Alice, you've got to come on Monday and do the exam with me.'" But Alice was dispirited and reluctant. "I don't think that's a good idea, I really don't," she told her friend. "If I fail, that's another blame on my part. If I pass, who's going to pay my transportation? How am I going to get to Ethiopia?'" Besides, she didn't even have a pen. Jackie pulled one out of her purse, threw it at Alice, and said, "I'll see you Monday." Alice was still unconvinced. She went back inside the car repair shop, where she had a job translating paperwork into English, and said to herself, "I don't want to bother, I don't want to put myself through this." Public university was out, and a private one was far too expensive. "I didn't see myself going back to school. I thought that was the end of it."

But Monday morning came, recalls Alice, "and something woke me up around seven. I remember thinking, should I go take that exam?" She was living with a cousin in the capital of Kigali, and when she walked out the door—and before she could change her mind—a minibus happened to pull up, right in front of her. She got on, but the other passengers told her the bus didn't go to the right place, so she got off and hailed a motorcycle, arriving at the exam "crazy and confused" from her ride. But when she saw Jackie waving at her, she calmed down and went inside. The test lasted three days, and instead of going back to her cousin's house when they were finished, she traveled to her mother's village of Mutara, not telling anybody what she had done: "I did not want to be embarrassed, that I had failed the exam." After a few days helping out on the family farm, she returned to the city. Her cousin greeted her with the news. Someone had stopped by to congratulate her. She had passed.

Rwanda's minister of education was Jackie's uncle. When he went over the test scores, he had noticed the first-place finisher. "Who is this girl?" the minister asked his niece. "Her name is Alice," replied Jackie, and the minister had said: "You tell her to come to the ministry, to my office. I want to meet her." When Alice showed up the official was rushed. I have to leave, he said, but talk to the secretary. There are some other good scholarships that just came in, for full-time students, a four-year degree, in America. "I think you deserve that," he added. "You beat all the boys in mathematics."

The scholarships were sponsored by the Pacem In Terris program, based at La Roche College, a small Catholic school in Pittsburgh. They were aimed at young people from war-ravaged regions who would study in America and then return home and help rebuild their countries. Alice was stunned. "In America, you express more, and now I would hug him around the neck. But then I just couldn't do that. So I just said, 'Yessir, yessir.' And that's how I got the scholarship." Forms were filled out. Faxes were sent. A professor at La Roche, Patricia O'Donoghue, was taking over as president of Mount Mary, a women's college in Milwaukee. Of the twenty-three scholarship winners only two were females, and she said, give them to me. So when Alice went to get her visa, and encountered her godmother's brother, an employee at the American embassy, she told him, "I'm going to this place called Wisconsin." He replied: "Wisconsin is a state. It's cold there and they have cows." But the weather report did not dim Alice's excitement. The Tutsis are herdsmen. Her brother had cows. "As long as they have milk," she said, "I'll be fine."

Alice is a tall woman, with a soft voice and a dignified bearing, but she grew animated as she told the story. She needed passports, tickets, visas, shots: "Everything was happening, boom-boom-boom-boom." And then she realized she had to tell her mother. But there were no phones in Mutara, not even a telegraph. "I rushed to my mother in the village, I remember it was a Thursday, and I said, 'Mom, I'm going to America on Saturday. Good-bye.'"

Today Alice lives in Grafton, a suburb of Milwaukee. She graduated from Mount Mary, married a man she met there, and now works two full-time jobs, selling shoes and cleaning a church. She sends home at least half of what she makes and supports seven relatives—grandmother, mother, two sisters, a brother, a niece, and a nephew—plus various family friends and orphans from the genocide. The entire clan occupies a four-bedroom brick house that Alice financed, back in the village where she told her mother good-bye. She occasionally feels guilty about staying in America, and she admits that life in Milwaukee is far more comfortable than in Mutara, where the family home still lacks electricity and running water. But her conscience, and her reasoning, are clear: "I always thought I would go back and work for my country and help my country. But I feel like I do more good being here. The money I send does help the country, and helps my sisters get an education. They're better off with me being here. That was a tough decision, but I knew I wasn't going to make it, or accomplish my dreams, by going back to Rwanda."

This is a common story. Many immigrants come to America thinking they'll return home, but never do. They find partners, raise children, build careers, create communities. However, often they send money back to family members who remain behind. Even a small check by American standards makes an enormous difference in a poor country like Rwanda, and modern technology makes it possible for an immigrant like Alice to stay in closer touch with her homeland than ever before. When her sisters need something they call on their cell phones or send an e-mail from an Internet café. "Coming to this country has saved me and changed my life completely and made me a completely new person," says Alice. That is not completely true. Yes, Milwaukee is a long way from Mutara. But like many immigrants she brings the values and loyalties of the "old country" with her. She wants to become a U.S. citizen and vote in an election—for the first time in her life. But her ties to tribe and family remain strong. She lives in America, but her devotion, and her dollars, flow back to Rwanda.

Alice's story begins during Africa's colonial era, when Germany and then Belgium ruled the region that is now Rwanda. The occupying powers deliberately nurtured rivalries between the three local tribes: Hutu, Tutsi, and Twa. They issued ethnic identity cards and installed the Tutsis—a distinct minority but a wealthier and better-educated elite—as their overlords and tax collectors. The wave of nationalism that swept Africa in the 1950s reached Rwanda and inspired the Hutus to arm themselves and rebel against Tutsi rule. The Tutsi king died (or was assassinated) in July 1959 and by November a violent Hutu uprising, known as "the wind of destruction," had killed thousands of Tutsis and sent many others fleeing for their lives. Alice's parents and grandparents were among the refugees.

Her mother's family, the Izagirizas, ended up in a camp in Uganda. It was a miserable place: poor land, no streets, no houses. It wasn't even on a map. The refugees had to cut down trees to create living spaces. They built mud huts with thatched roofs for shelter, but there was no electricity, no water, not even outhouses. Diseases such as malaria, cholera, and sleeping sickness spread rapidly. There was no medical care and many died; so did most of the livestock the refugees had managed to bring with them. "When they left Rwanda they lost everything, they had nothing," says Alice. But the Tutsis were driven and determined, and "little by little, people got out" of the camps. They had to learn new languages and customs, and often they changed their names, trying to pass as Ugandans, who called them "snakes" and "cockroaches." Alice's uncles left first, but her mother, Melaniya, had to stay behind, lashed to the back-cracking work of camp life: cooking, cleaning, farming a small plot of beans and corn, scrubbing pots with grass because there was no soap or water. As a practicing

Catholic (the Tutsi king had converted in the 1940s), she also taught Bible classes to camp children. When Melaniya was twenty, a cousin came to her and said, let's get out, there are jobs in the city. They plotted their escape in secret, and since they couldn't carry suitcases, they put on several layers of clothing at once. "She didn't want her mom asking where she was going," says Alice.

The young women made their way to Kampala, the capital, where Melaniya got a job as a maid for wealthy foreigners. Four or five months later she returned to the camp. Alice picks up the story: "She got her salary, and bought plates and blankets and spoons. She was excited. She went to visit her mom, and found them in really bad shape. She was the first one who had actually found work in her family." She stayed a few days and returned to Kampala. On the way back, her bus was in a serious accident. Most of the passengers were killed. The doctors wanted to amputate Melaniya's injured leg but she screamed in protest. Rwandans, notes Alice, "really care about beauty, and if you lose your leg your life is gone." The leg was saved, and one day, while he was doing his rounds, a young security guard named Philibert Rutabayiru noticed Melaniya's name on the door of her hospital room.

Philibert was seven or eight during the "wind of destruction." As the Tutsis fled their country in terror and chaos, the boy lost contact with his family and was taken in by strangers, who settled in Tanzania. Refugee children would go to work and be paid in food, and Philibert found employment in a mine owned by an Arab man. A woman friend of the mine owner was visiting one day and overheard the boys who worked there talking among themselves. When one spoke Philibert's name she realized he was her nephew, her brother's son. "She kind of took him in and raised him for a while," says Alice, "but she was an alcoholic and it didn't work out." At sixteen he joined the Tanzanian army, but it was a rough life for a foreigner, so Philibert deserted and ended up in Uganda. With his military background he found work as a security guard, which is why he was patrolling the hospital corridors when he noticed Melaniya's name. Their daughter tells the story: "He said, 'This sounds like a Rwandan name,' but it was tough to approach someone and ask if they were Rwandan, because many of them would say, 'No, I'm not.' They tried their best to change themselves, to call themselves Ugandans, find a job, and be accepted into the community. But when he read Melaniya's name he said to her, 'Are you Rwandan?' And that's how they met. I like it when my mom tells me that story."

Philibert and Melaniya were soon married, and in 1975 they named their firstborn child Adelphine. But as a young girl she was so strong-willed that she picked up the nickname "Alice," in honor of Alice Lakwena, a legendary guerrilla leader. Philibert found occasional work as a guard or policeman. One of his jobs was combating the flies and mosquitoes that cause so many diseases in central Africa, and that involved taking his young family to distant corners of the country. Wherever they landed, the first thing Philibert did was find a school for his children. "Some places were so remote you had to sit under a tree and the teachers would teach us, or the parents would get together and put up a shack," Alice recalls. Everything was strange. Christianity had not reached many of these areas and the children were frightened by traditional religious practices. The food was different, with no cows, only sheep and goats. "In my tradition we don't eat sheep, but we had to eat it. We don't drink goat's milk, either, but my sister Lillian got sick, with malnutrition, and I remember my mom had to feed her goat's milk. That was kind of the last straw."

Philibert never went beyond elementary school but he knew education was the answer for his children. Sometimes they had to walk miles each way, through forests and across rivers, but school always came first. "I remember crying. I was scared of the other kids, but my father insisted, 'You have to go to school,'" says Alice. She was a quick learner, and even as a little girl, she recalls, "I would go to these Ugandan schools and I'd be able to count and the teachers were surprised, but my father would teach me from home; he always loved education." One day her mother came to pick up Alice and found her perched on a classroom desk, teaching everybody how to say different words in the Rwandan language, Kinyarwanda. In a country where Rwandans were called "snakes" and "cockroaches," identifying so publicly as a refugee was not a good idea. "My mom was scared but I was laughing. I didn't realize how dangerous it could be."

Their life in Uganda ended one day when a gang of poachers accused Philibert of fingering them to government authorities. He was summoned to a traditional court in the center of the village, presided over by a teacher who had seven wives. Melaniya feared he would be killed on the spot and told Alice, "If anything happens, grab your brothers and run to the pastor; go there and hide." Alice was about five at the time, and she sneaked out of the house to see what was going on. She remembers "a big fire burning" and men with spears. For some reason the court decided to adjourn for the night and resume in the morning. Philibert didn't wait. He took his family and fled through the darkness, leaving most of their possessions behind. When they reached a city he had only enough money to buy one ear of corn from a street vendor. He tried to break it into pieces for his children but couldn't do it. So he picked out the kernels, one by one, and fed the family.

By this time Philibert's parents were dead but he had two brothers and a cousin who had returned to the family's hometown in Rwanda, Rwamagana. Philibert and Melaniya decided to join them, but it was a difficult transition. "My father was so poor, so poor," recalls his daughter. "When we came back to Rwanda we had nothing. We had to start all over again. I remember telling my father, 'I will study, and I'm going to buy you a bicycle. With my first salary I'm going to buy you a bicycle.'" But she had another dream as well: "I always told them, 'I will go to America and I will work and I'm going to buy my own bike.' That's what I was always saying, and it happened."

Eventually there were five children, three girls and two boys, and

Philibert supported them working at a rice factory owned by Chinese émigrés. He rose to the job of night manager, but he and Melaniya "had some misunderstandings," and she decided to return to her family, in the camps of Uganda, taking the youngest child, Emmanuel, with her. Philibert remarried, but one Friday morning he came home early. "I went out of the house to see him, and his face was all smashed and bruised, like he had fallen down," Alice recalls. "I went to school but I couldn't study. I came back and things were bad. My stepmother says, 'Your father is very sick, very sick.' He was shivering and sweating and talking things I didn't understand." As Philibert deteriorated his second wife left. Within two months he was dead, leaving Alice alone with three younger siblings. She was thirteen.

The day after his burial, Alice went to the local priest and said, "My father just died, my mom is in Uganda, we have no food, and I want to study in your school. Are you going to charge me school fees?" No, he said, no fees, and if you come every Saturday I will give you food. Alice's godmother wanted to separate the four remaining kids and distribute them to friends and relatives but Alice refused: "I said no, we can't separate, I always thought things would happen." They lived that way for almost a year, by themselves, spending Christmas alone. "I don't know how we did it," says Alice, but she knew her responsibilities: "All Africans, when you are the firstborn, it's like you are another mother. You have to take care of your siblings but also your father. You cook, you clean, you find firewood, and I did all of that. It's what's expected of a child in Africa."

There was no mail or telephone service in the refugee camp where Melaniya was living, so she remained unaware of her children's plight. The only form of communication was radio. People would submit messages that were read over the air on a Rwandan-language station, in the hope that someone would hear them and relay the news. A construction worker in Uganda heard a broadcast saying that "some kids were calling their mother to say their father had died." The worker knew Alice's aunt and recognized the family name, and the aunt delivered the word to Melaniya.

"My mom went crazy," says Alice, and decided to return to Rwanda and rescue her children. She needed money from her brothers—for buses and bribes—but they warned her against making the trip. War fever was rising in the region. Exiled Tutsis were organizing a rebel army, the Rwandan Patriotic Front (RPF), to retake control of their country, and there was "no way she was going to make it." But Melaniya went anyway, crossing the border into Rwanda on foot, deep in the forest, where no guards patrolled. Alice remembers the day that her mother arrived. She was at school, her brother John was home sick with a bad case of malaria, and her cousin Robert came looking for her: "Now I'm scared to death. When I saw him I thought something was wrong with John. I said, 'Is John dead?' And he said, 'No, it's your mother.'" And then she saw Melaniya: "I just looked at Mom and couldn't believe it. I didn't even cry. She looked so horrible, so worn-out, so skinny. She looked so bad."

The four children returned with their mother to Uganda, but crossing the border again was not easy. Melaniya and John went back through the forest. The three girls—Alice, Lillian, and Theresa—pretended they were just going to sell milk at a farmer's market on the Ugandan side and a guard let them through. The two groups met up at the market and headed back to the refugee camp. It took them four days, sleeping on the streets between buses.

Camp life was harsher than ever. With Philibert dead and no money coming in, the family lived on their small garden plot and handouts from Melaniya's brothers. But there was a spirit that Alice remembers fondly: "One thing I cherish about being in the refugee camps—there was such a sense of togetherness, of community. Every person there was your cousin or your uncle. You didn't just sit in your own house eating your own food. You lived in extended families. You ate whatever you wanted to eat, wherever you were."

The camps were a prime source of recruits for the RPF, and Alice was an eager convert to the rebel cause. She had seen kids beaten or thrown into rivers, just because they were Rwandan, and she wanted to return to her homeland. Because she could read and write well, she joined a cadre of young people who circulated secretly through the camps, reading messages from the rebels and raising money. Many of the older refugees "had lost hope, lost their identity. The elders never thought going back to Rwanda was possible." The mission of the RPF was to "tell them what it is like to live in a free land, not in the refugee camps." Unlike most of her fellow recruits, Alice had actually lived in Rwanda and knew a lot about her native culture. She taught other kids traditional dances and put on shows at weddings and festivals. She also took a secret code name—which she won't reveal, even to this day—and received basic military training. "They brought in rifles and showed us, this is how you open it and this is how you close it." But they couldn't shoot the guns, because that would alert their neighbors. "We'd meet secretly in the camps and post guards outside to make sure the Ugandans didn't know about it."

Meanwhile, Alice was going to school, and like many "camp kids," she studied hard, because she knew education was her ticket out: "We didn't have anything else to take our minds out. We weren't going to watch TV or go out in the streets. We didn't even worry about someone else wearing shoes that were better than we had because we were barefoot. We didn't even have uniforms." The camp kids did so well in the national exams that the Ugandan government "had to send soldiers to see if we were cheating." But they didn't need to cheat; they had plenty of motivation: "When you are Rwandese, when you're a refugee kid, you want to make a mark. They would tell you, you have to study or you'll end up on the farm."

Alice took the exams for secondary school but never got her grades. The camp still had no mail or phone service. Her uncle, who worked in the city, checked the lists but couldn't locate her. She had used her given name, Adelphine, and he didn't recognize it. "Thank God, nobody had the same last name as me," she says, and eventually he found her. She had passed with flying colors and had a place in Kyebambe, one of Kampala's best schools. Her uncle rushed to the camp, gave her the news, and offered to pay her fees. Hurry, he said, the term has already begun. But there was one problem: that same day she was scheduled to ship out with other recruits from the camp for advanced military training. The guerrilla war was heating up and more troops were needed on the front lines. When Alice's commander heard about her exam grades, he made a decision that changed her life. "I remember him calling me aside and saying, 'Don't leave with us.' He saved me. He knew what was best for me." Many of her friends went off to war. Some didn't come back. Alice went off to high school in Kampala.

"I was scared. I didn't know what to expect," she remembers. "You're from a camp where nobody wears shoes, there are no cars, and now you have classmates whose parents come in cars to pick them up." On the first day, the new girls were asked to sing a song. She chose one in her native tongue, Kinyarwanda, and did a traditional dance along with the tune. The other girls laughed at her. She was a refugee kid. A misfit. A lonely misfit, cut off from her family and the "togetherness" of the camps. When she did return home for holidays, she worried that rain pouring through the thatch roof of their hut would ruin her books and homework. Classes were very strict and taught in English, which she had to learn quickly. She had one uniform and one pair of shoes. When it was time for tennis she didn't have the right gear. She remembers going to exactly one dance in four years, and that's because she was a prefect, a student leader, and had to go. "Other kids would go in the corner and cry, but I didn't cry. I would always say, this is my dream, I'd better get it right."

In those years she grew close to her younger brother, John. When she arrived home for holidays he would meet her at the bus, his wide smile beaming happily, and walk with her for miles from the stop to the camp, keeping her safe. The genocide against the Tutsis, the triumph of the RPF, and the downfall of the Hutu government happened during her last months at Kyebambe school. The camps emptied virtually overnight, as the Tutsi refugees rushed back home. John returned to Rwanda and sent her a letter, listing all their friends and relatives who had been killed. It went on for three pages. "I cheated the genocide," she says now. If her father had lived, and the family had stayed in Rwanda, they almost certainly would have been massacred.

Her uncle found her at school and said, you can't go back to the camp, everyone is gone. So when she finished the term she boarded a bus with other Rwandan students and headed for home. "I remember when we reached the border they were supposed to check the bus, but all the students got out and just started running, running, running. We wanted to see who could cross the line first. Some of those children had never seen Rwanda, never stepped foot in Rwanda, so we're all rushing and the soldiers are saying, come back. But we're students, we didn't listen, we crossed the border and started jumping and rejoicing."

But Rwanda was a country filled with ghosts. "It was emotional, too emotional. There was a lot of disease and dead people everywhere. In the middle of the street there were dead bodies lying around." People wandered around looking for relatives. Many orphans found none. The survivors had trouble facing each other. Alice's godmother and seven children had all been murdered, and one day Alice met the woman's husband. "I just started crying," she says. Another day she saw the father of a childhood friend: "I approached but I didn't know what to say. Then this voice came out of me and I said, 'Sir,' and he turned around, and I said, 'Can I talk to you?' and he said, 'Sure.' I asked where his daughter was, and his eyes opened so wide, and he just walked away." A girl cousin survived a grievous wound, but the rest of her family died, and she carries deep scars, emotional and physical, that will never go away. "That's why I feel guilty when I talk about my stories," says Alice. "Because there are many stories that are worse than mine."

Her brother John had moved to their father's town, Rwamagana, and started working at the local hospital. The rest of the family settled in Mutara and became squatters, taking over a house owned by a Hutu clan. Eventually the Hutus returned to their property: a widow and three children. Melaniya offered to share the house with the woman, and the two families crowded into the small dwelling. The Rwandan school system follows a British model and after high school, there are two additional years called "A levels" before college. Alice enrolled in a new school, the grandly named Rwanda International Academy, founded by a returning refugee on the site of an old technical college. It was there that she learned to avoid the land mines that still littered the school grounds. "Education wasn't stable then," she recalls. "We did not have enough teachers, schools, dormitories, food. All dormitories had no windows or doors or running water. Classrooms had no chairs. Everything was chaotic." No wonder she didn't pass her exams for college. She got the part-time job at the gas station after graduation and thought about returning to Uganda to look for work. She was just about out of hope on the day her friend Jackie told her about the scholarships to Ethiopia.

When she left for America, Alice had never been on an airplane before, and the journey was filled with new impressions. At a stopover in Kenya, "I remember seeing a little Japanese girl sleeping on the floor with torn jeans. I had never seen torn jeans, I didn't know it was a fashion, and I thought she was homeless. All of a sudden I looked around and she was on the same flight with us." Alice had no pocket money and during a nine-hour delay in the Kenya airport she couldn't buy any food: "I remember being so hungry." When they finally boarded the plane, "The flight attendant gave us snacks before dinner, then cookies. I kept begging her to bring me more. I was calling them pancakes!"

Alice was traveling with a girl named Priscilla, the other student headed for Mount Mary, and they were met at the Milwaukee airport by a delegation of nuns. Her first impression was of a vast green land, filled with trees and grass: "We used to think that all of America was skyscrapers and big buildings, that people grew tomatoes in pots on the tops of their homes." When they got to the campus, "I remember looking at the grounds and thinking, my mom would be so happy here; she would plant something in that ground." Alice "just fell in love" with the school and the country, but the adjustments were not easy. Her fellow students knew little about Africa: "They would ask questions like 'Did you walk around naked?' and 'Did you live by the fire?'" Alice had never lived in a building with running water, let alone a washing machine: "I took my clothes downstairs. I had seen my girlfriends washing, so I put my clothes in a machine, shut the door, and left. Forty-five minutes later I came down and they were not washed. I didn't realize you had to put money in till one of the nuns helped me. Everything was a learning experience."

Rwanda is a tropical country, so Wisconsin's changing seasons, as fall turned into winter, confused her: "When it was snowing all the trees looked dry, like they were dead. I remember looking out the window and thinking, there's a lot of firewood out there. Then all of a sudden that tree is blooming again. I thought it was dead. How come it's growing back leaves again? I didn't get it." Student customs also confused her: "I got fascinated by jeans. I used to think that jeans were a uniform for students, because I would see everyone wearing them. In my school we used to wear skirts and I thought, now I have to wear jeans for a uniform? My classmates used to ask me, 'Why are you always dressed up?' because I would wear skirts and dresses to class." She couldn't understand students wearing bedroom slippers or bringing food to class. Above all, she couldn't understand them talking back to the teachers: "I had an English teacher, a nun, and I remember a student getting up in class and saying, 'I don't like this.' Honestly, I just wanted to disappear. I had never heard a student talk to a teacher in that tone of voice. In my country you'd be thrown out of class and beaten."

She adapted quickly, however, to one part of American life: making money. About a month after arriving on campus she offered to help out in the school kitchen, serving a meal at a catered event, and was surprised to receive a check for twenty-one dollars. "I was really excited, but I didn't know what to do with it," she recalls, and a classmate, a woman from India, suggested she open a bank account. But twenty-one dollars wasn't enough to do that; she needed fifty. So the woman lent her the extra money—they trekked down to the local branch of Wells Fargo—and Alice joined the American economy. "I started working in every job that was open to me at Mount Mary," at the library, the admissions office, the kitchen, the fitness center. "I told everybody, 'I need hours, I need hours.'" When the school couldn't produce enough work she cleaned houses for professors. Soon she started sending money home, but the envelopes often got lost or stolen. Then someone told her about Western Union. She'd wire the money and send a fax to John, at the hospital where he was working, to pick up the cash. If she earned $200 she'd send $120 home.

Work and school left little time for fun. Classmates would invite her home for holidays but the visits were often awkward: "I'd see what they do at Christmas, and it made me envious sometimes, all the gifts and the food." One Thanksgiving, Alice and Priscilla were visiting a friend's family: "We were sitting in the living room and nobody's talking to us. In my culture, you don't just leave guests alone. The girl had gone to talk to her mother and we were there all alone, watching TV, and I was so hungry. I said to Priscilla, 'Are we allowed to look in the refrigerator?' I remember thinking, I want to go back to school, I miss my room." On another holiday one of the nuns from Mount Mary invited the two African students to spend a week at her old convent in Springfield, Illinois. There were few nuns left in the five-story building "and we had a whole floor to ourselves," Alice recalls. "We could go downstairs and have ice cream in the middle of the night. That was the funnest time I ever had."

After a year or so in America, the nuns at Mount Mary gave Alice money to return home. Work had already begun on the new house she was building in Mutara and she was eager to see it. She was also eager to see John, her favorite brother, who was meeting her at the airport. But when she arrived, "I was looking at everybody and couldn't see John. He was tall, but I couldn't see him, and right there I knew John was dead." On the way to the airport, the minivan he was riding in had crashed, killing nineteen passengers and the driver. The camera she had brought, to record a joyous homecoming, instead took pictures of grieving relatives at John's funeral. She knew John had a daughter, but at the funeral, she noticed a woman holding a baby boy. "Whose child is that?" she asked a relative. "You don't know?" came her reply. "That is John's." So now she had a greater burden than ever, taking care of her dead brother's two children along with everyone else. "It would have been a disgrace if we hadn't taken in John's kids," she says. "They're ours. That's all we have of John left." But her dream of returning to Rwanda died with John. When she showed me the album of photos from his funeral, her eyes filled with tears: "My life changed completely. I hated Rwanda. I started looking for people to finish up the house. I moved my mother in and the next day went back to the U.S."

Back at Mount Mary she had little time for a social life, and besides, the girl who had gone to only one dance in high school found that men were one more thing about America she didn't understand: "From my upbringing I didn't know how to date." But she was now alienated from Rwanda by John's death, and committed to a life in

America, so she was ready for romance when friends introduced her to Cliff Schaut, a computer engineer who already had children from a previous marriage. They dated for more than a year and got married shortly before her graduation, partly because the American custom of living together was just not for her: "I didn't want to move into a man's house if I wasn't married." No one from her family could afford to come to the wedding, and that explains a lot about her decision to get married: "I don't think people realize how tough and lonely it can get for someone in this country without a family member near you or without someone you really trust to talk to, laugh with, share your thoughts with, help you go through tough times, support and listen to you when you need to share your past horrors. Life in America would have been more complicated for me had I not met Cliff. I am glad I found a soul mate."

After graduation Alice moved into Cliff's house in suburban Grafton, but without a car or driver's license her employment options were limited. After a week she couldn't stand the idleness and was walking around the town looking for jobs when she saw a brochure for St. Joseph's, a local Catholic church. "I went to the priest and said, 'I just moved to this area. I'm looking for a job. Is there anything at all? I have my degree, I have a wonderful GPA, but I need a job.'" For a while she did some data entry work but an unpaid volunteer took the slot. "They said, 'Alice, we don't have a job for you anymore,' but I remembered that a woman who cleaned the church was quitting. I said 'I will take it,' and they said, 'Are you sure?' and I said, 'Yes.'" Since Alice grew up cleaning pots with grass in a refugee camp, cleaning church floors with a mop was not beneath her, and she likes the peace and quiet: "I go there late at night, when nobody's there. I walk in the hallways and talk to myself and sing out loud. I just feel calm."

She kept her night job at the church after finally landing a day job, selling shoes at the Allen-Edmonds factory outlet. She works entirely on commission, and she admits, "It's difficult sometimes, when you have so much going on in your brain; you don't really want to talk to customers. But I do my job well." (So well that when George W. Bush was campaigning for president and stopped at the store, Alice was assigned to take him around.) It's an exhausting schedule that wears her down at times: "I look at my paychecks and I can't believe I work all those hours. I just pray I keep healthy because I get scared. If something happens to me, what's going to happen to my family?" As the only source of income for the entire family back in Rwanda, she pays for everything—food, clothing, bus fare, medical bills. And her obligations keep expanding: "At my mother's house you never know who lives there. There are a lot of orphans that need a place to live and she's also taken in a girl of about nineteen who just had a baby boy." Some months the money doesn't go far enough, and she has to call her sisters' schools and say, "I'm sorry, I'm not able to pay the school fees, excuse me for a month." She's taken out credit cards and pays the overdue bills first, sometimes barely staying afloat, and the future doesn't look much brighter. Sister Lillian has emotional problems, so her medical bills are high and her job prospects dim. Sister Theresa had polio as a child and walks with the aid of braces and crutches. "Thank God she's not growing anymore," laughs Alice. "When she's growing you have to buy new braces, but I haven't bought new ones in a year now." Theresa's in college, but she has to walk long distances on her crutches—often in the rain—to get to classes and the library, so Alice bought her a laptop computer to make studying easier: "She has these huge calluses on her arms, she walks so much." Alice's dream is to buy her sister a motorized wheelchair, and since elevators in Rwanda are scarce, she hopes Theresa can find a job where she doesn't have to climb stairs, as a teacher perhaps, or in a bank. "But it's going to be tough; even normal people can't find a job."

After eight years away, Alice's bitterness over John's death had softened enough for her to return home for Christmas. She and Cliff wanted to go together, but they could only afford one ticket, and even then she had to borrow money from her retirement account at Allen-Edmonds to finance the trip. She showed me a video she took of the visit, and she has a lot to be proud of—a solid brick house, a grateful family, a deep sense of accomplishment. But in a situation like this one, where a family back home depends so heavily on remittances from America, a certain amount of resentment is unavoidable. Watching the video, I sensed an undercurrent of tension at family gatherings and Alice confirms that "we were constantly fighting." She's an American now, and she says of her sisters, "I've trained them to do things the American way. Organized." Tell me ahead of time when your fees are due, or you need bus fare home. But her sisters don't always appreciate her "American way" of doing things: "I remember being home and saying, 'Quick, quick, quick,' and my sisters would say, 'Relax.' But I didn't know how to do that. I didn't know what to do with my free time."

Alice also doesn't know how to cope with all the requests for help that are constantly pouring in: "Most people, from any third-world country, believe that once you reach America, it's a safe heaven. An answer to everything. Some of those, who know I'm married to a white American, think I have all the potential to help them. They think I am rich and I have it all. They don't know that I have to work twice as hard to maintain my life and my marriage and also care for my family needs in Africa. It really feels overwhelming, knowing that you're at least living in conditions better than most, and yet you are not able to help them all. It is sometimes hard to say no. I have made so many promises, which have caused me some emotional breakdown. You know you love them, you wish them well, you would do anything to help, but you can't. How do you show them you still love them, even though you can't afford to lend the help they ask you for?"

These pressures have strained her marriage, as well as her emotional well-being: "Getting married was the hardest thing I've ever done. It's not easy when you get married to someone from another culture. Every day's a learning experience." One sticking point between them has been her fierce determination to send money home, even though cash is always scarce. Her two salaries are both modest; Cliff's computer repair business had to close; and paying lawyers to regularize her immigration status strained their budget to the breaking point. "It's tough for my husband sometimes to understand my way of living," says Alice. "I can tell because of his upbringing, the American way. You work hard and your money is your money. It was tough to get Cliff to agree until I said, 'There's nothing that's going to stop me from helping those unfortunate people.'" Cliff was also paying child support to his former wife, and writing the checks made him angry until Alice told him, "These are your obligations; this is what you do for family." "I can tell how much he's changed," she jokes. "I tell him sometimes, 'I'm going to change you into a Rwandese.'"

Like most immigrants, Alice today is a creature of two cultures. Her Rwandese side keeps her tied to Mutara, to all the people who need her back home. So she sells shoes during the day and cleans church floors at night and doesn't get much fun out of life. This is a woman who had to take responsibility for three siblings at age thirteen, and she says, "You don't really miss what you never had." But her American side prods her to think big, get ahead, improve herself. "To be honest," she admits, "I'm not really content with my career right now." She always wanted to be a doctor, and while that goal faded long ago, she still hopes to go back to school, and earn a master's degree in health-care administration. And she still wants children of her own. "I don't know what the future holds for me, really," says Alice. "I just try to be better, try to do what's right. Day by day."

3.

Eddie Kamara Stanley, Marie Stanley, and Mabinty Kamara

SIERRA LEONE

I was assigned to cover the war areas and we fell into a rebel ambush. They pointed a gun for me, and then they shot, but it went into the other person's head, the person that was behind me.

When Eddie Kamara Stanley first arrived in the United States he was homeless. It was September 1995, and Stanley had fled the brutal civil war in the West African nation of Sierra Leone. He had no money, no job, no friends. A distant cousin arranged for him to be picked up at John F. Kennedy Airport and dropped off in New Brunswick, New Jersey, but after that he was on his own. "I went to a black man's house," he recalls. "I was sleeping in a house with broken windows and he was telling me I should pay, but I don't even have anything for the place, and he kicked me out. He drove me from the house. I don't have another place to go." One day, as he was wandering around town, he saw a Catholic church and went in. "I started going but I sit in the back of the church," says Stanley, who was born a Muslim. "I was not even baptized but I go to pray, because I believe the Lord has saved me."

Stanley was lucky. The church he picked, Sacred Heart, had a long tradition of welcoming outcasts. Its website features a "Prayer for Migrants and Refugees," which reads in part: "Lord Jesus, today you call us to welcome the members of God's family who come to our land to escape oppression, poverty, persecution, violence, and war." That certainly described Stanley, whose father and brother had been murdered by rebels six months before he started praying in a rear pew. Over time he met church officials, who helped get him through the winter, and on Easter Sunday he was baptized. That same day a retired couple, Joyce and Arthur Delaney, who had once lived in New Brunswick, decided "almost on a whim" to return to their old church for Easter services and sing with the choir. The Delaneys were up in the choir loft during Stanley's baptism, Joyce recalls, and another choir member said to her, "I think they're looking for a place for him to live." That day, the church bulletin had advertised for a family to take in Eddie for two or three weeks. So, when the Delaneys got home, Joyce turned to her husband and asked, "Are we going to give this guy a room or not?" Arthur agreed: "We had an empty nest and plenty of room. Before you knew it, two weeks turned into a year. It was just one of those things."

That year had some rough moments. "To be honest," says Arthur, "at times I was a little resentful" of Eddie's constant presence. But the family forged a deep bond with their houseguest that continues to this day. "The Delaneys are a very wonderful family," says Stanley. "They gave me an under-the-table job because while I was seeking asylum I was not allowed to work." The job was taking care of a family friend, a ninety-two-year-old man: "They were paying me four hundred dollars a week and they were letting me save this money; they were opening an account for me; even if you buy water they don't like that. They want to give you everything." Stanley had left a wife and two children back in Sierra Leone and the Delaneys "made my family call me collect and they paid the bills." They also helped him press his case for political asylum, return to school, and navigate New Jersey: "At times I'd get lost. I didn't know how to get back home, and Joyce would look out for me." When Eddie saw snow for the first time, he tried to wash it off the family car with a garden hose. And when he tried to buy his own car he was bilked by an unscrupulous dealer who took his paycheck but kept the vehicle. "I went in there screaming" at the dealer and demanding a refund, Joyce recalls, because Eddie was a "very gullible" customer who did not understand American business practices. "The culture from which he came was so different," she says, and he was too trusting of people. But his trust in the Delaneys was not misplaced. Eddie came to love Joyce's Italian cooking, especially spaghetti, and when he moved out, he asked her to write down all his favorite recipes. They stayed connected by more than pasta sauce, and in 1998, the Delaneys helped Eddie bring his family to America. A few years later, when the Stanleys produced a new daughter, they named her Joyce and asked their American friends to be her godparents. His experience with the Delaneys and Sacred Heart Church has deeply influenced Eddie's views toward race and he warns his children to resist any antiwhite sentiments they hear in the black community: "I always tell them, 'Don't judge anybody because of a person's color. You came here because of white people, you are fed because of white people, you went to school because of white people.'"

Eddie Stanley has walked a twisted and tangled path since that Easter Sunday in 1996, when the Delaneys witnessed his baptism from the choir loft. His polished brown head still looks like it's been carved from a piece of mahogany, but illness and anxiety have hollowed his cheeks and halted his step. He has earned several degrees but few paychecks in America and the family subsists mainly on the meager wages that his wife, Marie, earns as a nurse's aide. They've been evicted several times and their last house, in the suburbs south of Philadelphia, often lacks heat and hot water. The civil war in Sierra Leone got worse after Eddie fled and Marie's horrific experiences ("You see people killed every day; you wonder if you're going to live the next few seconds") have left her deeply traumatized. The couple does not sleep in the same room because Marie at times "just flips up," screaming in terror from her nightmares and jumping out of bed. Eddie, who was diagnosed with cancer in 2003 and has almost died twice, mordantly calls himself "a living ghost." Yet he remains, in Joyce Delaney's words, "a cockeyed optimist [who] really believes in the possibility of what we call the American dream." Eddie agrees: "Thank God I'm here today, in the civilized world. When people talk against America I don't feel happy. I would be the last person to criticize America, the last person."

A cold, shabby house outside of Philadelphia represents a vast improvement over where Eddie Kamara was born—a one-room hut made of palm leaves, built on a termite hill in the middle of a swamp five miles from the nearest village. Eddie's father had quarreled with his own family and moved to a remote region, deep in the African bush, where he tried to grow rice, maize, and beans on scrubland nobody else wanted. The Kamaras had nine children, and even after several left home or were adopted by relatives, that still left two adults and five kids to share the tiny space. At night, the family clustered around the only source of heat, an open fire in the center of the hut, and slept on mats woven from palm leaves. The Kamaras essentially existed outside the cash economy, consuming most of what they grew or caught and trading the surplus to other farmers. "Most of the selling is like a barter system," Eddie recalls. "If you have hens or chickens or whatever, when they grow up, if you want salt to put into the sauce, you send somebody to the market and exchange it." His mother owned exactly one garment, a simple piece of cloth she used to cover the bare necessities and carry the latest baby on her back. When I asked if he had been to school Eddie laughed at the question: "There was no way I would go to school because there is no money to pay [the fees]. We don't even think about that. I lived in an area where you would not know anything about school." Had he ever read a book as a boy or even seen one? "No. Read what? I could read my mind, I could interpret my mind, what I see, but not in an academic setting." In fact, most of Eddie's relatives have no idea when they were born, but he does: March 18, 1952. His mother remembers that she gave birth on the same day that the "paramount chief" for their tribal district was crowned: "That is the only thing that made me to track it; I went into the records. Other than that I'd have no way to know my birthday."

The Kamaras lived off the land. They fished in nearby streams using homemade nets woven out of fibers extracted from the stem of a palm leaf. They caught small game in primitive traps fashioned from sticks. As a boy Eddie joined a communal work gang, moving from farm to farm during the harvest season: "They only provide you food, they don't pay you for the labor." When I asked if the work was hard he lacked a frame of reference: "It's hard, it's hard. But you would not know it's hard because it's a traditional culture. It's only when I came outside, I begin to compare other jobs I had and I begin to realize it was something hard. It's something I have to do, so I would not know the difference." Did he feel hunger as a child? "It's hard to tell because I had nothing to compare it. I feel this is the way everybody is living." But now he is appalled at the waste he sees in the West: "The food that is dumped here, if you take it to where I come from, there would be no hunger." Until he arrived in America, "I didn't realize I had been living in miserable poverty." In Sierra Leone he had been making $22.50 a month, with fourteen people to feed, and yet "those who didn't have jobs saw me as a well-to-do person." So when he made $5.15 an hour at his first job here his reaction was, "Why should I go back?"

The Kamaras belonged to the Limba tribe. Their district was called

Tonka Limba and they spoke one of thirteen tribal dialects. The nation of Sierra Leone was a distant concept. Life was defined by tribal custom, not civil law. As a new year dawned, elders would sit around a large fire, "telling stories until midnight [about] animals interacting with human beings," and playing instruments made from the ubiquitous palm leaf. Then everyone was expected to plunge into an icy stream for a ritual bath: "The year's finished, the year is beginning, and they say you are cleaning yourself, but this is one thing I hate about my family setting. That's cold, a very cold time, but you can have no objection, you have to do it." Since few tribal members could read or write, customs and lessons were passed on through an oral tradition of song and story. Eddie recalls a verse about a wayward boy who ran into the forest and was eaten by animals disguised as human beings: "This is one way to tell kids to obey their parents." Even now, when he calls his mother back in Africa, he sings that song to her: "She's too old, she tends to forget my voice, but when I sing that song she remembers." He also sings a ditty he once made up, about a boy who has trouble opening his eyes in the morning and cannot find a place to urinate: "Any time she hears that she laughs and knows it's me. I'm the only one that sings that."

As Eddie sings those songs in the Limba language, and repeats the refrains of his childhood, his voice turns sweet and happy. But he recalls with horror other tribal customs, including one imposed on the parents of a deformed child. They are expected to take the infant to an old woman, a "soothsayer," who performs a ritual killing deep in the woods and buries the body in an unmarked grave. When the Limba see a crippled baby "they say this is a devil," says Eddie, and the soothsayer "will return that baby back to the devil; nobody will see that baby again. That's the practice in my country." Stanley is even more outraged at the "Bondo society," the secret and sacred rites that mark a young woman's coming of age. Induction means instruction in such topics as cooking, menstruation, and child rearing. But for the

Limba it also means genital mutilation, the surgical removal of the female sex organs: "They take the kids to the forest, to the bush, and when they slice they make a big noise—*whooo, whooo, whooo*—so nobody will hear the girls crying. That is what happens. They keep them there until they are healed, and during the process of healing, they take clay, they rub them with clay, and when they are healed they run from house to house saying, 'I am mature, I am a woman.'" No man is allowed to witness the ceremony or even talk about it: "In my country I cannot discuss that. You automatically offend every woman; it's taboo." But he stubbornly insisted that "my children would not go into that society," and his daughters avoided the surgery.

A chance meeting changed Eddie Kamara's life, but since time is an elastic concept in a world with no clocks or calendars, he is not quite sure when it occurred. He was probably in his late teens when a British surveyor named Joseph Stanley came through the district and his father met him in the bush. Stanley needed help carrying his equipment and young Eddie was assigned the job. The surveyor saw a spark in the lad, "and when we came to the township, to the village, where the paramount chief was, Mr. Stanley expressed his desire to help me go to school. He took care of everything, and the paramount chief put me in school through that Mr. Stanley." In his honor, Eddie took the surveyor's last name: "That is how I got the Stanley, because of that man being so helpful. We are all Kamaras. I am the only Stanley in the family." When I asked why the surveyor decided to help, Eddie had no clear answer: "I don't know what motivated him, to be honest." Perhaps he saw Eddie's father "struggling with a lot of kids." Or he wanted to "remove people from the bush or thought education was important for Africans." Whatever the reason, Eddie suddenly found himself in the first grade of the Bubuya District Council School, a mud brick building twelve miles—and an entire world—away from his family's hut.

The first problem was distance: the school was too far for Eddie to make the round-trip every day. So he stayed in the village and cut the commute to seven miles each way. "I have no shoes and the road is so hard," he recalls, so he would wrap palm leaves around his feet to ease the pain. The second problem was his age. When he showed an aptitude for school he was quickly advanced to the third grade, but when he proudly told his parents of his promotion, his father was furious with him: "He said I was lying. How can I go three classes ahead? I'll never forget that because he gave me a serious beating. I was trying to run, but he hit me on the back and I fell down. Then he stepped on my foot when I was trying to move. My mum started crying and went to her people to complain." The third problem was dress. Not only did he lack shoes, he really had only one garment, a simple loincloth: "It's like underwear but it's not underwear." He was not alone, however, and sometimes he and his mates would go to a stream, wash their loincloths, hang them on a bush, and wrestle naked until they were dry. The wealthier boys had longer pieces of fabric, which they could fold double over their backsides to cushion blows from the teachers: "If you misbehaved or did something wrong the teacher has to flog you; you could get wounds on your back." One particularly stressful exercise was called "hot mental." The teacher would rapidly toss out questions—the multiplication table was a favorite—and "if you can't answer you are in trouble, you have six lashes. I only realized beating and flogging is not good when I came here to the Western world."

Eddie liked school and did well. "My handwriting was good," he recalls, and other students started asking him to copy their homework. He learned to play soccer and joined the school team. He skipped more grades and when he sat for the high school entrance exams, "I came with flying colors, the best record. The people started knowing about me." But a year later he had to drop out. His benefactor, Joseph Stanley, was long gone and his father could not afford the school fees. The elder Kamara had only one way to obtain cash: borrow it from a lender, then pay the loan back when his rice crop was harvested. But when the crop failed to cover the fees, his father kept falling behind. "At times I cry when I think of him," says Stanley. "He spent a lot of his resources educating me." Even today, cash is very scarce back home, and when Eddie scrapes together a hundred dollars every three months to send to his mother, "she considers it a very big thing."

After dropping out, Eddie had trouble finding work: "People are saying I have knowledge, I have a brain, but I don't have anything to officially support my understanding." He met a man with connections at a teacher's college in Freetown, the country's capital, but his application was rejected: "You are a high school dropout; I feel that pain all the time." For a long time "I had no fixed abode, to be honest, I was like the tide," flowing from town to town when he could hitch a ride on the back of a passing truck. Finally he found a job with an agricultural development project sponsored by the European Union, but he quarreled with his bosses, who treated the local help badly: "I told them they have to give us some respect, they have to talk to us like human beings. We do the work and they get the praise." He switched to another development project, and one day he was leading a team of workers—seventeen of them packed into two Land Rovers—when he spotted a young woman at the side of road. She was clearly in pain from a bandaged finger: "I said to my driver, Ali, 'Stop, let's give this lady a ride.'" But there was a problem: the government was cracking down on the abuse of official vehicles and had set up checkpoints along the road. So at each stop Eddie introduced the young woman, whose name was Marie, as his wife. She got off near her home and the Land Rovers continued their journey. The project was based in a remote, swampy area of the country but on weekends, Eddie was allowed to return to Freetown. His contract provided for a hotel room, but Eddie stayed with a relative and sent the expense money home to his family: "I had never been in a hotel; it cost too much and I am poor. Why should I sleep in a hotel when my mum and my family are sleeping in the dirt?" He had not forgotten the girl with the bandaged finger, and one day he was talking to one of his bosses about her. It turned out the boss and the girl came from the same village. Eddie convinced the man to go back home and ask Marie if she'd marry the fellow who had given her a ride. No promises, the boss replied, "I cannot make any decisions for her," but I'll make your case. Marie was still a teenager, almost twenty years younger than Eddie, but she accepted: "He went and negotiated and brought Marie for me." The young couple had little money and no place to live together, so Marie stayed for a time with Eddie's mother in the bush. After the development project ended, he found occasional work as a freelance journalist, providing small news items and photos to the official government press agency, but the pay was unreliable: "You don't even set the price. If it is published they give you something." In the south of the country, meanwhile, civil war had been flaring for years, and in early 1995, the conflict consumed the Kamara family.

Eddie and Marie were living in the provincial capital of Kambia. Their first son, Edward, had just been born, joining his older sister Josephine. The rebels, known as the Revolutionary United Front (RUF), had been moving north, terrorizing villages along the way and forcibly recruiting new troops. The RUF had developed a reputation for "enormous cruelty," according to one history of the war, and Stanley describes their tactics: "They don't ask your consent, they force you to join them or they kill you. If you don't want to be killed you have to follow them." Early on the morning of January 25, the rebels abducted six Catholic nuns on the outskirts of Kambia and then moved into the town. The Stanleys heard a commotion in the street, and when they looked out, they saw a boy named Elijah, the son of the local butcher: "We heard this noise, we heard him screaming. He was cursing, he said, 'The bad people have come.'" Elijah probably saved their lives. Eddie and Marie gathered up the children and ran: "I was just trying to protect the young ones close to me. I was trying to escape, that's the best thing you can do. You don't even have second thoughts. Your first thought is to run away." Fear and frenzy gripped the town. Some people jumped into a river and drowned. Others were hacked to death by the rebels. The Stanleys managed to reach safety, fleeing northward to the border that Sierra Leone shares with Guinea. Eddie's father and brother did not make it. "They were brutally murdered," he says. "Their heads were chopped off." Were they deliberately targeted? No, Eddie responded, the killing "was indiscriminate." Several cousins and other relatives also died that day: "We don't know if they drowned or were abducted and later killed."

The family resettled in Freetown, where Eddie found steadier work with the government press agency. The country had long been run by the All People's Congress (APC), a party dominated by the Limba and other northern tribes, but a few years before the APC had been ousted in a coup led by southerners and the Limba were no longer in favor. Stanley says that "one way to punish me [for being a Limba] was to give me life-threatening assignments. I have no options, I have to live." Six months after his father's death the rebels were still terrorizing the countryside: "I was assigned to cover the war areas and we fell into a rebel ambush. They pointed a gun for me, and then they shot, but it went into the other person's head, the person that was behind me." That bullet sliced through Eddie's finger: "There was no escape. I was captured and brutally beaten with gun butts." He managed to produce a press card issued by UCIP, a French acronym for the International Catholic Union of the Press, "and this is the card that saved me." Instead of giving him a death sentence the rebels gave him an interview: "They told me their story, they told me a version of why they were fighting. I should tell the world why they are fighting." Then they released him with a dark warning: "They would kill any other journalists that they met if I didn't publish the story."

Returning to Freetown, he sought help from the United Nations mission "but they said they couldn't do anything; they encouraged me to go back to my office." When he briefed his bosses at the press agency, "They said I'm a rebel collaborator. The word *collaborator* in Sierra Leone is tantamount to death without trial. I was warned I'm not supposed to write anything critical of the government, or anything favorable to the rebels, or they were going to get charges against me for that. There's no true independent journalism in that part of the world. If you want to be objective you find yourself in trouble. Journalists are being killed, or abducted, they would disappear. That is the penalty they would pay for being critical of the government." Eddie had become "a target on both sides." The government resented his talking to the rebels; the rebels were angry that he had not published their manifesto. One night in early September a friendly police officer who had been watching his house warned him "there were suspicious people in front." He escaped out the back, climbed a fence, "and went to the nearest police station." Officers returned to his house and captured the intruders, who soon confessed. They were rebel agents who had been "sent by their commander to get me dead or alive." Hours later Eddie watched as the police made the rebels dig their own graves and then shot them in the head. He knew he had to leave the country. He had no money for a plane ticket, but he'd been doing some freelance public relations work for Sabena, the Belgian airline, and he went there for help. The local manager "saved me a lot" by issuing a ticket good for a year. Eddie was still under police surveillance but he managed to slip away from his watchers, take a ferry to the airport, and board a plane for Brussels. Marie had been sleeping in another house on the night of the rebel foray and had no idea where he was. They would not see each other again for more than two years.

He had no documents, no passport or visa, and was forced to stay in the Brussels airport for two days. After obtaining papers Stanley traveled to the Austrian city of Graz, where he explained his story at a conference sponsored by UCIP. Then he took a train to Vienna but it was a "very uncomfortable" journey: "Wherever I went to sit, people got up. In Austria it's very different to see a black person. I have nobody to talk to, nobody understands." Once in Vienna he had only enough money to buy four small loaves of bread and a few oranges: "I eat the whole thing, even the skin, because I need to fill my stomach. I went from street to street. I could not speak the language. My God that was terrible for me. I was running out of everything." Finally an Austrian journalist put him in touch with a group of nuns who took him in. After six weeks he called Marie back in Sierra Leone, and she was furious with him: "The first thing she say is, 'Why you do this to me? You didn't even tell me!'" After he disappeared, Marie explained, she had gone to the ministry to collect his back wages but news had already spread that he was a fugitive in Europe and had spoken out publicly at the conference in Austria. "They refused to give her the money," he said. "They told her, 'Your husband has done things against the government.' An officer kicked her and beat her." Marie urged him to call a friend in the ministry and find out if it was safe to return: "She give me a number to call, so when I call he say, 'You're in trouble. It's better you stay, don't come. If you come here they're going to kill you, or you're going to be abducted and abandoned in the bush. The government is very angry about what you did.'"

At that point Stanley decided to seek asylum outside his home country. The nuns urged him to stay in Austria but he preferred America: "I believe America is the best. It's the nation of nations. You can see every nation in America. You can see everyone." When I asked how he had formed that impression, he said that while he was growing up, the left-leaning government in Freetown had ties with communist countries such as Russia and Cuba: "So most of the stories we hear come from those parts of the world; we don't hear much about America." And since Sierra Leone had once been a British colony, many of his countrymen yearned to move to London. But "by chance," Eddie had met a Peace Corps volunteer "who had told me a lot about America. [She said] there are a lot of opportunities in this country. It's difficult to come here but if somebody comes here you have many chances for progress." The American embassy in Vienna granted him a visitor's visa and said, make your case for asylum when you get to the United States. Still lacking money for a ticket, he went back to Sabena: "The first thing they said was, 'You make too many demands.'" But they offered him a deal: report here every day and if a seat opens up on a plane to America you can have it. Eventually one did, starting him on the journey that led to the rear pew at Sacred Heart and the spare bedroom at the Delaneys'.

His first problem in America was asylum. The Committee to Protect Journalists, based in New York, "joined hands" with human rights lawyers and Catholic activists to press his request. At first Stanley was turned down because Washington was not convinced that returning home would place him in danger. He filed an appeal, which was still pending when yet another coup deposed the government back in Freetown. "They called me over the phone and granted me asylum," he recalls. "They had refused at first but everything I told them was fact." Then the high school dropout decided to get more education. Stanley says it was Arthur Delaney's idea: "He say, 'Eddie, you have to go to school.'" But Delaney says, "Eddie's a professional student, he loves being a student." He attended an adult school in Plainfield, New Jersey, and took the GED (General Educational Development) test. A passing grade would have earned him the equivalent of a high school degree but Eddie failed the first time; his math score was too low. After finally qualifying for a GED he took classes at several local colleges and then applied to Rutgers, the state university, but failed the admission test. "I told them my story," he recalls. "I'm traumatized" by my experiences back home, "I have this problem, I can't concentrate. So they said okay. They made me repeat the entrance exam and I passed." Stanley concedes that Rutgers cut him a break: "I think they accepted me on the basis of something I don't even support, affirmative action. Even now I don't support that. That is reverse discrimination. People should not be accepted because of their color but because of what they are capable of doing."

Eddie struggled to get through school: "At my age, some people say you can't teach an old dog new tricks. I laugh, it is not one hundred percent true, but it is true enough. It is for me. My brain does not click like a clock. I'm carried away with so many problems, too many things to think about." He kept at it, however. He had not even seen a book until his late teens, but in May 2003 he earned his degree in labor relations from the Rutgers school of management.

After Eddie fled Sierra Leone, Marie's situation had deteriorated sharply. The civil war kept escalating and she reached a breaking point: "I have people who were checking on my house every day. They say they were going to arrest me. I have to escape. My God, it was not easy. People were dying; we crossed dead people on the streets. You see them, they put them on the truck, you see the blood flowing in the street. Our house was a target, they started shooting, we were so lucky. I was sitting there with my brother-in-law. He just got up, and a stray bullet fell right there. He would have been killed." After that incident, her brother-in-law urged her to flee: "When I was escaping he gave me some money. He said, 'You know what, Marie, I have my family here. I can't handle all of you guys; you need to leave this place.'" She packed up her two children and headed for the border with Guinea, where refugee camps had been established under international supervision: "Oh my God, the rebels were in the streets checking people. I wear tight pants to avoid the rape. They were harassing people; they would pull you out from the truck and beat you." A soldier hit her on the foot with a grenade launcher: "My foot was so swelling, but I just shut my mouth. I was waiting for him to release us; they kept us there for so many hours; we were standing there waiting. If they catch people they amputate their hands, they don't even care."

The Stanleys described to me acts of unspeakable horror. Their stories seemed even more surreal because they spoke while driving through a placid American suburb to pick up their kids from school. In one case, a thirteen-year-old boy was ordered by rebels to have sex with his mother. When he refused, says Marie, "They slaughter him. They didn't even use a gun. They use a knife; they start cutting him from the back, from the spine. They not use a sharp knife, they use a dull knife so he will take a long time to die." The rebels would seize a pregnant woman and bet whether she was carrying a boy or a girl. Then they would slice open her womb to see who was right. "I saw it," she says. "They'd use a knife and cut the pregnant woman and yell, 'I won, I won.'" Cannibalism was common: "They would take the dead baby and fry it like a meatball. They would kill people and take their insides and fry them and eat them." The mortuaries were so full "they don't have any more space. There would be like high piles of dead people. They would call everybody to go look for your own person. They kill everybody. They don't care."

Even the survivors were indelibly marked. The rebels would seize a victim and ask, "Short sleeve or long sleeve?" If he said short they would hack off his arm at the shoulder; if he said long, they'd sever his hand at the wrist. Rape was a constant danger and Marie says, "I was lucky because when they capture me, they don't have sex with me." Her "tight pants" made an attack more difficult. She also told the soldiers "Don't rape me, I have that sickness," meaning HIV/AIDS. Adds Eddie: "That's what saved her from being raped." His sister was not saved. She was captured by rebels and kept naked for days so that any soldier could easily assault her at any time. "She's almost dead," Stanley says now. "She cannot walk straight again; she does not see any man as anything again. She has no feeling." After his sister was finally released she went to see her mother, "but she could not stay home; she was very disrupted. Rape is seen as something sinful. You don't want anybody to see you because you feel you've been molested." His sister moved upland, to a remote corner of the bush, and the Kamara family "made a funeral for her. We made funerals for a lot of our people." Many years later, the scars and the shame of those days remain raw. Marie: "We don't tell people what happened, we don't tell everything." Eddie: "These are not stories, this is reality. Some things I have never said because I'm wondering how people will take a look at me." Marie: "I don't talk much about it, what I went through in Freetown. Even when I came here, I didn't tell my husband much of this stuff." Eddie: "We have lived a terrible life. When they tell me I'm sick and dying, I didn't take that as anything, because what I have undergone is more than the death that is threatening me."

Marie and the two kids made their way to the camps on the Guinea border but she never felt safe: "We were always threatened, we didn't stay too long in one place, the rebels were always around." The couple "lost communication for some time." Eddie finally tracked down his family with help from the Red Cross and Catholic relief workers and filed an asylum request on their behalf. "They granted my family asylum and I raised money" to help bring them to America, he said. The Delaneys and other families at Sacred Heart chipped in. In addition to his job as a caretaker, Eddie drove a limousine. The pay was only six dollars an hour, but when one of his customers heard his story, he gave him a five-hundred-dollar tip. The family was finally reunited in 1998 and Eddie started saving to sponsor other refugees. Joyce Delaney remembers visiting the Stanley household on the day her godchild was baptized: "The house was overflowing with people, mainly young people he brought here, children of relatives and friends. He wanted to get them out of that place and give them a chance." Adds Stanley: "The good side of the war is that it brought a lot of people to the Western world."

One of his favorites is his niece, Mabinty Kamara, his younger brother's child. She was living with her aunt and grandmother in January 1999 when shooting broke out early one morning. Everyone raced for the woods but Mabinty stayed behind to go to the bathroom. In an interview with her school paper at Northeast High in Philadelphia she told the story: "When I came out they had left me. I was so scared. I just stood there, in the middle of the street screaming. There was nothing around me to hide behind, so I just stood there screaming and crying. I was only eleven." Eventually someone took her to her aunt, who promptly slapped her across the face for getting separated. "I could have died," she recalls. "I just heard bullets all around." The Stanleys are raising Mabinty and call her their adopted child. "I had to claim her," says Eddie. "That's the only way I could help her to come to this country." Once she arrived, she was stunned by the sight of so many trees: "I wanted to cut them down and sell them because they are worth so much. There are no trees in Sierra Leone because you cut them down and sell them for firewood. And they're expensive." Mabinty has adjusted quickly to America. Her e-mail address is "Coolcat Mimi," and she plays doubles on the school's championship tennis team. She's also a good student and says, "I just like school. I like to learn." The other Stanley kids don't do as well "because they want to come home and play games on the computer, and I'm like, 'I have to type a report.'" She quotes Eddie as saying, "I'm going to focus on Mabinty because she's serious." After the family moved south of the city, she decided to stay at Northeast, and her daily commute requires several trains and buses each way. But then her uncle walked seven miles in bare feet over rough roads to get to school.

The Stanleys have disdain for some fellow immigrants, particularly those not willing to work hard. Marie tells this story: "One day I was working and I meet a black woman from Africa. She said, 'You come here from Africa; there's free money here.' I told her, 'There's no free money here, you know that. You see me here every day. I came here since 1998 and I work every day. I don't get free money.'" More troubling were several young men from Sierra Leone whom the Stanleys sponsored. Eddie is convinced they "started sexually molesting my children . . . and then they became my enemy." The abusers

were caught "red-handed," he insists, but authorities declined to pros-
ecute. The experience dimmed his enthusiasm for America: "The legal
system in the U.S. is very appalling."

His encounter with this country's medical system has been more
positive. In November 2003, not long after receiving his degree, he
was teaching a special education class in New Brunswick and suffered
a "serious attack." The diagnosis was terminal cancer of the stomach
and esophagus. When a priest came to his hospital room to adminis-
ter Last Rites he relates his reaction: "There is an error somewhere.
The Lord is not ready for me yet! I'm not going to accept it. You can
pray for me if you want but I'm not going to accept it." He would not
accept the diagnosis because he worries so much about his children:
"I think, what will be the fate of my children after me? This is why I
want to live a little bit longer. When I die, who will be able to help my
children stand by themselves? They need somebody to be there. At
times I get carried away; I put a lot of pressure on them for education.
I tell them why it's so important for them to learn." His condition
was so grave that one surgeon declined to operate, saying it was hopeless. Another agreed to perform the surgery and removed his entire
stomach and parts of other organs. He was cancer free for several
years until a tumor reappeared on his liver. Experimental medication
originally designed to treat leukemia has kept him alive, but pain
and fatigue have sapped his ability to hold down a steady job. He's
also caught in an odd trap. Because of his college degree he considers
many blue-collar jobs beneath him. But he's not really competitive for
white-collar jobs in, say, counseling or management. And he lacks the
proper courses to be certified as a teacher. "I haven't been able to get a
job," he told me. "That is the problem."

So he fills his time cooking meals, washing clothes, and driving
the kids to school. Marie supports the family and the Stanleys "have
never had real money," says Arthur Delaney. "They have a major
minus cash flow." Marie explains: "I am trying to look for something

else, but it's not easy. I was trying to go to school but I have all these kids. I have to pay babysitters, and it's hard to sit in class. I've got too much on my brain." Ten years after leaving Africa she remains edgy and nervous. She keeps a bag packed at all times, a "paranoid" reaction, in Eddie's words, to the days when she lived in constant fear of a rebel attack. "I just can't think about what happened back home," she says. "That's why you see me with a bag, because of the war. We always worry." At times she comes home from work and cannot face her family: "Sometimes I go to my room and lock myself in. It's so noisy here."

Eddie Stanley looks back on his journey and says, "I have not seen a country with more generosity than America." But he and Marie cannot put the past completely behind them: "We don't take things like many other people. The war has destroyed us—emotionally, physically, and financially." Every day is a struggle: to pay bills, find work, stay healthy, keep their kids in school, cope with the nightmares that will not die. "I always tell people," says Eddie, "I did not come to America on a pleasure trip."

Part II

THE
INTERNATIONAL
ENTREPRENEURS

For many immigrants, starting a small business has long been the best way to enter the economy. They raise a bit of capital from family or friends and pour their drive and determination into building something they own themselves. As a child in Bayonne, New Jersey, I could walk to Levine's fish market, Irv's candy store, Judicke's bakery, and a dozen other shops run by immigrant families. My friends' parents ran Kavula's bar, Wigdor's jewelers, and Cherow's hardware. The Petridis family sold hot dogs from a truck parked next to the DeWitt Theater on Friday and Saturday nights. And that tradition holds today. My local cleaners in suburban Washington was just bought by a Chinese family that barely speaks English. My bagel place is owned by a Nigerian. My favorite restaurant is run by an immigrant from Italy.

Some immigrants, however, are able to think beyond bars and bagels and take advantage of the global marketplace. It's a marketplace where new ideas matter more than old families, and the information revolution has been fueled by immigrants like Moscow-born Sergey Brin, who co-founded Google, and Andy Grove, the Hungarian transplant who built the giant chipmaker Intel. Moreover, many newcomers are well positioned to conduct business abroad; their knowledge of foreign languages and customs enables them to open doors and close deals a lot faster than their native-born rivals. Researcher Vivek Wadhwa documented the economic contributions of contemporary immigrants in the *Washington Post*: "Almost 25 percent of all

international patent applications filed from the United States in 2006
named foreign nationals as inventors. Immigrants founded a quarter
of all U.S. engineering and technology companies started between
1995 and 2005, including half of those in Silicon Valley. In 2005
alone, immigrants' businesses generated $52 billion in sales and em-
ployed 450,000 workers." One alarming trend: some of these entrepreneurs are returning home, particularly to China and India, where
booming economies are creating new opportunities just as America's
shortsighted immigration policies are making it more difficult for
immigrants to remain here. In an article for *Reason* magazine called
"Goodbye Chang, So Long Singh," Shikha Dalmia wrote: "They
can live the American Dream in their own country close to family
and friends."

Asis Banerjie exemplifies the entrepreneurs who are living and
working in a world where national borders are quickly disappearing.
He came to America as a graduate student in chemistry and returned
to India for fourteen years before moving back to a suburb of Cleveland. His factories make high-tech plastics in Medina, Ohio, and
Chennai, India, and he has joint ventures with companies in Japan,
Korea, and China. He describes himself as a "global citizen with an
address in Medina." But his real home might well be the first-class
lounge in a major airport as he does business around the world on
his iPhone and BlackBerry while waiting to board the next flight for
Seoul or Shanghai.

Tom Chan also came to America for an education. After he failed
the college entrance exams in Hong Kong, his father sent him to live
with an uncle in Oakland, California. He scrubbed pots in an Italian
restaurant to finance his tuition, and after earning a degree in accounting he followed a time-honored path, starting a small business
geared toward fellow immigrants. His first client was a restaurant in
San Francisco's Chinatown, but he had bigger dreams. As the Chinese economy opened to Westerners, Chan knew the right angles

and made the right connections, and today he is a major importer of fireworks made in China, the country his parents had fled in terror more than sixty years ago. But while the Chans are New World entrepreneurs, they bring Old World values to their business. When Tom faced a health issue and asked his son Herbert to leave his banking job and join the family firm, the young man never hesitated: "The way my brother and I were brought up, it's family first, no questions asked. We know what we have to do."

4

Wai Hung (Thomas) Chan and Kong Kuk (Maggie) Wong Chan

CHINA, HONG KONG

"PYROCPA" (license plate of Thomas Chan, formerly an accountant who now imports fireworks from China)

Tom Chan's parents left China in 1945, during the civil war that led to the communist takeover of their country four years later. "They were afraid of communist rule," he says, "because they had heard a lot of bad things about the communists." The Chans settled in Hong Kong with their two daughters and had three more children, including Tom, the youngest, born in 1954. When he was nineteen, he moved to California for college, majored in accounting, married another immigrant from Hong Kong, and made a modest living auditing the books of small businesses in San Francisco's Chinatown. Then one of those clients came to him with a deal: a contact in the Chinese fireworks industry wanted to enter the American market. Could Tom help him find customers? Bored by his job, and frustrated by his prospects, Tom eagerly accepted: "Chinese people are entrepreneurs. Even before the communists took over China, Chinese people are mostly doing business themselves; they're always thinking about how to make money. After Nixon went to China in the seventies, and Deng Xiaoping became the leader, he's really trying to open up China to the rest of the world and that created a lot of openings for people with ties to China. That's really how I started."

In 1990 Tom Chan made his first trip to China. His destination was Liuyang, a city in the mountainous Hunan Province that has been manufacturing fireworks for centuries. As Tom recalls, the trip "was not a pleasant experience." At the time, state-owned trading companies still controlled the economy and the system was both corrupt and confusing. "Our order was not very big and the trading company didn't give us the time of day," he says. Chan had grown up speaking Cantonese but the local language was Mandarin and he had trouble communicating. Liuyang was still very poor, energy supplies were unreliable, and the city lights "were very dim, very distressing." Since the city lacked any decent hotels, business travelers were forced to stay in the provincial capital of Changsha, one of China's hottest cities, where temperatures regularly topped 100 degrees. The trip to Liuyang took more than three hours each way over bad roads, and the business day often ended at two in the morning—in bug-infested rooms that lacked basic amenities such as toilet paper. That first trip left Tom thinking his parents "were correct to flee the country" when they did. "I'm asking myself, what am I doing here? I was just like a foreigner, even though I'm Chinese."

Today, Tom Chan no longer feels like a foreigner in China. As capitalism replaced the old communist system, his business flourished. He spends about two weeks a month in Liuyang, and is often joined by his son Herbert, now second in command at United Pyrotechnics, the family company. The Chans maintain an office with twenty employees in Liuyang, and father and son now both speak passable Mandarin. The city boasts a new hotel, the Grand Sun, and Tom is such a frequent guest the management saves him the same room, 1211. In fact his commute is so routine that it's almost like driving to China-town from the suburbs: a late-morning flight on United Airlines from San Francisco to Beijing, which arrives midafternoon the next day (his frequent-flyer account is approaching two million miles). If the plane is on time he can catch a connection to Changsha a few hours later. The road from the airport to Liuyang is much improved and after a forty-minute drive Tom can be sleeping in room 1211 by 9 P.M. Oc-casionally he has to go through Hong Kong on business but he doesn't like to: "For some reason, in Hong Kong I can't sleep at night."

In the old China, the Chan family enjoyed a privileged life. Tom's grandparents "had some money and some land" in Guangdong Prov-ince, a wealthy coastal region not far from Hong Kong, and Tom's father "really didn't have to work" as a young man. That changed quickly as the communists advanced. As Tom's sister tells the story, the family's escape was "a very horrible trip" with "nothing to eat." Once he arrived in Hong Kong, Tom's father found work with the British colonial authority as a prison guard: "It's a steady job and they provide you housing. He kind of settled down like that."

The pay was modest, however, and the elder Chan gambled part of it away playing mah-jongg, a game that resembles gin rummy but uses tiles instead of cards. "Chinese are notorious gamblers," says Tom. "Look at the casinos in Macao [an island long controlled by the Portuguese that has now reverted to China]. All the gamblers are from mainland China or Hong Kong." His memories of his father are tepid at best: "We don't talk that much. My father was never really home, he was at work or playing mah-jongg. We were not that close." But Tom's father did have a brother in California, a man who had immigrated many years before to work on the railroads and wound up running a laundry. That brother, Tom's uncle, would occasionally send money back to his family, usually during the New Year's holiday, and Tom recalls that the gifts "were a big thing to my father." They would prove to be a "big thing" to Tom as well.

As a boy he was baptized Catholic and sent to schools run by Catholic missionaries: "Even my name, Thomas, is given to me by the Catholic Church," although he never used it until he came to America. Growing up he loved soccer and loathed school and "never in my mind did I think I would leave Hong Kong." But life in the colony was a cutthroat existence and the elder Chan worried that his son was too timorous to succeed: "There are just too many people in Hong Kong, so they have to figure out who is better and who is not better. They have a kind of class system, and they group the better ones into a better class." The key test was for higher education. If you made it into the British university you'd likely get a government job "and your life was kind of set." But Tom failed the entrance exam: "I really wasn't up to taking the test; I knew at the time I wasn't good enough. I wasn't motivated." So the elder Chan asked his brother in California for help, the brother who had prospered enough to send money home at New Year's: "I think in my father's mind my future in Hong Kong was very limited. Without a university degree it was hard to make a living, and around that time everything in Hong Kong started to be very expensive. The way he thought was, I have a much better future if I come to America and study. I think that's how he approached my uncle."

The uncle agreed. He lived in Oakland, across the bay from San Francisco, and suggested that Tom apply to Merritt College, a community school known for welcoming immigrants. The paperwork took a year and Tom, now out of high school, filled the time in a menial job at a company that imported canned meat from Sweden. He still wasn't very excited about moving to a new country: "If my father

tells me to come then I come here—that's really the main thrust of it."
When I asked what he knew about America he answered: "Nothing,
nothing. I have no idea what I'm coming into, I really don't." After
Merritt accepted him, his father bought his ticket—a cheap one, with
many connecting flights. So he arrived in the middle of the night, to
be greeted by relatives he'd never met: "I think they recognized me
from my picture; my father must have sent them a picture."

His aunt and uncle lived in a two-bedroom apartment, and one
of his cousins was still at home, so Tom slept on a sofa in the living
room: "It's a strange feeling and an empty feeling. You really feel kind
of lonely and you're by yourself and you're living with people you
don't know. It's not really comfortable." Since Tom didn't know the
neighborhood, he seldom left the apartment, except for occasional
shopping trips with his relatives: "I'm not an outgoing person who
talks a lot; a lot of time I'd just sit there with them." But he did learn
something about America: "I watched a lot of football at that time.
My uncle was a big fan" of the Oakland Raiders.

Once classes started he found college confusing. Under the British
system back in Hong Kong, students were generally told what to take,
so Tom was unprepared for the choices he faced at Merritt: "When I
came to America I had no idea I had to pick classes myself. I had a
terrible time my first few days because I didn't know what classes to
pick. I talked to other people from Hong Kong and they knew—but
I didn't." Tom's uncle paid his first-year tuition bill of eight hundred
dollars, but the newcomer still had to work to support himself. Since
he didn't have much time to study he "just picked the easy subjects"
where he could get good grades with little effort. He quickly found
a job, stocking shelves and delivering orders for a grocery store in
Oakland's Chinatown, but the pay was "really pitiful," and he soon
decamped for a chance to wash dishes at an Italian restaurant called
Vince's. The pay was better, $1.25 an hour, and it came with an un-

usual perk: Vince's was a favorite hangout of the Raiders' coach, John Madden, and the team owner, Al Davis. Tom recalls the scene he saw from the kitchen: "Every time [Davis] got there, the manager would put a phone on his table." Cleaning plates wasn't so bad but Tom despised one job, scouring out the pots used to make soup: "They've got all kinds of things on the bottom, and you actually have to scrape them." Often he had to use a putty knife to finish the job: "That's really the thing I hated the most."

Tom worked seven days a week, and after morning classes at Merritt he'd leave campus: "I was a very strange person. I don't talk much, I don't socialize much. I went to class and after lunch, then I'm gone, I'd disappear." But he wasn't entirely invisible. The Chinese students would sit together in the cafeteria, and one of them, Maggie Wong, noticed the shy boy who seldom spoke. Maggie's parents were also refugees from mainland China who had resettled in Hong Kong after the communist triumph. Her father, an esteemed carver of Buddhist figures, first came to California to work on a temple complex then under construction in the city of Ukiah. The elder Wong kept his workshop in Hong Kong but wanted his family to stay in America, away from the evil influences of that glitzy Asian boomtown. I had dinner one night with Tom and Maggie at their favorite restaurant in San Francisco's Chinatown, and she told me: "My father wanted my older brother to start over away from his friends." He did, eventually opening a jewelry store that led to a cluster of family-owned outlets. Arthur, the Chans' younger son, notes the irony: his uncles, sons of a man noted for crafting religious icons, ended up selling jewelry, "the antithesis of the Buddhist philosophy" of simplicity and spirituality.

Maggie's first impression of Tom was hardly positive: "He seemed like an arrogant person. He wouldn't socialize. We didn't know he had to get to work." But gradually they started spending time together.

"He was a very quiet person," says Maggie. "I didn't have to worry about working, and I admired the fact that he supported himself." Their dates were simple: "We'd go to the library; he couldn't afford to take me anyplace. He'd still be studying and I would doze off." Tom breaks in with a laugh: "That shows how attractive I am, right?" At Vince's he gradually moved up to busboy and then car parker, but when he finally managed to take Maggie out for a meal it didn't go well: "I took her to Denny's and she hated American food. I didn't know it at that time." He also bought a cheap used car and Maggie recalls: "He was so proud, he wanted to show off his new car, and he paid for the gas with all the dimes and nickels he had collected as tips."

After two years at Merritt, Tom went on to California State University, Hayward, a short drive south of Oakland, and studied accounting. He thought the skill would be "more practical" than marketing or business management and that he'd be able to find a job if he stayed in America. Meanwhile he left Vince's and went to work for FedEx at the Oakland airport, processing invoices. The pay was better, there were no soup pots to scrape, and he could occasionally see Maggie after leaving work at eight or nine in the evening. Tom still lived with his aunt and uncle so the young couple had little privacy: "I can't afford to move out and they didn't ask me to move out." There was talk of marriage but Maggie's parents were reluctant: "At first my parents didn't like him that much. They were wealthy and he wasn't. They told me I should have a better choice." Eventually the Wongs came around, but just barely. During Tom's senior year at Hayward, the couple drove to Reno, Nevada, one weekend: "We didn't have a wedding. We just registered. Her father came with us." The Wongs owned a small apartment building on Grant Avenue, in the heart of Chinatown, and let the youngsters use one of the units. Since Maggie had a green card, making her a permanent resident, her new husband qualified for one as well. "After we got married I probably made up my mind to stay here," Tom remembers. He never even bothered to tell his parents in Hong Kong: "I don't talk to them that much." After graduation he joined a small accounting firm in Chinatown and started building a new life in America.

The firm's specialty was doing audits for government agencies and Tom hated the work: "Auditing to me is a waste of time. You can't find anything wrong with the books unless they're stupid enough to let you find it, especially with government contracts. It's a really boring job." Two years later he went out on his own with two partners: "It was a big risk because we had no clients; we were trying to do our own thing." A new restaurant in Chinatown finally hired them, and "that place provided the starting point for us." But still, clients were "hard to come by," as Tom explained: "At that time you were not allowed to advertise, and people don't change accountants that often. Once you use an accountant—unless he's negligent or doesn't care about you—you tend to stick with the same one year after year. They know your thinking, and your books. We never made a lot of money with accounting. It just provided us with enough money to pay our mortgage."

That mortgage was on a small house in San Leandro, a working-class community near Oakland. The elder Wongs had given the couple five thousand dollars for a down payment but they were still struggling financially and looking for new sources of income. One of Tom's accounting clients was a Swedish bakery in downtown San Francisco and when the owner retired, the Chans bought the business. It was a backbreaking routine. Tom and Maggie would get up at four-thirty, sometimes stopping at a produce market on the way in to buy lettuce and tomatoes for sandwiches the bakery sold at lunchtime. "In the winter it was pretty bad," he remembers. "You really didn't want to get up at four-thirty; it was pretty cold." But as Tom put it, Chinese people "are always thinking about how to make money," and this was their chance. The Chans would arrive at about five-thirty (the bakers, who were all Chinese, started several hours earlier) and get the shop ready for a seven o'clock opening. Business was brisk—the homemade Danish pastries were a hot item—but profit margins were thin. A coffee and pastry sold for $1.35, "and when we tried to raise the price ten cents everybody started screaming." Once they got to the shop, Tom didn't do much ("I would sit there and wait for the Danish to come down. I still kind of miss it.") and at nine he would leave for his accounting office. Maggie manned the sales counter and Tom admits, "She works harder than me. It's probably in her family blood; her whole family works very hard." After the morning rush, Maggie would leave at ten and go to her brother's jewelry store. Often the Chans didn't return home till six-thirty or seven at night, just your typical fourteen-hour workday. As their son Herbert sums up the family philosophy: "It's work first, play second. If there's time."

The Chans closed the bakery when the rent tripled and bought a coffee shop in Berkeley but "it didn't go well," says Tom. The bakery had a stable staff of experienced workers who turned out the same recipes every day. The coffee shop kept losing cooks and driving the Chans crazy: "The restaurant business is tough. It's the most difficult business, unless you know how to cook. If you don't know how to cook you're at the mercy of your cooks. If they walk you're dead." The Chans abandoned the coffee shop and Tom looked around for a new business opportunity: "I always had something going on. I was trying to find some way to make some money."

At that point, "a very strange thing" happened. One of Tom's accounting clients imported goose down from China, which was used to fill pillows and comforters. Most of the down came from Hunan Province, so the businessman had been traveling there for years and had "very good relationships" with local traders. And it was this fellow who brought Tom into the fireworks business. "I talk to him a lot," Tom recalls, "and he knows I always want to do other things. So he asked me to explore what I could do." I asked Tom if he knew anything about fireworks and he answered frankly, "No, I didn't even know how they work." But that did not stop him. His entrepreneurial instincts kicked in. He did some research, found a trade association devoted to fireworks, joined up, and went to their convention in New Orleans. But the man who disappeared from the cafeteria at Merritt College and seldom socialized with other Chinese students was not exactly a natural gladhander: "It was such a boring trip. I didn't know anybody. I didn't know who to approach." Eventually Tom engineered his first deal and it was a disaster. He imported a load of fireworks for the Lummi Indian reservation in Washington (reservations are the biggest retail market in the country because local laws don't apply), "but we didn't know the business and we didn't know what they were looking for." Much of the inventory went unsold and Tom lost three hundred thousand dollars: "It was a very expensive lesson. We really didn't think the whole thing through. We figured we could sell everything we brought in. We never thought, what if the product you brought in is not right?"

Then he caught a break. At the industry convention the next year he met a man named David Burda, whose family owned Phantom Fireworks, a company based in Youngstown, Ohio. "They stayed in the bar all the time," Tom remembers, "so I stayed in the bar drinking beer with them." Looking back on his meeting with Burda, Chan says, "I don't know why he gave me a chance. He and I just clicked. It's very strange: he doesn't have to give me a chance, but he's helping me tremendously." Burda helped in two ways: he gave Chan an order from Phantom, but more important, he told Chan the exact price his company was willing to pay. And that information gave Chan an edge in negotiating with the traders back in China. "Without that information there's no way I could get into the business; it was very valuable information," he remembers. If he didn't know Phantom's bottom line he would be at the mercy of the Chinese sellers: "If you don't know them, and you ask for a quote, they will jack it up two or three times. They're not looking for a long-term relationship, they're looking at how much we can make from this deal."

That meeting with Burda led to Tom's first trip to Liuyang, and even though it was a dispiriting journey, it was a productive one. Most American retailers such as Phantom used brokers based in Hong Kong, and Tom was able to offer a different service: "Our selling point is, we're in the States; you don't have to wait for nighttime to call Hong Kong and talk. You can call us in the States during business hours. Then we can solve the problem for you at night, when you're sleeping, and then we report back to you in the morning." But more than convenience, Chan was selling trust. China was then, and in many ways still is, a free fire zone when it comes to commerce. There's no such thing as a legal code, says Tom, so contracts can seldom be enforced in the courts. Personal relationships are everything, and over the next few years he built up his contacts on both sides: sellers in China and buyers in America. "If you want to buy things from China you have to be careful," he says. "Which source is more reputable? More reliable? Which one gives you the product you want?" Gradually Tom became an expert in answering those questions, and by 1995, five years after his beers with Burda, he signed up his biggest client yet, Ingram Enterprises, a major retailer based in Missouri. "After that we really took off," he says. "It took many years to recoup the money we had lost—we learned our lessons the hard way—but after that everything ran pretty smooth."

The fireworks business has changed dramatically since then. The state-run companies that once controlled the trade have disappeared, and Tom and Herb now deal directly with the factories, about 650 of them, located in Liuyang. Their office there is constantly looking for new suppliers and testing new products, and while consumer demand remains strong, the industry faces many challenges. Making fireworks is a dirty and dangerous job, and with garment and bio-tech factories springing up in Liuyang, finding workers is a grow-ing problem. "Our industry is kind of fading," says Tom. "We're at a crossroads." Pricing is also a problem. Titanium produces the gold color in fireworks displays, copper oxide creates a blue effect, and worldwide demand for these minerals has quadrupled their cost. Retail prices are up 25 percent and Tom says that "if we keep raising prices we don't know if the consumer will continue to buy." The in-dustry has imposed stricter safety standards on itself, but some risk is unavoidable and product liability insurance is costly. Fireworks, Tom admits, are "not a product you use on Sunday, they're a product you use after a whole day of partying," and even a drunken idiot who blasts off a finger can still sue. The other issue is shipping. Many freight lines will no longer carry fireworks, particularly after a con-tainer bound for Europe caught fire a few years ago and scuttled the entire vessel: "We're down to a handful of lines, and if one day they decide they don't want to ship fireworks, the whole industry would be dead." But the core of the business has not changed. After mil-lions of frequent-flyer miles and countless nights in room 1211 of the Grand Sun hotel, Tom Chan is well tuned to the business mores of his parents' native country: "The advantage is that I know how these people work. I know how they will skim things to cheat you." Her-bert is even harsher about his ancestral homeland: "The people over there would screw over their whole family if it meant more money. That's the problem with China right now."

As the fireworks business grew, so did the Chan family. Herbert was born in 1980, Arthur in 1985. With their parents working such long hours, the boys spent a lot of time with a Chinese-speaking babysitter. "My brother and I never lost the ability to speak Cantonese because she didn't speak English," says Arthur. "Our family would always be speaking Chinese." In fact Herbert didn't speak English until he entered school at age six. On Saturdays the whole family would drive to Chinatown, where Tom went to his office and Maggie worked at the family jewelry store. "I would complain about it," Arthur recalls. "My friends would talk about sleeping in or watching cartoons, and I was the one in the car on the way to Chinatown. Saturday was just another day at the office." The Chan household ran on the Old World principle that children obeyed their parents and didn't require an explanation. When Herb protested that other kids didn't have to take piano lessons or spend Saturdays with their parents, the response was curt and clear: "You're taking piano and you're going with us to Chinatown and that's the way it is." Adds Herb: "When we were growing up we were taught, never talk back to your parents. Whatever they say goes. So that's what we did; we just followed."

It's a common pattern in immigrant families for parents to impose strict rules on the older children and then loosen up as younger ones come along. As Arthur recalls, "My brother wasn't allowed to go to high school dances. My parents were under the impression there were lots of drugs and alcohol at those dances." Five years later, Arthur went to all of his school events, even though substance abuse was actually a bigger problem during his high school years than during Herbert's. Another story illustrating the Chans' parenting style: Herb was scheduled to play in a basketball tournament, but his parents said he could go only if he finished his homework. "I said, 'Yeah, yeah, I got it done,'" recalls Herb, so the family drove him to the game. "My parents on the way over figured out that I didn't do it, and they turned the car around and said, 'You're not playing, you're going home.' My mom has a way of figuring out the truth and I can't lie without giving it away. Which means I can't play poker." That same sense of self-discipline also applied to family finances. "I don't necessarily think money was ever tight," says Arthur, "but I always had the sense we were saving or scrimping or not indulging ourselves." They shopped for clothes at discount stores and were always looking for a bargain, says Arthur: "I joke with my mom that every time we went shopping we'd look for the little red signs that tell you there's a clearance." When Arthur started playing tennis he badly wanted a new racquet, just like his friends, but his parents refused, saying the old one was good enough: "It was a lesson in not caring what other people were going to think. It was something they taught me: it's not worth your time to care about something like that."

Eventually the Chans moved from San Leandro to Tiburon, a fancier suburb in upscale Marin County. As in many immigrant families, the parents stayed rooted in their traditional culture, leaving their children to explore wider horizons. Says Arthur: "My parents didn't have any connection to Tiburon. It was just the place we lived, because it had good schools. A lot of our anchors were in Chinatown, in terms of economics or family, even for something as simple as food. If my parents wanted authentic Chinese food they're not going to go to the Chinese restaurant down the street, they're going to drive across the bridge to a Chinese restaurant in San Francisco." The Chans had little in common with other Marin parents and seldom saw them socially. Most of Arthur's friends had mothers who "stayed at home and drove their kids to soccer practice and played tennis on Wednesday morning, but my mom never did that. She was always working. It never occurred to me until a lot later that it would have been very uncomfortable for them to try to be friends with my friends' parents."

Tom and Maggie's sons, however, straddled two worlds: Tiburon and Chinatown. Both boys associated "with lots of white kids" and Arthur recalls going "to like twenty bar mitzvahs in middle school." Racial taunts were rare and Herb laughs: "The only knocks I got were, you must be really smart because you're Asian and you wear glasses. That was about it." But racial identity was never far below the surface. "I think someone from Chinatown, who looked objectively at my life, would say I was whitewashed," says Arthur. But at the same time, he adds, "I would have my feet in Chinatown," attending family dinners or hanging out with cousins. "Our experience is Chinese-American. It's not like mainstream America, but it's not like my parents transported China or Hong Kong into our home, either. It's very much a distinctive hybrid of the two."

When I asked Arthur which place felt more like home, Marin County or Chinatown, he paused before answering: "Is neither an option?" Then he told a story to illustrate his point. Before his high school prom, a bunch of guys and their dates gathered at the home of Arthur's best friend to take pictures and have a meal. His friend's mother laid out a buffet of Asian foods, from sushi to chicken sate, and then pulled Arthur aside and whispered, "I brought in all this food for you." For years, he recalls, this family had "treated me like just Art, not Art the Asian," but at that moment a sense of difference, of separateness, leaked out: "I knew it was well intentioned, so it wasn't like I was upset at her for thinking of me, but the execution wasn't quite there."

When it came time for Herbert to enter college, his parents preferred Cal State–Hayward, Tom's school. It was even close enough for him to live at home. But he rebelled. He'd been accepted by the University of California at Santa Cruz, about two and a half hours away, and the fellow who had spent every Saturday at his father's office in Chinatown wanted some space, some distance from his family. "My parents thought Santa Cruz was a slacker school, that you couldn't accomplish anything there," says Herb. When he showed them the engineering and business courses the school offered, they finally relented, but his parents still expected him to come home most weekends for family dinners: "There was some tension there. My parents thought I was getting away from them, but actually, I wanted to hang out with my friends. I was going to go back—I just didn't want to do it every week."

It was always expected that Herb would "go back" and join the family business. But he wanted to prove himself first, so he got a job after graduation with Wells Fargo, the big California bank. "People could see that I actually could get a job," says Herb, and not just trade on his father's connections. "It gave me some street cred." He thought he would have at least three or four years out on his own, but after only two, his mother called with a stern message: we need you now. "My mom just said, 'It's time for you to come back,' and that was all they needed to say," recalls Herb. "I said 'Okay, just let me finish out the quarter so I can make my bonus and then I'll be back.'" Tom had suffered an attack, similar to vertigo, and he was worried that he could no longer keep up his grueling travel schedule. Maggie says that when she called Herb, "I told him that he had no obligation to work for the family. If he didn't like it, I didn't want him to feel regret that he worked for his dad." But Herb heard the conversation differently. His obligation was very clear: "I felt it was my duty to help him out, so he could enjoy life a little. The way my brother and I were brought up, it's family first, no questions asked. We know what we have to do."

But Arthur, the younger son, did ask questions and chose a different direction. Even in high school he viewed his heritage more through an intellectual lens than a practical one. He volunteered for a program called Crossroads, teaching civics to immigrant children and using video to help them tell their stories. "At Crossroads," he once told an interviewer, "my video production students believed they had no story to tell." So they were shocked and delighted to realize "they were central, not an afterthought" to the American narrative. When it came to college he turned down the University of California at Berkeley to go east to attend Georgetown University—the first member of his generation to leave the state. By this time Tom Chan had expanded his business interests far beyond Chinatown and he saw the value of his son's decision: "Dad always had a very curious thing about learning to deal with white people. For him going to Georgetown was better than going to Berkeley. Berkeley wouldn't teach me how to interact with white people and Georgetown would." At the same time, adds Arthur, "I was not supposed to lose any touch with my Chineseness. So for them it was a big move, but at the same time it was a smart move." When he left home he took a small figurine of Buddha with him: "It was less a religious thing and more a reminder of home, of comfort. I put it in my pocket every exam I took, and I had it on my desk, a small token from home."

Arthur stayed connected to his "Chineseness," but as he left his hometown behind, he redefined his identity. At college he joined groups that celebrated a broad notion of cultural diversity, including a Latin American dance troupe, and felt part of a larger community of racial minorities: "That was all new to my parents, being Asian as part of a general minority, empathizing with the experience of black Americans or Latinos or other marginalized populations. It wasn't just about being Chinese. That was something new." So was his interest in filmmaking. The family business is business—importing fireworks, selling jewelry, running restaurants (his uncles and cousins own several). So when he applied for a graduate fellowship to Ireland and described his interest in cinema, his mother was stunned: "It was so out of left field that my mom thought it was a ploy to win the scholarship, that I had decided to brand myself a filmmaker so that I would have a compelling story. I was like, no, that's what I'm actually thinking about. Then we had to have this conversation about careers."

Arthur is also thinking about law school, but he is definitely not interested in joining his parents and brother at United Pyrotechnics (Maggie now keeps the books for the company). "I actually told this to my mom," he says. "Part of the reason you guys came over here was that I wouldn't have to join the family business, that I could actually go out and choose what I wanted to do. That was part of the incentive, that was part of the reason I didn't go to Berkeley, and why I'm looking into law school. All those things are to give myself options." Herb never felt he had options, and doesn't seem to regret that. His world is his parents' world. His lives in the same building, in a downstairs apartment. He dates a girl from Taiwan who speaks Chinese. He regularly pops into the family jewelry stores in Chinatown and chats with his cousins about the tribulations of working for your parents. "I think we're all waiting to see what we would do when the reins are finally handed over to us, to see how we would handle things," he says. "That's the common thread: Okay, well, we're just in waiting." When I asked if he was happy he responded: "I'm happy with it. It's a great business to be in, working with my parents. When we're in China we're often together. We talk business most of the time and that's fine with me. I'm trying to get as much knowledge as possible from my dad while he's still boss. I want to follow in my dad's footsteps. I want to keep his legacy going on, especially with the company he built from the ground up. That's what drives me, to keep it going, and try not to screw it up."

The matriarch of the family remains Maggie's mother, Herb and Arthur's grandmother. Her late husband, the Buddhist carver, is buried back in China and she spends several weeks every spring in his home village. But the center of her life is Chinatown, where she still lives in her own apartment, right across the street from several of the family stores. She's never learned to speak English but she doesn't need to. As Herb describes her daily routine: "She goes to the park and does her tai chi, then she has some dim sum. After that she makes the rounds of the jewelry stores, and then goes and plays mahjongg." Her two grandsons have chosen divergent paths. One lives a few blocks way from her, the other in New York. One wants to make money, the other wants to make movies. One felt an obligation to his family, and came home; the other felt an obligation to himself, and left home. Both young men reflect the immigrant experience, the transition from foreign-born parents to native-born children, just in different ways. As Herb says of his grandmother, "Everyone in her family is out doing their own business, which is almost like the American dream." He pauses and adds: "It *is* the American dream."

5.

Asis, Indira, Priyanka, and Piyali Banerjie

INDIA

When I go through the American security system, going abroad to China, the lady knows: she's looking at my American passport. Still, by mistake she writes Indian. So by paper I'm an American. My future is in America; that's where I'm working hard to get the jobs. But no matter what I do, people want to look at me and say, "Dr. Banerjie, he's an Indian." So I am both.

Asis Banerjie worried about the time. It was Sunday night, and he was still in New York, attending a party for a family friend who had just finished her doctorate in chemistry from Columbia University. He had earned the same degree a year earlier at Case Western Reserve University, and now he faced a long drive home to Lancaster, Pennsylvania, where he was working in his first job. As he said his good-byes and walked out the door, a family was coming up the steps. The daughter was carrying a cake, and someone said to Asis, "Why don't you stay back, because we're going to cut that cake." He reluctantly agreed, and as the delicacy was served, a cassette tape was providing background music, a Hawaiian guitar playing Indian songs. Asis was talking to the cake-bearing family: "So I asked, 'Who is playing this guitar? Whose recording is this?' And you know, the father is always proud of his children. So he says, 'That's my daughter,' with a British accent." The guitar player was Indira Ghosal, a student at Queens College, but if Asis was turned on, Indira was turned off: "I looked at him and said, 'Oh, my God, what a hippie.' He had long hair down to here!"

When Asis returned to Lancaster he told an older friend, Dr. Amit Mitra, a fellow immigrant from India, "I found the girl I'm going to marry." This conversation followed: "He said, what's her name? I don't know. What's her address? I don't know. What's her phone number? I don't know. So how, Asis, are you going to find her? I said well, I know she's Indian, she plays the guitar, she goes to Queens College. I can find it out." Asis was a determined fellow. A small, wiry man with a machine-gun personality, he had planned his life meticulously from an early age, and now that he had a degree and a job, a wife was next on his list. "If I like something, I pursue it aggressively," he says. "That's the way I know." He also got lucky. A friend from student days in India, who was working in a chemistry lab at Queens College, knew Indira and provided her number.

So the next weekend the ardent suitor pursued his target: "I called and spoke to Indira's father, and I said, 'I met you in that place, and now I am visiting my friends in Queens, and if you don't mind, I'd like to stop by.' " This was 1978; the culture was exploding in all directions. But not in the ethnic neighborhoods of Queens, and certainly not in the Ghosal household. Here customs were trapped in 1958, the year Indira's father first left India, and the courtship rituals of his home country were still observed. A young woman had very little say in choosing her husband. "Oh my goodness, from the age of

sixteen my parents started looking," Indira remembers, and their goal
was not just an Indian son-in-law, but one of their own kind, a high-
caste Brahmin from West Bengal. Asis fit that bill, so when he asked
to stop by, he was warmly encouraged. On that first visit he talked
almost entirely to Indira's parents, not to her, and when he offered to
drive her back to campus, she was petrified: "My father is telling me
to go out with this guy and he didn't even know him. I actually went
into the kitchen and asked my mom, I said, 'Is it all right for me to
go?' and she said, 'Yeah, yeah, yeah, he seems like a nice fellow.' So I
go with him, and I got into this huge Monte Carlo, and I stuck to the
door. I was frozen."

Dr. Mitra, Asis's friend from Lancaster, called Indira's father and
"intentions were expressed." When the aspiring groom came to visit,
either Indira's brother or a young married couple served as chaper-
ones: "We couldn't go anywhere without someone being present
there." Indira was twenty-one, an American college student with
dreams of medical school, and she chafed under the Old World traditions imposed by her parents: "I said to my father, 'I'm too young to
get married, I don't want to get married until I finish college.' But my
father says, 'He happens to be such a good chap, he's so well educated,
from such a good family.' It was basically a lot of brainwashing. I
was pushed into getting married by my parents." The wedding took
place less than a year after Asis had first heard her play the guitar.
Since then, the Banerjies have had an adventuresome and prosperous
life together. They moved back to India for fourteen years and then
returned to America in 2002, settling in Medina, an Ohio town about
an hour south of Cleveland. But they both know that the "brainwashing" of her parents exacted a high price. Indira dropped out of Queens
College and never made it to medical school, and Asis says, "I tell you
truly, her potentialities were lost because of my coming into her life."

Indira today is still a beautiful woman wearing gold earrings and a
warm smile that masks an iron will. Drawing on her own experience

she sends very mixed messages to her daughters. In one sense she desperately wants them to follow the old ways, to do what she did and marry within the tribe. Says her younger daughter, Piyali: "My mom flat-out told me, she looked me in the face and said, 'If you ever marry someone who's not Indian, don't call me mother again.'" But Indira also resents the weight of custom that crushed her own hopes, and she adamantly wants her daughters to be independent women with their own degrees and careers: "I want them to have a profession. As I told Piyali yesterday, 'Don't make the same mistake I did, never make the same mistake I did. Never make the same mistake that your grandmother did.'"

That grandmother, Maya Rani, was only seventeen and living in Calcutta when a freshly minted university graduate named Dinonath Ghosal applied for a job in her father's office. As Indira tells the story, the older man, an accountant with the city government, thought the job seeker "was very handsome, and said, 'I have a daughter who may be a good match for you.' And that's how it all started." Dinonath "fell in love at first sight" with Maya and found every excuse to visit her parents' house at teatime, but the young couple barely talked to each other before the wedding. The girl's family had money and since she was the oldest child she received lavish wedding gifts—jewelry, furniture, even pots and pans. According to custom, Maya moved in with her husband's family and plunged immediately into a highly stressful situation. Dinonath was the oldest of nine children, and his mother was bedridden with tuberculosis: "It's a very sad story, when my mother tells it she still cries. She was seventeen, eighteen years old, and now she has to act as the mother of all these small children." Dinonath's father had dropped out of medical school to join the state railway system, and he took out his disappointments on his family: "My father's father was an extremely picky person. If the food wasn't properly cooked he would throw it."

Indira was born a year after the wedding, and six months later her father decided to leave India for graduate school in London. Her mother's jewelry was sold to finance the trip, but there was only enough money for one ticket, so wife and child stayed behind in India. The little girl would not see her father again for nine years. After his departure, Indira's mother returned to her own parents' house, leaving her plate-tossing father-in-law to fend for himself. It was a large house, divided in half: an aunt, uncle, and five cousins occupied one side, while Indira and her mother moved in with her grandparents on the other. She was a pampered child, even more so after her mother left for London four years later: "Everybody sort of sympathized with me because I didn't have a mother or a father." But her idyllic life ended at age nine, when her father returned to bring her back to England.

Bengalis refer to London as "Bilat," so a *bilati* is a foreigner, and that's what Indira's father was to her, a *bilati* who wanted to steal her away from her beloved grandparents and the only home she'd ever known. Indira describes the scene when he arrived: "I remember this huge crowd of people and there I am, this tiny skinny little girl, standing on the veranda which looks out on the road. Looking down, I see this huge blue Mercedes stop right in front, and I see him coming up the stairs from the courtyard, so I run to the bathroom and lock the door and start playing with the water, because I loved playing with the water. And meanwhile no one knew where I was, because here's this son-in-law who's come from England and everyone is busy with him and making tea and this and that." Indira remembers that her father asked, "Where is my daughter?' but Asis says that he really asked, "*Which one* is my daughter?" a more revealing turn of phrase. Finally, an aunt tracked her down in the bathroom, where she had taken off all her clothes, and insisted that she get dressed and greet her father. "I don't want to see him," the girl yelled through tears. "I don't want to have anything to do with him." She finally calmed down, but the reunion did not go well: "I'm looking at him and thinking, oh my goodness, I'm supposed to go and be with this man? Who I don't even know? He's a foreigner, he's wearing a three-piece Savile Row suit, he even speaks funny."

That uprooting was the first of four times Indira would leave one country to live in another, but that's not unusual. Once émigrés have cut their connections to home they are set loose in the world and often keep moving. By the time Indira landed in London her younger brother had been born, but her father's job at the Indian embassy did not pay well and as the eldest son, Dinonath was obliged to send a chunk of his check back home to his own "extremely picky" father. The expensive suit he had worn back home to pick up his daughter was an extravagance, designed to impress his relatives and mask his modest means. The Ghosals could only afford two rooms on the third floor of a house owned by a Polish family. When the child got there she went looking for her mother: "I will never forget this: as I walked up to the second floor I could smell this horrible smell. I didn't know what it was; I had never smelled it before. A Polish general used to live there and he used to drink twenty-four hours of the day, and I was smelling brandy or rum. It turned me off so much." When she reached the third floor the stench dissipated a bit and she saw a woman holding a baby. The woman beckoned but the girl held back: "I said, 'I want my mother,' and she said, 'I am your mother,' and then I went running to her and she hugged me and she was crying and I said, 'When are you going to send me back to my grandmother? I want to go back tomorrow.' So she said, 'Okay, we'll send you back tomorrow, but don't you want to stay a little while and see the baby? Look, this is your brother—don't you want to spend time with him?' And I said, 'No, I want to go back to my grandmother tomorrow.' And that's how my life in London started."

It didn't get much better: "When I moved from India to England I hadn't crossed over the bridge. I couldn't accept that life. I spoke very little. I had this constant longing to be with my grandparents and cousins and uncles and aunts." Her father's degree was in marketing and advertising and four years later he got a job in New York, working for Procter & Gamble, the large American company that inspired the term *soap opera* by sponsoring daytime radio dramas. Indira arrived in America at age thirteen, and the family settled in East Elmhurst, a Queens neighborhood filled with Jewish, Irish, and Polish families. Her father took the subway to work in Manhattan, and she entered the local public school. It was quite an adjustment from St. Mary's, the Protestant school she had attended in London: "I saw these kids chewing gum, with their feet on the desk, throwing spitballs at the teacher. I was in a state of shock. Oh my goodness, it was a nightmare going to that school. My homeroom teacher was this little old lady, she must have been in her seventies, and the students had disrespect for her. I couldn't get over that. In England you couldn't even slouch in your chair; we had to sit up all the time. You couldn't speak in class unless you were told to speak." But the lack of rules was also liberating: "I felt so free. I didn't have to sit up straight, I didn't have to keep my mouth shut, I didn't have to write with a number-two pencil all the time. I didn't have to carry around an ink pen and an ink bottle and blotting paper."

The Ghosals tried hard to keep their culture alive. Indira's mother always spoke to her in Bengali, and helped the girl compose letters to her grandparents in their native tongue: "I would sit at this little table in the kitchen while she's cooking and she'd tell me the spelling and how to write it and construct the sentences properly." There weren't many Indians in East Elmhurst, so on weekends the Ghosals would often travel around the New York area, meeting other Bengali families. They would talk politics, sing songs, cook food, trade gossip: "They were the first generation, they had to cling on to something, they clung on to their old heritage." At festival time the families would sometimes gather at Columbia University, which provided a free hall: "We would have our little cultural dances and singing and rituals pertaining to the Mother Goddess."

Of course food and music were not the only items on the menu when Bengalis gathered. There was also marriage. The parents would introduce their children to each other while trading cautionary tales of wayward girls who had strayed from the fold. "What happened to a few of the other girls, they got involved with non-Bengali, non-Indian fellows, and that was devastating," says Indira. "There was such a huge cultural gap in those days. One girl got engaged, and then she had to break her engagement, because she never got along with the guy. Another girl, something terrible happened to her, she was involved with somebody. Another girl got involved with drugs. Blah-blah-blah. My parents had this fear, I think. They always said, 'You're not going to marry anybody but a Bengali and a Brahmin.'" Family pressure, even from thousands of miles away, could not be avoided. "'Your grandparents are still alive,'" Indira was told, "'and as long as they're alive, and your uncles and your aunts, what are they going to say?' It was constant." But not all Bengali Brahmins were good enough: "I remember even amongst us, the families, my parents were very careful to say, 'You know, that fellow is not that good and that family is not that good. That fellow is not really involved in his studies, that fellow is going to get nowhere. He's vagabonding about, not studying enough, we don't know what kind of future he'll have.'"

One summer during college Indira was teaching swimming on campus to a group of autistic children, and another counselor, a Jewish boy, showed an interest in her: "He started calling me at home, and my father and mother would listen in on the other end while I was talking to him!" Her father was furious: "He said he shouldn't be calling, 'Why does he call you after you come home?' That was the end of that. I think he understood. He said, 'Your parents don't approve of me calling you. Are they afraid we'll get involved or something?' And I said, 'Yes, so don't call.'"

The boy went off to medical school in upstate New York, but their meeting left a mark. While Indira was not ready for marriage, she was ready to leave her parents' house and look for her own identity. She had already lived in three countries, on three continents, and she didn't feel completely comfortable in any of them. Asis, too, had traveled a long way in a few years. He was born in a rural part of West Bengal, far from Calcutta, in a tiny village called Kudra that did not appear on any maps. Several generations before, his ancestors had been sent to the region by the king of Uttar Pradesh, another Indian state, to manage his vast landholdings. The village had no school, no electricity, no running water. But Asis's grandfather knew that education, not land, was the key to his children's future. His sons all earned graduate degrees, mainly in science and engineering, and one spent time as a postdoctoral fellow at the University of Illinois. Schooling for the girls was a much lower priority, but all of them married into "established, educated families." Asis figures that his grandfather has more than two hundred descendants scattered around the world and Indira says, "That man must have had fantastic genes, I tell you."

In the family compound, separate buildings for living, cooking, sleeping, and housing farm animals clustered around a central courtyard. Indoor toilets were considered "dirty, not religiously clean, because gods were living in the temple of the home." Indira relates a tale told by her mother-in-law: "The basic bathroom was in the field. Women had to get up very early, when it was still dark, to go to the bathroom, so nobody could see them. The women would go in groups, within vocal reach of each other, so they could talk to each other. And if a man came everyone would hear." Even more scary than men to the squatting women: snakes that lived in the field. The nearest school was ten miles away, and the only means of transportation were bullock-drawn carts, ungainly vehicles with huge wheels designed to plow through muddy tracks during the monsoon season. Since the journey could take three or four hours, students often lived at school and saw their parents every few months.

Asis's father was a lawyer who had joined the freedom struggle against the British and spent time in jail. But he was the eldest son, and bound by tradition to return home: "All the other sons started leaving, but my father could not desert his father. He was his only support." When Asis was about five or six, his father made one concession: moving the family out of the countryside and into a nearby town. The boy's life had been so sheltered till then that just seeing a bus was a novelty. But Asis had inherited his grandfather's drive for success and his uncles' talent for science: "They were our models." For ninth grade he won a scholarship at a Hindu missionary school, and after that, "There was no looking back. I never paid a penny for my education." He proudly lists the honors that followed: third in his class at the University of Calcutta, first among masters' students in chemistry at the University of New Delhi. Several older relatives were already interested in polymer science, the structure of plastics, and he followed their lead. Case Western in Cleveland, not far from the rubber capital of Akron, and a leading center of polymer research, offered him a full scholarship. He arrived in August 1974 with $250 in his pocket, and had to spend $220 of it on an apartment. He earned his degree in three years and explains, "I used to sleep once in three days time; that's how I finished so quickly." He contracted bleeding ulcers, which almost killed him several times, but he was in a big hurry: "From when I was in high school, I knew exactly what I'm going to do with my life. I figured it out, and I did not deviate a millimeter." By early 1978 he had taken a job with Armstrong World Industries, a leading maker of flooring and other building materials, in Lancaster. In March of that year he met Indira and by December they were married. It was all in the plan.

Tagore, the Bengali writer, was renowned for his pithy sayings, and this one captures Asis Banerjie well: "I have become my own version of an optimist. If I can't make it through one door, I'll go through another door—or I'll make a door. Something terrific will come no matter how dark the present."

Asis always had the goal of returning to India, and he made that clear to Indira's parents: "I told them, I will marry your daughter provided she will go back to India. You might think, well, after marriage I would be changing and I said no, that's not going to happen, because I am determined." It took ten years to make the move. Armstrong led to other jobs at other companies in other states. But Asis was a door maker—he wanted to start his own company, and he could not do that in America: "This country was not ready for an entrepreneur with my background." With little capital and few connections, he couldn't attract the investors he needed. But in India he was a hot property: "Having a degree from the U.S., experience from the U.S., those are the things that India wanted. India wanted people like me to come back and set up things there." Drawing on his background in polymer science, his plan was to make "designer plastics," high-tech components for everything from medical devices to farm equipment. "We brought something new to the country," he says, and both public agencies and private banks were eager to lend him money.

The question was where to locate. His native state of West Bengal was plagued by power outages, and he worried that the machines in the factory and the air-conditioning at home would not work efficiently. Besides, "there were strong communist unions in most of the companies in West Bengal," and Asis was not the sort to deal patiently with worker demands. So he chose the city of Chennai (formerly Madras), the capital of the southern state of Tamil Nadu: "They really embraced me. This guy has come from America, he doesn't speak our language, he could have gone to Bengal, instead he's come here. That was a big, big plus factor for me, for the local people, for the local government, for the bank."

After her marriage, Indira finished her degree at Cleveland State, found work as a medical technician, and occasionally taught yoga to suburban housewives, but most of her time and effort was invested in her two little girls, Priyanka and Piyali. So nothing was holding her back when Asis proposed the move: "I've always wanted to go back because I had those fond memories as a child, of being with my grandparents." But her motives were more complicated than that. Indira had never felt fully at home in America, and when I asked why she replied, "I think the culture, the culture. When I started living here, I just felt that I didn't belong here. I thought maybe I'll fit into India much better, and that basically is why I wanted to move there so badly." She also wanted her children to know their heritage: "I knew that living in this country I could not have taught them all the various languages, all the various cultures of India. I wanted them to know about India. I wanted them to love India the way that I loved India." There was another reason as well. Indira's parents still lived in America (although they've now retired back to India), and the young couple was obligated to spend many weekends with them. All her married life, Indira had walked "under [her] father's saddle," as Asis put it, and he felt oppressed by the same burden: "We didn't grow up." So ironically, the couple had to leave America and return to India to escape her parents' Old World influence. "When we went to India we had independence," he says, and Indira agrees: "There was a thread that was cut."

The business Asis built in Chennai was very successful. The family had cars, drivers, servants of all kinds, a walled house by the beach far bigger than the one they now occupy in Ohio. In some ways a West Bengali in Tamil Nadu was a *bilati*, a foreigner. "I didn't know the language," recalls Indira. "The culture was totally different, the attire was totally different, the food was totally different. I didn't know anything or anybody." But Indira made her way. She found peace in her homeland, starting two nursery schools in Chennai and enjoying a "spiritual growth" that had eluded her in America.

"Everyone asks me this question: How could you be brought up in England and America and go back to India and make yourself so comfortable?" she says. "And I say, number one, I always wanted to go back to India. Number two, when I got on the plane with my children and my luggage, I said to myself, I leave America behind. I'm going to a new country and I'm going to adopt their ways of doing everything. And I never looked back. If I did, I'd be like a lot of Indians who went back to India, and tried to settle down, and couldn't adjust to their environment and came running back to America." Indira describes a common pattern: Indians who dream of returning home and don't like it once they get there. "These people," says Priyanka, referring to her parents' generation, "when they're in America they're like, Americans don't have the same values as Indians. When they go back to India they're like, nothing happens in India, India is so dirty. When they're in India they want to go back to America, when they're in America they want to go back to India. They just drive people crazy." Indira chimes in: "Yes. Yes."

After eleven years Indira moved the girls to Calcutta, where they could attend better schools and absorb the Bengali culture. Asis commuted from Chennai on weekends and started a new business project in Bengal so his travels could become "a profit center, not a cost center." Indira continued her yoga teaching and volunteered for a nonprofit organization that brought medical services to the slum dwellers of the city, mainly Muslims "who had never seen a doctor." The older Banerjies were happy but the younger ones were not. It was 2001. Priyanka was getting ready for college and the pull of her birthplace was growing stronger. If Indira felt that she "didn't belong" in the United States, her daughters felt the same way about India. "I grew up in India and I love India but I knew in my heart I was an American citizen," says Priyanka. "As a kid my mom said, 'You have to be proud to be an American, everybody in the world wants to be an American. You're so lucky.'" In school she read the classic American novel *To Kill a Mockingbird* and "I was like, yeah, that's my country!" She studied the American War of Independence and identified strongly with the rebels "who seemed so heroic." (It helped that India and America had both won their independence from the British, so they had "bad guys" in common.) Indira occasionally made pizza and other American treats "and we'd be so happy about it." She gulped down American TV shows, from *Small Wonder* and *Friends* to *Buffy the Vampire Slayer* and *Beverly Hills 90210*: "You'd watch those shows and be like, you want to live there. Everybody wants that. I always used to think, maybe it would better if we lived in America because America was a cool place to be. So if I'm an American, why am I here? I should just move back there. It's cooler."

Asis was not exactly into "cool" but he agreed that his daughters should study in America. He had returned to India "for selfish reasons," he admits, but "they were born in America, and both Indira and I realized that when the time comes, we must give them an exposure to America also." The Indian tradition of paternal power was still strong, however, and Asis decided that Priyanka should attend Calvin College, a small, conservative Christian school in Grand Rapids, a furniture-making town in western Michigan. He thought his daughter "would be well taken care of" on a religious campus, far removed from the temptations of city life, and that she could find "an alternative father to me" among the faculty. It was a bad choice from the beginning. "Every day she'd cry on the phone," recalls Indira: "I've got nobody here, there's nowhere to go for the summer, nowhere to go for the holidays." Adds Priyanka: "It didn't seem right. I'm American, my parents are American, we're all American. But they're not here. It just seemed wrong. Loneliness is something that really gets to me."

She wasn't the first college freshman to miss her parents, but the distance made the separation worse. So did her roommate: "I had a really crazy roommate, it was really hard living with her. There's an episode of *Buffy*, where she gets a demon roommate, and when I went to college I remembered that episode and I thought, I really hope I don't get a demon roommate. And guess what? I did! I did!" A small college in a small midwestern town was not the right place for a *bilati*, a foreign student with a dark face and a strange name: "You realize, everybody else is white and I'm the only one who is brown and that's something I never thought of." Her background evoked the "craziest questions" from fellow students. One example: "Like, you're from India, do you have cows?" Her response: "First I was just shocked. I was like, we live in a city like you guys. In fact my city in India is much bigger than Grand Rapids. I don't know what you're talking about. Cows?" Then there were the elephant questions. Do you own one? Do you ride it to school? "I got tired of telling them the truth so I would say, yeah, me and my sister would share an elephant."

Instead of finding an "alternative father" at Calvin, she found religious intolerance: "It's a very small Christian college and they really teach their beliefs. But their beliefs were not my beliefs. That really confused me about who I was. It was kind of a scary thing." Then there was the racism. An old tradition at Calvin involves the male students serenading the females and everybody holding hands while they sing. "There were three boys," says Priyanka. "They could have held my hand but they didn't. So I'm like, why aren't they holding my hand? You know, I just felt really hurt that none of them came forward to hold my hand." Eventually she "kind of cracked under the pressure" and Asis could see what was happening. He had escorted his daughter to America just before 9/11, and after the attacks he had trouble getting back to India, so he wound up spending several months in the United States, watching Priyanka decline: "I could see she is going down every day. Every day. We were beginning to lose her. Not because she was becoming bad, but she was getting disturbed. Her studies. Her mind." So Asis made a decision: the family would move back to America. As he told Indira: "Priyanka needs a home in America. Thanksgiving time she doesn't have a place to go. Christmastime is coming, her roommate is gone, she wants to go home. So I think we need to move here and to be near them so they feel at home."

But Indira had found her home in India and was "dead, dead op-
posed" to moving back. "Believe me," says Asis, "I had to go through
a difficult time. I had to say yes, we are going. But she is determined.
Come what may, she's not coming from India." Once again, however,
a man made a decision for her. "I said no, we have to go," says Asis.
"Priyanka was crying every day, and as she was crying my energy and
power was getting more and more. I must do it." In December 2001
he started trying to sell his business, but found no takers. Finally he
unloaded the land and buildings he owned and was able to pay off his
debts. But money was a big problem. In exchange for the loans he had
received when he started the company, he had promised to keep his
profits in Indian rupees, so he could export very little cash. "We were
starting from ground zero, absolute zero," he recalls. They sold some
household goods and shipped the rest to America, but they had no
address, no destination. An old family friend lived in Urbana, Illinois,
so that's where they told the moving company to send their belongings. In September 2002, they flew back to America.

The Banerjies landed in Urbana, and with the help of their friend,
a respected doctor, they were able to rent an apartment and enroll
Piyali in high school. But just a few days later, Asis went to Cleveland
and met with executives at PolyOne, a major plastics manufacturer.
When they offered him a job he took it. He still owned a company
in India but he was cash poor, and this "allowed me to earn money
from day one, American dollars." So he called Indira and said, "I am
coming back to unwind everything." They broke their lease, took
Piyali out of school, bought a secondhand car, drove to Grand Rapids
to see Priyanka, and the next day arrived in Avon Lake, the Cleveland
suburb where PolyOne was headquartered. But finding a place to live
was not easy. Apartment complexes wanted references that Asis did
not have: "I had no credit history. I thought it would be easy but I had
nobody to stand by me. I had a company in India, but who cares?"
Finally they saw an ad for an old farmhouse on a large estate. The

owners were less concerned about references and the Banerjies took it. One week in America and they'd already moved to a new state. "We spent days in that empty house until our belongings came from India," remembers Indira. But the family member making the biggest adjustment was Piyali, who found herself in an American high school for the first time. In describing her reaction to Avon Lake, Piyali used virtually the same words her mother had used about her arrival in Queens thirty years before: "All of a sudden we moved here and you put me in this alien country, filled with different-looking people. Kids are chewing gum, they have their feet up on the desk, they don't stand up and say 'Good morning, ma'am' and wait for the teacher to say, 'You can be seated now.' It's your choice. They can't force you to perk up and say 'Good morning,' and I was like, teachers don't demand respect in this country. Kids don't really have respect for their teachers. I didn't think that was cool. I thought it was weird, ignorant. I don't want to say 'uncultured,' but what do they value then?"

The answers to that question stunned her. She met an eleventh-grader who was eight months pregnant: "She looked like she was from a good family; apparently she used to be a cheerleader, which means, I don't know, she might have been middle class or upper middle class maybe. Her boyfriend looked like a rich person, too, because he drove a nice car, like a brand-new Mustang. I just didn't understand how they could do this. I was in a state of shock." Then there was the pretty girl in her advanced biology class who showed her pictures of a bunch of boys: "I said, 'Are these your boyfriends?' and she looked at me and she's like, 'I wish.' So I'm like, 'Oh, what do you do with them' and she's like 'Oh, I just sleep with them,' and I'm like, 'Why?' and she's like, 'Because' and I say, 'I don't understand,' and she says, 'Welcome to the terminology of friend with benefits.'" The girl explained the meaning of the phrase: "Whenever we feel like it we just call" and have sex. "I had no idea. I thought she was lying to me. How was that even possible? I just sat there for the rest of the class in a state of shock, staring at the wall. Does my teacher know these things exist? Do guys know that these things exist? Does a freshman know these things exist?"

Everything about the school was intimidating: "I was just scared. These kids were so tall, they talked really fast, I didn't know what to talk to them about. They'd always use the phrase 'I don't care' in place of 'I don't mind' and that seems so ignorant to me. I didn't understand their vocabulary. I didn't understand why they took some pills called Adderall [a drug prescribed for attention deficit disorder] for fun. Weed was really big in American high schools. Everyone was doing it, from the jocks to the prettiest cheerleaders. I'm like, they're doing drugs and their parents don't even know about it! Why are they doing that? It doesn't even feel good! I tried it one time. I remember coming home and my mom says, 'Are you okay? Your eyes are red,' and I'm like, 'I'm so tired.' I went to bed and I'm crying, oh my God, this is the worst thing ever.

"When I moved here I was seventeen and I didn't know who I was," says Piyali, almost six years later. "There were so many options, it was like a basketful of fruits. I could be an apple or an orange or a banana. I could hang out with the kids who liked punk rock or the kids who had pink and green and purple hair, and I'd be like, wow." Piyali's classmates were also confused about this *bilati* in their midst. Some weren't sure what kind of Indian she was and would ask, "Are you the dot or the feather?" (The "dot" refers to a *bindi*, a forehead decoration worn by some Hindu women.) Others "asked me if I lived in a tepee and if I knew Gandhi. I didn't even know what a tepee was." She was nicknamed "Pocahontas" and asked if she had a pet raccoon. Others called her "Princess Jasmine" from the Disney film *Aladdin* (which was set in a mythical Arab country). Some of the girls wanted to know what kind of tanning lotion she used: "I thought they were making fun of the fact that I was brown. I didn't realize they didn't think I was a naturally colored person. Some of them just hadn't seen anything like me before."

Piyali's parents were as confused as her classmates. They didn't understand the high school vernacular and Indira remembers: "My biggest question was, what does this word 'hang out' mean? Would they be hanging from trees?" The Banerjies were very strict parents. "My big fear was that she'd be mixing with the wrong crowd," says Indira, so Piyali started hiding things: "I used to smoke cigarettes and I lied to my parents for a really long time." Indira would sniff her clothes when she got home and recalls a common exchange: "'I can smell cigarettes. You've been smoking, right?' 'No, I haven't.' But I knew she was."

After graduation Piyali went off to Kent State University, in northeast Ohio, and like her sister had a rough freshman year. Fellow students wanted to party on Thursday night, and even though she had an early class on Friday, she'd go along: "I lacked the discipline my parents brought me up with. I was disappointed in myself. I ate bad food, maybe two meals a day, just garbage, like pizza. For once I didn't have my mom shoving vegetables down my throat, I didn't have anybody telling me when to go to bed, and I think, deep inside, most foreign kids miss that feeling of their parents telling them what to do." She had a room on the first floor, and students could easily climb in the window. One night at 3 A.M. a group barged in after a night of drinking and tossed a handful of condoms around her room. "I was never one of those clean people," says Piyali. "I was used to my mom cleaning up after me, or in India a maid would clean up. So I didn't clean up the condoms." That weekend, her parents visited and found one: "They were like, what is this? They flipped out on me." Indira: "Oh yeah, I flipped out. I said, 'What's this condom doing here? Are you sleeping around? This is not good. This is not good. You're not telling me the truth.'" Piyali's grades plummeted, and to a father who loves to recount all the honors and degrees earned by his family, her academic record was devastating. Indira describes the family dynamic: "I think there was a gap, a lot of distance between all of us, and I was caught in the middle. She would tell me a lot of things she would not feel comfortable telling Asis. So I would listen to her, and keep my mouth shut, and then listen to him. I felt like I was the mediator. I'd tell him about her but I had to screen out a lot of things." Even a censored version of Piyali's life enraged her father: "He's blunt with his words, and I would say, 'You can't speak like that to her.'"

The simmering tensions finally boiled over. Both daughters agreed to leave their schools, move back home, and enroll at Cleveland State. To Piyali the arrangement was a godsend: "I just wasn't doing well, I was slacking, I just felt I needed someone to say, Piyali, wake up, time to go to class. Piyali, it's twelve o'clock at night, go to bed. I just needed a little push, so I moved back here, along with my sister. We basically had zero friends; it was just her and me. We'd plan when to go to school every day. We had a little schedule: when we'd hang out, when we'd meet up for lunch, stuff like that. I knew I could talk to her after class and I would wait for that moment, so I could just hug that person who was familiar to me." Cleveland State was a far more diverse place than either Calvin or Kent. "We weren't the only Indians walking through campus," says Piyali, and she liked passing the spot on campus where the flags of all the students' home countries were displayed: "Your flag's up there and it feels good." When they did make friends, they gravitated toward other foreign students who understood what it was like to deal with old-fashioned parents. Piyali's best friend is Albanian: "She calls me up, and tells me how her parents won't accept the fact that she really likes this Venezuelan guy. She's just bawling out crying, and she's like, my dad yelled at me, he gave me the whole line like, 'We moved to this country for you, I'm going to hang myself if that's what you want to do.' And I'm like, 'Yeah, I've heard that one before. How long did it last?' 'About fifteen minutes.' 'Well, that's better than the thirty-five-minute one.'"

The sisters lived at home for a year and the change of scenery worked. Priyanka graduated and is now studying for a master's in geography at the University of Akron. Piyali is majoring in criminology, getting top grades and aiming for law school. But if they have found their professional callings, they are still searching for their personal identities. In fact, young Indian immigrants have a term that conveys their dilemma, "ABCD," or "American-Born Confused *Desi*." (*Desi* is a slang name for a South Asian immigrant. "ABCD" is such a common catchphrase that several longer versions have been coined, including "American Born Confused Desi, Emigrated from Gujarat, House in Jersey." One wit has even added K through Z: "Kids Learning Medicine, Now Owning Property, Quite Reasonable Salary, Two Uncles Visiting, White Xenophobia, Yet Zestful.") When I asked Priyanka to explain "ABCD," she replied: "We're just confused about if we're Indian or American. We have to deal with both aspects. Most people in my generation, who are born here, their parents like just came from India. They still have the Indian values and stuff. But in school our friends are American, so we develop American values as well. So we're both."

One sign of this cultural turbulence: Piyali has four tattoos, much to her parents' dismay. But one is a Hindu peace prayer, another is the sacred Hindu symbol Om. Her father did not know about the one on her stomach, a Japanese icon, until she was rushed to the hospital with food poisoning after a trip to Taco Bell. While the emergency room nurse was examining her, Asis noticed the latest addition to his daughter's body art: "He'd be like, 'That's never going to come off you, is it?' I was like 'No,' and he's like, 'Is that what you call a tattoo?' And I'm like, 'Yeah,' and he just looks at me like 'You're a weird person.'"

The core of the tension between the Banerjies and their daughters comes down to one word: *marriage*. When I ask Indira why it was so important for her girls to marry Indians she answers: "Because of the culture. I have seen so many couples, in the last fifty years of my life, because of the cultural gap they have broken up, or they've had something devastating happen to them." The subject is so touchy that Priyanka has "deleted the 'M word' from my dictionary" and she explains: "I grew up watching Disney movies. In *Cinderella* it's not an Indian guy who falls in love with her, it's a white prince. So I never grew up thinking my Prince Charming is going to be Indian. It's not like I don't like Indian guys, I find people from different races attractive, but every girl has her Prince Charming, and I always imagined him being white for some reason." Both young women also worry that Indian men would demand too much obedience and not respect them as equals. "When I was a kid," says Priyanka, "I realized I don't want to be the wife who will take off the shoes, and take care of the husband. No, I'm better than that." Piyali adds that Indian men "expect a woman to be good at cooking and cleaning and nurturing the kids. I'm willing to do both cooking and cleaning, but I want a little help from my husband." Priyanka cuts in skeptically: "You are going to clean?" Piyali laughs: "I would, except for the bathroom . . ." Both of them believe a lot of Indian men are not ready to help out at home, but their issues go deeper than dishes or diapers. "My dad is like, 'You want to marry someone who can provide for you,'" says Priyanka, "but I have this thing. Why should I be dependent? You don't have to be dependent on a man at all. Why aren't we good enough to provide for ourselves?"

This family debate has raged for years, but it came to a head when Piyali took up with a new boyfriend, the son of a Lutheran minister from Wyoming, an Anglo of German ancestry who already has a child. In Piyali's view, her parents don't understand that she's an American now, that meeting "our kind of Indian" and falling in love is not very likely. And it's their fault: "You bring me to a foreign country, there's a good chance I might like someone who's not Indian, and when that happens my parents are just so unaccepting of it. Like right now, Mom won't even accept the fact that I genuinely am interested in somebody. She will always tell me, don't make commitments, but I'm old enough. I've dated guys, smoked cigarettes, gotten drunk, been in bad company. Right now I have a grip on my life, I can do things on my own."

Modern technology is now serving ancient customs. While Indira's parents searched for her mate among the Bengali families of New York, the Internet has created a worldwide marriage market for young Indians. "That's how people are meeting now," says Indira, and she notes approvingly that one of her nieces recently married a man she met online. That story triggered the following conversation between mother and daughter:

INDIRA: "You can't tell me today, 'You don't mix with Indian people, so how do you expect us to meet Indian people.' There are so many Web pages that you can go to, if you really want to meet an Indian person."

PIYALI: "I don't want to meet an Indian person, I want to meet someone who's nice and treats me good."

INDIRA: "So you're saying Indian people are not nice and won't treat you good?"

PIYALI: "I haven't met any Indian guys who are willing to do that."

INDIRA: "Have you met anybody?"

PIYALI: "I've met some, I'm not interested at all."

INDIRA: "Maybe because you didn't give them a chance."

PIYALI: "I've met someone else."

INDIRA: "That's it. Just say that then. Say, I did not give myself enough time or enough chance to meet anybody who's Indian."

PIYALI: "Why should I close an option?"

INDIRA: "Why not open another door?"

PIYALI: "I don't think so."

If the "M word," *marriage*, deeply troubles the Banerjie family, the "B word," *business*, is a source of great satisfaction. After eighteen months working for PolyOne, Asis went off to start his own company. The landscape had changed considerably since 1988, when a foreign entrepreneur had trouble attracting investors. Now, venture capitalists were willing to back him, and in August 2004 he started Ovation Polymers, occupying an abandoned industrial site in Medina, a pleasant city of about twenty-six thousand. Today he has about forty employees making the same kind of advanced plastics and alloys produced by the Indian company he still owns. The key to his business is creating the right materials for very specific industrial uses. As he told the trade publication *Plastics News*, "taking headaches away from our customers" is his goal. "I'm not the most intelligent person but I can find a gap. I can find a small area and have some technological success. I can find a pothole in the road and fill it."

Asis believes that American manufacturers can still prosper in the global marketplace: "When I came to this country, definitely one of my goals was to create jobs in the U.S., to create an example." But, he admits frankly, many of those jobs are filled by immigrants. American bosses find that "they're not getting the results from their countrymen, and they cannot accept lackluster performances." That's particularly true in industries that are competing against products from low-wage countries. He drives himself relentlessly, boasting that when he travels to Asia, across the International Dateline, he can work "more than twenty-four hours" in a single day. And he pushes his employees just as hard: "My guys have to perform and so somebody has to drive them, and this driving goes beyond eight-to-five. For me, in my life, you can negotiate anything but time. Real time doesn't stop." He prefers managers from India, younger versions of himself who are willing to trade an ulcer for a degree—or a sale: "They understand my mood. Those who work hard, they don't even take half a day off, because they know I'll be very upset. Something is going to suffer. I have told them I want production, yield, efficiency, consistency, quality, and you don't get that if you sleep at night and leave it to the workers. Only by hard work can you be competitive. You can't become competitive by relaxing here, when people in India and China are working hard."

A recent Duke University study found that one out of four American businesses in technology and engineering are founded by immigrants. And Norman Tien, the dean of engineering at Case Western, told Cleveland's *Plain Dealer* that foreign-born entrepreneurs like Asis "are an economic engine" fueling the American economy. But to be successful, these entrepreneurs often have to ignore national boundaries. When rising fuel prices boosted the cost of making goods in Medina and shipping them overseas, Asis negotiated joint ventures to open plants in China, Japan, and Korea. He's a patriotic American but describes himself as a "global citizen with an address in Medina." He understands that capital and information are like ocean currents, flowing constantly across frontiers. His mother still lives in the tiny village of Kudra, yet he can talk to her regularly by cell phone. But he's also learned that global citizenship can breed its own kind of discomfort and discontent. Like his wife and daughters, Asis lives in many worlds and struggles to define his own identity: "When I go through the American security system, going abroad to China, the lady knows: she's looking at my American passport. Still, by mistake she writes Indian. So by paper I'm an American. My future is in America; that's where I'm working hard to get the jobs. But no matter what I do, people want to look at me and say, 'Dr. Banerjie, he's an Indian.' So I am both."

Part III

THE
BUSINESS
OWNERS

I was interviewing a Chinese-American woman for a teaching job at George Washington University and asked about her family. If you were Chinese in New York, she answered, you ran one of two things: a restaurant or a cleaners: "We were cleaners." She laughed when she said it, but her answer revealed a basic truth: many immigrants get their first toehold in the American economy by opening a small business (and then their kids become college professors). Often they start by hiring relatives and catering to other members of their ethnic community. That's what my grandparents did around 1920, when they rented a small stand in an amusement park in Bayonne and opened a gambling game aimed at other immigrants from Eastern Europe. What was true then is true today. A couple from Mexico, Jesus and Miriam Zavalza, opened Xochimilco Flowers in Tucson, Arizona. As Jesus told the *Tucson Citizen*, "I called all my friends and said, 'This is Jesus. I just opened a flower shop and it's almost Mother's Day. You love your mother, right?'"

Jonathan Bowles, author of a report on immigrant business for the Center for an Urban Future, called these newcomers "entrepreneurial sparkplugs" and described their impact on New York: "Foreign-born entrepreneurs are starting a greater share of new businesses than native-born residents, stimulating growth in sectors from food manufacturing to health care, creating loads of new jobs and transforming once-sleepy neighborhoods into thriving commercial centers." The reasons are clear: these immigrants are risk-takers, or they would not have made it to America in the first place. "They really just put themselves on the line," says Farhana Huq, who helps low-income women start businesses in San Francisco. While many newcomers don't have the education or English skills required in the corporate world, small business owners can utilize their foreign origins to connect to their neighborhoods and their customers. Maggie Wong Chan works in her family's jewelry shops in San Francisco's Chinatown. And while she has an American college degree she speaks Chinese to many of her clients, and understands their tastes. The mother of a former student emigrated from Portugal and now sells handicrafts imported from back home to the Portuguese community in Riverside, New Jersey. What many immigrants bring to the table is time, not a title; drive, not a degree, and small business ownership exploits those assets. Paula Stuht of the Tucson Metropolitan Chamber of Commerce told the *Citizen*: "Unlike in their homeland, they have the opportunity to work hard and put in the hours many of us born and raised here don't want to put in. They are working 18 to 20 hour days. It's all sweat."

Sam and Pete Kourtsounis know from sweat. They also know from food, the first business venture for many newcomers. Sam came to the United States at age fourteen in 1955 and started out washing dishes in Greek-owned diners in Queens. Pete came thirteen years later and followed the same path. The brothers shared a bedroom in their sister's house to save money, but it was not until 1983 that they could afford to open their own place. When they moved to Baltimore in 1994 and opened the Towson Diner they stayed open from 6 A.M. to midnight, seven days a week; they didn't take a single day off for a year and a half. Meanwhile, they both married women from the old country who shared their belief that in America, the streets were not paved with gold, but with stones you had to shape and set yourself. Says Pete's wife, Eleni, "The restaurant we put before everything else, to tell you the truth. The good times, the holidays . . ." But their children are not interested in the diner and Eleni is proud of that: "Our kids are not staying in the restaurant business; we educated them."

The Reyes family from El Salvador also started a restaurant—El Tamarindo in Washington's Adams Morgan district—but their story has a different twist. The Towson Diner serves American food with a slight Greek accent (I love their chicken souvlaki with garlic-spiked yogurt). El Tamarindo, named for Jose Reyes's hometown, specializes in Salvadoran dishes. Beti Reyes started making tamales at age eight and selling them door-to-door in her home village. When the Reyeses opened their first place, a beer-and-billiards hall, she'd make tamales at home, then bring batches to the business and sell them to the players. And while her two sons want to be rock musicians, her daughter, Ana Rosa, inherited her mother's work ethic. Ana helped out in the restaurant as a child, filling salt and pepper shakers, then went off to college for a business degree. But unlike the Kourtsounis kids, she returned home and is now managing El Tamarindo. "I like being here," she says. "It's like second nature to me."

6.

Sarantos (Sam) and Ioanna Kourtsounis, Petros (Pete) and Eleni Kourtsounis

GREECE

When the children were here last summer I was crying all the time. When my son asked me why I was crying, I said, "I'm thinking about the time you're going to leave me again."

Stavroula and Paraskevas Kourtsounis lived in Skoura, a small village outside of Sparta in southern Greece. I met them in November 1975, when I was a correspondent for the *New York Times* and writing a story about immigration to America. Their stone house was filled with modern conveniences, from kitchen cabinets to a new bathroom, all sent by their three children living in Freeport, Long Island, a suburb of New York City. Stavroula proudly poured me a cup of American coffee and said, "We have lots of bread but we don't have the children. When we had the children, we didn't have any bread."

A neighbor complained that since there were so few kids left in the village, he had to fetch his own cigarettes: "It's an old-age home here, with green dollars."

The oldest Kourtsounis child, Sarantos, moved to America in 1955 at age fourteen and started calling himself Sam. Four years later, Panagiata, the only daughter, followed. Petros, the youngest, was the last one left, and his parents offered him the family farm if he stayed. But when he finished his military service in 1968, he went anyway. "We had over five hundred good orange trees," says Petros, known as Pete in America. "Maybe once a winter it would freeze. You get disgusted. In some parts of Greece, God helps you, but not in Skoura. You'd go into the village at night, have a coffee, play cards, but what else was there?"

In May 1974, Sam and Pete returned to Skoura, looking for brides, and within six weeks they got married in a double wedding ceremony. A year later their wives had babies a week apart, and the brothers returned to the village, to introduce the children to their grandparents. One day Sam was stunned to find his mother sobbing in the kitchen. With the whole family back together, he told her, you should be happy, not sad. But when I talked to her six months later she offered this explanation: "When the children were here last summer, I was crying all the time. When my son asked why I was crying, I said, 'I'm thinking about the time you're going to leave me again.'"

Over the years I've always remembered Stavroula's words, because they summed up a central story of immigration. In searching for a better life abroad, young people had to leave their loved ones behind in villages like Skoura. No matter how many toilets or toasters or dollars they sent back home, it was never enough to fill the void created by their departure. Mothers all over Greece—all over the world, really—weep in their kitchens, thinking of their children in America. Many immigrants dream of returning to their birthplace, and the Greek word *nostos*, the root of *nostalgia*, literally means homecoming.

The theme has pervaded Greek culture and literature since Odysseus made his torturous journey back from Troy to his native island of Ithaca, but few modern transplants have followed his model, and the first reason is money. As George Mavrakis, a Spartan journalist, told me, "When they go over there, they get taken over by the sickness of the dollar. After ten years they've made a certain amount, and they think, Why not stay and make some more?" But the more important factor is family. If the choice is between parents and children, the past and the future, the future almost always wins. "Before long their hair turns white," said Mavrakis, "their children have grown up in America, and it's hard for them to come back."

When my story ran in the *Times*, a second article from Freeport ran with it, interviewing the children of the parents I had talked to back in Skoura. It was illustrated by a picture of nine immigrants, clustered around a table in a Greek-owned diner. Sam and Pete were two of them, and when I started this book, I decided to track the brothers down. I put their names into Google and quickly found a Sam and Pete Kourtsounis owning the Towson Diner in Towson, Maryland, a suburb of Baltimore. They were probably the same guys, but I wasn't sure. So I called the diner, got "Mr. Pete," and started explaining to him who I was and what I had written. Yes, he said, those were my parents you interviewed, and we've always kept your article displayed in our restaurant. A few weeks later I met the brothers at their diner, a glistening chrome tribute to the glories of cheeseburgers, cheesecake, and the immigrant work ethic. After they opened the place in 1994, they didn't take a single day off for a year and a half. "If I didn't have a wife who was born in Greece," Sam said, "she would never have stood for this type of life, she would have divorced me." Now in their sixties, the brothers take great pride in the business they've built and the children they've raised—three boys and three girls, all college graduates. But they know they've paid a very high price. "The restaurant we put before everything else, to tell you the truth," says Eleni. "To

be successful these days you have to put this business above every-
thing else. The good times, the holidays . . ." As her voice trailed off,
Sam's wife, Ioanna, chimed in with one forceful word: "Everything."
Eleni repeated it for emphasis: "Everything."

The odyssey to that diner in Towson started when Paraskevas, a
poor shepherd, married Stavroula, the daughter of a blacksmith. She
brought a piece of land as a dowry to the marriage, and her new husband, who never cared much for herding animals, sold his flock and
settled down to a life of farming. When I asked the brothers if their
parents had an arranged marriage they laughed out loud. Of course,
they said, that was the only kind. In fact, if you married someone
from another village, "they would say you married a *xeni*," or foreigner. Life was hard and simple for the newlyweds. Neither one had
gone beyond the fourth grade in school. Their house had no indoor
plumbing; water had to be carried from faucets scattered around the
village. When World War II broke out, Paraskevas was conscripted
and sent to the Albanian front. The army commandeered the family's
animals as well, particularly the mule, which was needed to carry
supplies across treacherous terrain. That left Stavroula at home, with
no husband to provide income, no mule to plow the fields, and a new
baby, Sam. "The mule was part of the family," says Pete. When the
Greek army was defeated, Paraskevas walked home from Albania
to find his village occupied first by the Italians, and then the Germans. Sam remembers the Germans as relatively benign rulers ("they
would take me for rides on their motorcycles, in the side carriages")
who "wouldn't touch anybody unless you bothered them." But they
had "zero tolerance" for disobedience and showed "no mercy" to
anyone who defied their edicts. If the resistance movement attacked
a German soldier, three civilians would be shot in retaliation. Many
villagers were reluctant to give up their firearms to the Germans and
one relative hid a pistol underneath a large dining table. When the
occupiers seized his house as a headquarters, the man was "scared

to death every day," fearing his pistol would be discovered. "What if they found it?" recalls Sam. "They would shoot him."

The pistol remained hidden till the Germans surrendered, but then things only got worse in Skoura. A civil war erupted between guerrilla bands, many of them communists who had fought the Germans, and the conservative government in Athens. But since everyone looked the same, it was a very confusing period. "You didn't know who the enemy was," recalls Sam. "You'd be walking down the street, you'd meet someone, and you didn't know if he was a communist or a right-winger." Skoura occupied a key spot along the Evrotas River, controlling a valley near the mountain hideouts of the guerrillas, known as Andartes. "Our people in the village started buying arms in the black market, a couple of submachine guns, a couple of rifles," says Sam. One villager, a military officer, organized fortifications: tunnels, pillboxes, barbed wire, booby traps. Two houses were fortified as strongholds. During the day the villagers would work in their fields, and at night they would take turns manning the outposts, watching for invaders. In 1946 and 1947, three battles were fought in Skoura, killing about ten villagers, but the Andartes could never break through. Sam recalls one attack, when his father had been out feeding his animals and couldn't make it to the main garrison. All he had was a shotgun, fit for hunting birds and rabbits, but he raced to an upstairs window and started blasting away at a guerrilla a hundred yards away. "So now this guy realized what was going on and he turned and started shooting [at my father] with a machine gun. You could see the rounds hitting the side of the window." But soon the Andartes withdrew, leaving Paraskevas and his shotgun—if not his window—intact. On another occasion a wounded guerrilla was dragged by his comrades into the Kourtsounis house, where he died. The dark red bloodstain on the floor never quite washed away.

The guerrillas were eventually defeated, with British and American help, but the civil war left many stains on village life. "It killed us," says Pete, who was born in 1946. "After the war was finished, it was still a mess. There was a lot of hate between families. Even now some people don't talk to each other." The area was devastated economically as well. The boys wore homemade pants, woven from goat's wool, and Pete says, "The material was so itchy and hard. We didn't wear underwear because we didn't have any. That was the only cover we had, but it was so itchy!" Shoes were so precious that the village kids would carry them over their shoulders in good weather, trying to extend their useful life. Paraskevas could seldom afford a whole pack of cigarettes so he would give Pete two drachmas, about fifteen cents, and ask him to buy a few smokes at a time. Then he would cut each one in half, just enough to satisfy his nicotine habit. There was no medication ("we didn't know what aspirin was"), not even handkerchiefs. When Pete had a cold he'd punch himself in the nose to loosen the phlegm.

By the early 1950s, says Sam, "Things were getting a little better, but still, there were too many people, too many mouths to feed. So that's when the immigration started." If you had a relative in America who could sponsor you, that's where you went; if you lacked a sponsor you went to Canada. Stavroula's brother agreed to sponsor Sam, and when I asked about his decision to leave, Pete answered: "It was not his decision; he was forced to leave. My father begged him to leave." Sam agreed: "Back in the fifties in Greece, the father decided; you didn't have your own say at all." By leaving, Sam reduced the family's expenses while increasing their income. Even at fourteen, he was expected to work and send money home. "It was part of his responsibility to support the family," says Pete.

Skoura was emptying out. "I remember the buses leaving; it was sad for the village," Pete recalls. "People were leaving every day; [their families] would escort them to the bus stop, and their mothers would be crying." When Sam's turn came, his youth made the departure especially wrenching: "Of course I was crying. I didn't have a clue where I was going." He'd never been away from home, never farther than Sparta, less than ten miles from Skoura. When he boarded a ship in Athens for the three-week journey to New York, "it was a completely new world for me." The seas were rough but the teenager was unfazed: "It never bothered me. I never got dizzy. I was the only person who went in for chow; I never missed a meal." The food was good, far fancier than standard village fare, and Sam gained three pounds on the trip. Half a century later he can still remember the fish soup served on board. He had no friends and used to spend hours, even in stormy weather, on the prow of the ship, peering into the future. "Go west, young man," he says now. "That's what we did."

Sam moved in with relatives in Freeport, already the chief destination for Skoura immigrants. He couldn't speak a word of English so he started school in the sixth grade, with much younger classmates. After school he walked several miles to a bakery, where he had a job washing the pans, cleaning the machines, and sweeping the floors. He also picked up work at construction sites and one day his fellow workmen left him alone to finish a job. He was terribly thirsty, and went to ask the neighbors for a drink, but couldn't communicate what he wanted. "To tell you the truth it was difficult," he says of those first years. "At age fourteen you still need your mother, so sometimes I would cry in my sleep." In 1961 he was drafted into the army and sent to Germany, where he finished his high school diploma. Once, on leave, he was able to visit his parents in Skoura, and his mother urged him to go to confession. No, he said, I've done nothing to confess. All he ever did was work hard and send money home. Pete remembers: "Sam was a kid—how much could he send?—but my father did expect it. When he'd get a letter from the United States, red and white, air mail, you knew it was something." Everyone in Skoura knew what was in those letters. When they came by registered mail, and required a signature, the postman always lingered, expecting a tip. The family had extra cash now.

When Sam left the army he concentrated on learning the restaurant trade, working mainly in diners owned by fellow Greeks. Back in Skoura, Pete was dropping out of high school. He saw no point in continuing, because college was out of the question: "Who would pay for this? It was something impossible." He worked for his father and learned a lot about olives, Greece's premier crop. His father insisted that wild trees were hardier than farm-raised seedlings, so the two of them would sneak into local forests (some publicly owned, others in private hands) and dig up young trees they found growing there. Sometimes forest rangers would stop them but Pete shared his father's outrage at the authorities: "If you go into the forest what are you stealing? Somebody's trees? They were wild!" But the uncertainties of farm life, and the regular failure of the family's orange crop, were deeply discouraging. Moreover, Greece was dominated by a rigid, class-based structure, and without the right family or political connections, Pete knew that he'd always be shackled to the land.

The final incentive came from the earlier immigrants to America, the ones who had left their mothers crying at the bus stop. Many were taking vacations in Skoura and making a big impression: "The village was going crazy in the summer." The visitors were called *Brooklis*, a play on *Brooklyn*, and Pete remembers the villagers gossiping: "This guy, he's a *Brooklis*, wow, he's rich." The *Brooklis* boasted of owning cars at a time when there were no private vehicles in town, only a few taxis. "The idea that you'd have your own automobile, it was something huge, you couldn't believe it," Pete recalls. And then there was the way they dressed. No goat's wool pants in sight: "We'd see them every day, and we got so jealous. You could tell they were from the United States; their hands were soft and tender, and we had calluses everywhere." The locals hid their roughened hands in embarrassment, not fully realizing how hard the *Brooklis* had worked for their nice cars and fancy clothes. "We didn't know the other side," Pete says now. "We looked at them like tourists; we thought they don't work."

He tells the story of a Skoura father going to America and visiting his son, a short-order cook. The father asks where he takes a siesta, the after-lunch nap beloved in Greece. The son points to the hot grill and says, "This is my bed."

In 1955, Stavroula and Paraskevas had directed their oldest child to leave. Thirteen years later they begged their youngest to stay. He was their social security plan, notes Pete: "The culture was, whoever stays, takes care of the parents." Adds Sam: "I think my mother expected my brother to stay there. She regretted his going to America." But Pete was determined: "It's the greatest country here; don't fool yourself, it still is. How can you refuse to come?" Sam sponsored him and the brothers moved in together, sharing a room in their sister's house in Freeport. Pete got a job as a dishwasher making thirty dollars a week and the Kourtsounis family was now firmly rooted in America. (Their sister, Panagiata, had come to America a few years after Sam and settled in the Freeport area. There she met and married an "islander man," as her brothers called him, who came from the Aegean island of Skyros. That practically made him a *xeni* to the boys from Skoura, but they had one thing in common: they all worked in the diner business.)

Six years went by. Sam was thirty-three, Pete twenty-seven, and they were both ready to get married. Pete had felt uncomfortable courting American girls ("I never communicate right") and he convinced Sam that while they could never find a job in Skoura, finding a wife was a better bet. If you married a *xeni*, an outsider, Sam explained, "the customs are different, most of the time religion is different, so therefore it becomes problematic." Pete makes a similar point: "Somebody who marries outside, you don't see them as much. They marry nice women, good wives, but it's not the same. We've got our own music, our own language. We teach our children early." Marriage, adds Sam, has nothing to do "with love and all that stuff."

So in May 1974 they returned to Skoura. "We arrive, two single boys," Sam recalls. "We didn't say anything, about why we went to Greece, but all this nosing around, they started the gossip." Pete: "They knew, they're not dumb. Besides, for my mother, it was like heaven. Why are the boys here? They want to get married. You have any *nifi* [brides]? Then the word spreads around the next day."

Pete went first. His sister's goddaughter, Maria, lived near his parents and thought her friend Eleni would make a good match. At seventeen Eleni had finished high school and was hoping to attend college in Athens. Before the mating dance began, Maria established the ground rules with the possible *nifi*: "The first question was, Are you willing to go the United States? Otherwise it didn't make any sense." When she said yes, the dance moved to the next step, and Eleni picks up the story: "My girlfriend says, 'Eleni, come to Sparta, come for coffee, and I'm going to meet you with Petros.' So I say all right. My mother screams at that time, 'No, no, you're not going anywhere, you don't have the money to spend.'" She went anyway, but the rules were rigid. The couple could only exchange looks, not words. "If you have an interest, then you continue," explains Pete. They both were interested, and the next day Pete and Maria went to Eleni's house in the nearby village of Goritsa. The pretext was borrowing a book, but as Eleni remembers, "We got a chance to talk. We went just to walk a little bit." The couple was never alone and Pete says the custom protected the girl's reputation: "You use the third person as an excuse. If you just go by yourself you create gossip. It's a small community, you can't afford it, her name has been around." The third meeting was back in Sparta, at a coffee bar, and Eleni describes the scene: "Peter says, 'Eleni, I think I like you,' and I say, 'I like you, too.' And that's it. Finished. The whole thing." Clearly "love and all that stuff" was not a high priority. They went to Goritsa and told Eleni's mother: "My mother says okay. We knew a lot of people from Skoura; they say nice words for him; he's a nice guy from a very good family." Sam:

"Family played a very big role in this." Pete: "If your family had a history they would know about it; they would pass it around."

Meanwhile Sam "was losing interest" in the project. He'd left Skoura at fourteen and found the ritual unnerving. "Then he started changing his mind," says Pete. "I knew if he didn't get married he's done, he won't ever get married, it would be too late. I said if you miss this now, and you go back to the United States, you miss the boat. And he decided to adopt the custom." The brothers' cousin approached her hairdresser, Ioanna, who had three sisters in Australia and was already planning to move there. "She says just go and meet him," Ioanna recalls, "and I say no, I'm not interested." But the cousin was persistent: "She says, just meet him, you have nothing to lose, so finally I say okay." Same dance, same steps. Sam and a bunch of his cousins show up at a café in Sparta ("in Sparta all the marriages happen in the café," jokes Pete). The couple looks but doesn't talk. "The next morning he came over to my house, in his car," recalls Ioanna. "So we went for a ride, and that's it."

ELENI: "And that's it."

SAM: "Very simple."

ELENI: "Very simple."

When I asked the two women why they were willing, at age seventeen, to marry strangers and move to a strange country, they offered similar reasons.

IOANNA: "I couldn't live in Greece because my mother was so strict. Don't go here, don't go there. It was a very small community. You weren't allowed to go out of the house after seven o'clock at night. You feel like you're suffocating. So I was ready to leave, to go to Australia. I'm leaving anyway."

ELENI: "There was too much gossip. They saw you talking to a boy and automatically they put you in a bad name. I want to be free! I want to be free!" College was not a popular idea at home: "My mother don't want me to go to Athens and find a boyfriend." So when Eleni broke her wrist, she delayed applying for a year: "All that year my mother took me to pick olives from the trees. So I say, 'Oh my God, I can't do that anymore. I can't. I have to do something else.' I know in my heart I don't want to stay in our town. There's nothing there for me. I had enough." And like Pete years before, she had met the *Brooklis* coming back to Greece "with movie cameras, with the nice clothes, with the jewelry, with the money to spend. And you say, look at them, and look at us."

On June 16 the two couples were married. After a brief honeymoon in Athens, the brothers went back to their jobs in America, and their brides moved in with their parents in Skoura. Then politics intervened: a coup overthrew the government of Cyprus, the Turks invaded the island, and the Greek military government collapsed. All Greek airports were closed for days, and when they finally reopened, Eleni and Ioanna grabbed a flight to New York.

They sent a telegram, notifying their husbands, but it never reached them. Eleni remembers arriving at Kennedy Airport: "We look outside for Petros or Sarantos and nobody's there. So I say, 'Oh my God, Ioanna, what we going to do?' She says, 'Take a taxi.' To go where? We have so much panic." They had no American money so a stranger gave them a dime and helped them make a call. They reached their sister-in-law: "We say we're here in Kennedy but they didn't believe us." Finally Panagiata and Pete showed up and collected the petrified girls. "And then everybody is coming over to the sister's to see the brides," says Ioanna. "The whole cousins and everybody." When she tells the story to her children they express disbelief: "My youngest son says, 'You came to America, you were seventeen years old, to follow Daddy? Were you nuts?' But they don't understand, the children, how strict it was back then. Today, everything's freedom."

The adjustment was very hard. The brides spoke no English and their husbands worked all the time. Ioanna hated the food and ate only French fries drenched in salt. If you served her a piece of rare meat she'd "freak out."

IOANNA: "I didn't know Sam. I had to learn his habits. He was a stranger to me." She recalls one evening shortly after she arrived. Sam said they were going to visit a friend for coffee and the man pulled out a large black case: "I thought he was going to play the guitar for me. How romantic!" Wrong. The case contained a rifle Sam had left with his friend for safekeeping. Sam had a sports car at the time and Ioanna was in the habit of slamming the front door shut. So he'd race around and open the door for her. Again, she thought he was being gallant. Again, wrong. "Before you know it," he was thinking, "that door will be flying somewhere." It got so bad that Ioanna sent a letter to her sister in Australia saying, "I want to leave, send me the money, I don't want to stay here." Why not return to Greece? "Not Greece. I was afraid of my mom. If I go back to Greece alone she would have killed me."

But she stayed, and gradually life improved. The brides watched soap operas (*Days of Our Lives* was a favorite) and read comic books to learn English. They took buses to nearby shopping malls and discovered Bloomingdale's. The two couples found apartments in the same building, a floor apart. And both women became pregnant at the same time. "I started to like it when I had my first child," says Ioanna. "Then I got busy with the baby, and I learned to drive." But even that process was not easy. For Greek drivers, stop signs are a mere suggestion, not a direct order, and after one harrowing lesson in the parking lot at Jones Beach, Sam gave up trying to teach his wife American rules and sent her to driving school.

The brothers sent their parents a hundred dollars a month but their neighbors back in Skoura were getting other gifts from their kids in America—bathtubs, washing machines, fancy faucets. "My father say, 'You have to send,'" says Pete. "You know, there was some jealousy." So with their sister Panagiata they went to Astoria, a Greek neighborhood in Queens, and bought appliances that ran on European electric current. The big project was a new bathroom, and Sam points out that in Greek tradition, toilets were built far away from the house: "They thought it was a dirty thing." So some villagers were appalled when the Kourtsounis house acquired an indoor facility.

PETE: "They'd say, 'You put this in here?' They couldn't comprehend the idea." Once the bathroom was finished, the elderly couple kept the door closed, hiding the "dirty thing" and confounding their kids. Sam: "I say, 'You have to leave the door open. Otherwise how do you know if anybody's in there?'"

In 1980 the idea of *nostos*, of homecoming, was still flickering. Eleni inherited some land from an aunt and she and Pete packed up the kids and moved back to Greece. They were still employees in America, not owners, and Pete saw a chance to open his own restaurant in Sparta. Eleni agreed: "I thought it would be much easier at that time to go back." They were wrong. The business opportunity never materialized and Pete decided the venture was "a waste of time and money." He explains: "It was impossible. The problem was, you compare it to here. Why should I kill myself when you already had it better in the United States? It was a mistake so we came back." The old obstacle that had driven the boys away in the first place resurfaced: without the right connections, even drive and ambition did not guarantee success in Greece.

ELENI: "If you're a very hard worker you have a lot of chances here in America. There you have zero." But there was something else: they were no longer Greek, they had become *xeni* themselves, foreigners in their own land. Sam: "It's the mentality, they think differently. You used to do the same things when you were there, but once you move, you see other things, your mentality changes, and you can't have both. Either you're going to be like them or you're going to be an outsider. So it becomes difficult." Eleni summed up: "It's a good thing we went. Now I know I can't live there." Transitioning to a different culture didn't work the other way, either. After their mother died in 1981, the brothers invited their father to live with them, but he was always a *xeni* in America, says Pete: "Where would he go? He couldn't communicate; it was like he was in a cage. He'd stay a couple of months and go back. If you don't come here by the time you're thirty or thirty-five, it's very hard to adapt."

By 1983, Pete and Sam had saved enough money to buy their own business, a small diner in the Queens neighborhood of Bayside. They brought in their sister's husband as a third partner and ran the place for eleven years, but then the brothers decided to sell out and move out. "Economically New York was not a good place to be," recalls Sam. "There were too many restaurants, too much competition, it was not a good idea to invest money." Pete: "We were making a living but we didn't have any future." They found a restaurant for sale in Towson and after some repairs, opened for business in the spring of 1994. "We came with the mentality of New York," he says, and it didn't work. For one thing, summer is tourist season in New York and the brothers expected an immediate influx of business. "Here it's the opposite," says Pete. "Everybody goes to Ocean City in the summer; the town's dead." Then they put dishes on the menu that were popular in New York—cheesecake is a good example—but unknown in Towson. Sam: "We used to make the cakes and sometimes we'd throw them in the garbage can. I'd say to the salesperson, Spiro, 'What the hell's going on? Why don't people eat the cakes?' And he says, 'Sam, you're not in New York. This is Baltimore. You have to educate the people.' So most of the time we'd give the cakes for free, so people could try them out. This is how we got started."

Business was so slow at first, says Pete, that "we got scared. We had no credit, nobody knew us here." They fired most of their staff and did most of the work themselves, from cooking and baking to fixing the air-conditioning equipment. "I used to work the line, short order, sixteen to seventeen hours a day," Sam remembers. What saved them was their years of experience in the business, says Pete: "We know what it's all about. If somebody didn't know, they'd never make it. We didn't panic because we knew we could stay ahead." But there was another factor as well. They had no other option. Sam: "We couldn't possibly leave. We sold everything in New York. Where were we going to go? Back to New York?" Pete: "There's nowhere else. It's here. It had to work." And eventually it did. Fall came and students returned to nearby colleges, Goucher and Towson State. A good write-up in a local paper helped. But the toll was brutal. The place served seven days a week, opening at 6 A.M. and closing at midnight. The brothers would get three or four hours of sleep a night and never took a day off. They were grateful that their wives were "from the old school" and tolerant of their schedule. Pete: "Our wives understood what we went through." Sam: "She's not going to tell you, 'I want to go out Saturday night,' because she knew you were tired, that you were working your butt off. Somebody who didn't understand the concept would say, 'I don't care, I want to go out,' but they understood how we felt."

They did understand, but Ioanna felt like a widow at times, especially when it came to the kids. "They play sports and there was never a dad there," she says. "My oldest son, his soccer games, he was on travel teams, he would travel everywhere, and his father was never around. Sometimes it's hard to explain to my son why his father was not there. There were a lot of things I had to do by myself." The families seldom went to church together, or shared holidays. Eleni: "So many Easter dinners we ate with no father at home . . ." Sam: "Nothing's free. You have to work. To accomplish things you have to work. The restaurant is busiest on weekends; you can't just say I'm going to take off. But the kids, they don't understand. They say, 'Where's my father?' I say, 'He has to work.' It's hard, you know." Eleni: "It's a very big commitment." Ioanna: "Big-time." Even now, when the business is thriving and life is a bit easier, Eleni is surprised and alarmed when Pete comes home early: "What's wrong? You left the store? What's the matter with you? It becomes a habit. Oh my God, you left the store all by itself? What's going to happen there? We put all our life in here, you know." Pete: "You can't fool people. This is not a summer place, where I might see you or not see you. All our business is here, everybody knows us, some customers come in two or three times a day, and they think everything goes well if you're here. The employees, too. We proved that from years and years. We have to be here."

Sam left Greece young and feels increasingly separated from his homeland. He last visited there eight years ago and Ioanna recalls: "Three weeks was okay, but the fourth week, my God, I have to go home." Pete feels closer to Skoura and has built a vacation home there, but in many ways he's now a *xeni*, even in his village. Dealing with Greek workmen, for instance, drove him crazy: "It's a joke, really. They drag on for years to build." His answer: send all the materials and appliances from America. "Even the cabinets are from Home Depot," he boasts. "You know why? It cost me cheaper and faster." The politics are just as aggravating. Greeks can be relentlessly anti-American, blaming Washington for siding with their archenemy, the Turks. "You get in a cab in Athens," says Pete, "and they ask, 'Are you from America?' You say yes and they say, 'You think you police the world!' What the hell, I'm a passenger, but this is the mentality. They criticize all this but they're jealous, too. After the news in Greece, everything is American TV. I tell them, 'Why you have this on? If you don't like this coffee, why you keep drinking it?'"

As a result, most of the *Brooklis* who return to Skoura in the summer associate with each other, says Pete. "The locals are different. They're occupied with something else; they can't mix with us." Politics is only part of the reason. The transplants can no longer put up with the Greek schedule, which involves little breakfast, a late, heavy lunch, and dinner at ten-thirty or later. "We live on Tums and Rolaids," says

Pete. "The customs are so different. How can you possibly get up at seven, drink a small coffee, then go up to one o'clock [before eating lunch]. The whole stomach is going nuts." Pete and his expat pals often hang out at a café called El Posto in Sparta, and they urged the owner to adapt to American ways, especially at breakfast: "Some of us went out and said, 'You've got to put omelets on the menu.'" Pete estimates that as many as thirty-five families return to Skoura in the summer and the village "is booming, there are cafés everywhere. But in the winter, no good. By Thanksgiving no one is left." As Sam notes, the lure of *nostos* goes only so far: "Every Greek-American has faced the same problem. You go for the summer, a month, some two, some even three. But they always come back to America because of the kids, their grandchildren. You're going to leave your children and go to Greece? It doesn't work that way."

Both families were determined to pass on their heritage to their children, speaking Greek at home and attending Greek Orthodox services regularly. Sam and Ioanna's oldest boy was "a good altar boy, he never skipped church," and when she babysits for her first grandchild, Ioanna whispers to him in the language of the old country. Says Eleni: "If we don't talk to them in Greek, that's it, it's finished." But for the next generation, maintaining their identity is not easy. Of the four who are married, two picked Greeks but two found Italians, and their two cousins, Panagiata's children, have both married Jews. So now they have relatives who celebrate Passover along with Greek Easter.

What the families don't want to pass on to their children is the diner. One boy is a dentist, another a state trooper; the women are in finance, insurance, or sales. Eleni: "Our kids are not staying in the restaurant business. We educated them." Pete: "We are the last generation in this business. After us I think there will be very few. For us, uneducated guys, immigrants, it worked. But I'm glad my son is not involved." For one thing, the older generation doubts that their children would put up with the hardships they endured. Ioanna: "The new couples, I don't think they can do the restaurant, because they want their husbands together. You raise the kids, you go to the movies, how are you going to work in the restaurant?" Eleni: "Their wives are going to leave them." Because they marry women who are not like their mothers, not "from the old school," young Greeks who do take over family restaurants can cause problems for their fathers. "If you have members of the family here you never retire," says Pete. "We see this from a hundred examples around. The father works and the son goes away." Besides, both families have so much of their wealth tied up in the business, they can't afford to give it to their children. Financially, they'd be better off selling it to strangers. "We have so much expenses," says Eleni. "We pay the college, we pay the weddings, we help them with the houses, we have no money left for us. So this is our money, this is our retirement." The *nifi*, the new bride who came to America at seventeen, not knowing what a dime was or how to make a phone call, continues: "We went through very hard times with this business. That's why they say, if they'd married American girls, they would have divorced them a long time ago. Now we have a good life. Our kids they finish school, which is very important to all of us. They have their own jobs. We have our cars, our nice houses, we have a better life. But really it was very hard work. We missed a lot of stuff in the younger years. Like I explain to my daughters today, you know something, we came from Greece with one bag, with nothing. We started from zero."

7.

Jose, Beti, and Ana Reyes

EL SALVADOR

They put five people in the trunk of one car and they tried to cross from San Diego to Los Angeles. I felt the car running like crazy, I felt that something was happening, and then I hear a knock. It's Immigration. They opened the trunk, we were all stuffed together, and they kept me for three months in jail.

Since 1982, Jose and Beti Reyes have run a restaurant in the Adams Morgan section of Washington, D.C., specializing in the dishes of their native El Salvador. The name, El Tamarindo, comes from Jose's hometown, but it's Beti who always had the head for business. When she was about eight, she would help her grandmother make tamales, two or three hundred at a time, and then the girl would peddle them all over her small village. "You want tamales? You want tamales?" she would chant as she made her rounds. "We are a very busy, very working-hard family," she adds in her fractured English, and that has not changed. For many years, the Reyeses had a rule: one of them was always present to supervise the restaurant. Beti would work the first shift, getting the place ready to open for lunch at eleven. Jose would stay till closing: 2 A.M. on weekdays, 5 A.M. on the weekends, leaving only after the last stragglers had departed the neighborhood bars and dropped in for a *pupusa* (a thick corn tortilla stuffed with cheese, beans, or pork) before heading home.

The four Reyes children have reacted very differently to their upbringing. Ana Rosa, the youngest, got a degree in business from Florida International University in Miami and came home to manage the restaurant. "I like being here. It's like second nature to me," she says. The other sister, Evelyn, owns her own hair salon. But the two brothers, Erick and Javier, want nothing to do with running a small business, says Beti: "They say, 'No, no, I don't plan to live my life the way that you live, just working and working and working.' That's what they say." Instead, says Ana, with a mixture of pride and bewilderment, "both of my brothers want to be rock stars."

If the boys are not selling tamales, they are following a different family tradition. Jose, too, has always wanted to be a star. "In the beginning I didn't know anything about music," he told an interviewer from *Hispanic* magazine. "But we all have a dream, and I wanted to sing. I was a businessman, but I also needed to do something to express myself, my emotions. So I took singing lessons." Then he started writing songs, and recording them at his own expense, and like his wife's cooking, his music is deeply rooted in his homeland. The video for his song "El Tamarindo," a tribute to his birthplace, is set on a beach. Shots of Jose in a variety of silk shirts, trying very hard to look like a Latin lover, are interspersed with young girls writhing rather chastely to the beat. Another song, "La Batea," takes its title from a shallow wooden bowl that has long served in Latin cultures as both a washboard and a percussion instrument. The lyrics are equally simple:

Now the whole world is dressed very beautifully
Because we're going to dance in the rhythm of the washboard

Look for your partner and let's dance
Because in this party, you shouldn't miss out

The boys have not exactly taken up the washboard. Erick (on bass) and Javier (on electric guitar) play with a band called the FIF that combines a variety of ethnicities (Haitian, Filipino, and African-American besides Salvadoran) and musical styles. While it's primarily a hip-hop group, they add dashes of funk, R&B, and rock, creating what one reviewer called "a musical gumbo of sorts." Listening to three of their songs posted on YouTube, one hears a lot of "niggers" and "motherfuckers," frequent references to urban violence (bodies in Dumpsters, knife slashes "from hairline to throat"), and a suggestion that the best way to make money is selling dope. That doesn't seem like the lesson the Reyeses were trying to teach their children by working eighteen-hour days at the restaurant. But Jose is proud of his boys and their music even if he doesn't understand it: "It depends on how much emotion you put into it. If someone puts a lot of emotion in, it's going to sound better, it's going to be good music." He even fantasizes that he and his sons will one day play in the same concert. But, he concedes, "I don't think that's going to happen."

Jose's father was a tenant farmer, and the boy left school at about age ten to help grow the corn, cotton, and watermelons that sustained the family. His favorite job was preparing the oxen to plow the fields. Dropping out was no big deal, since continuing classes meant walking an hour each way, and his parents "didn't think I should go to school; they thought I was going to live the whole time in the country anyway." (Jose was illiterate when he arrived in America, but he took night classes and learned to read and write. His English is still so poor, however, that our conversations were conducted in Spanish, through a translator, and he keenly feels his lack of education. Proudly, he showed me a poster-sized blow-up of a check for $1,860, money he raised to help build a library back home.)

The family house had no plumbing or electricity, and it was Jose's responsibility to fetch water from a nearby river. His contacts with the outside world were minimal: an occasional trip to a local market to sell crops, a passing truck that would stop and buy the family's watermelons stacked on the side of the road. "We didn't know any better, so it was fine," he recalls. But then he started learning about a world beyond his village, and life wasn't so fine anymore. El Salvador had been sending a steady trickle of immigrants to the United States for years, and one of them was a family friend. Jose recalls the impact the man made when he returned to El Tamarindo: "You could tell there was a change in him, that he had done well. When he got back to El Salvador he bought property, he bought nicer clothes, you could see the change, and that would affect anyone. It was happening all over El Salvador. Everybody was coming back and saying this is a place where there's a lot of opportunity, for work and success."

Even after electricity came to the village, poor families like Jose's could not afford to connect to the power grid, let alone buy a TV set. So little shops were opened where these families could go and watch television. From listening to a battery-powered radio at home, and seeing TV in those village shops, Jose remembers commercials sponsored by "coyotes," the smugglers who help illegal migrants negotiate the border: "The coyotes, they do the advertising. They let people know that if you want to come to the U.S., call me, I take you to the U.S." At about age fifteen, Jose says, "I started thinking about it. That's when I realized I could actually leave the country and do something different." It "happens over time, it's a gradual change," but soon Jose was saving money and planning his escape. When he turned twenty he told his parents. "My mother didn't want me to come here, she thought something bad would happen to me," but his father "knew I was already decided" and sold a cow for forty dollars to help finance his journey. On an April day in 1974, at five in the morning, he and a friend stood on the roadside to catch a bus to

La Union, the closest city. From there they crossed Guatemala and headed north through Mexico, changing buses often and reaching the border town of Tijuana in three or four days. They hadn't called any of the coyotes who had advertised back home, but it didn't matter. Smuggling undocumented migrants across the border was one of Tijuana's biggest industries. "It's really easy to find a coyote. People dedicate themselves to that," Jose says. He went to the hotel desk, told the clerk what he wanted, and was handed a list of phone numbers. He dialed one of them and the next day the coyote showed up and called his room: "It was just like a taxi driver, you talk and make an agreement." Jose had about six hundred dollars with him (what he had saved from working in the fields, plus the cow money). The coyote took two hundred dollars and guided a group of four or five people across the border that night. It took less than two hours and afterward, the travelers bedded down in an orange grove on the American side. "We couldn't see anyone," Jose recalls. "We didn't see any cars or lights; everything was really calm. I just walked across without any problems. I was very happy when they told us we were already in the U.S. I had achieved a goal I had set for myself."

The next morning Jose and his friend were driven to Los Angeles and put on a plane for Washington (for another $140 apiece). When they landed, they took a taxi to an address on Rhode Island Avenue, not far from St. Matthew's Cathedral (and practically next door to where I lived when I first arrived in Washington ten years earlier). A friend from home put them up for the night, and within a day or so they had found a room of their own in the Mount Pleasant neighborhood, the center of the Salvadoran community. "It was easy to find work," Jose recalls, and he got a job washing dishes at Blackie's House of Beef, a famous Washington landmark. A few weeks later he switched to another restaurant, near the city's waterfront, while his friend found work at a Mexican place. They thought they were safe, but they were not.

Three months later, immigration authorities raided his friend's workplace, seizing all the illegal aliens and escorting them home to gather up their belongings. Jose was taking a shower when his friend arrived at their room, in the custody of federal agents. When the agents asked if he had papers, Jose had to say no, so he was arrested as well. The two men spent six days in jail. They were asked to sign voluntary deportation orders and they complied: "There was no other alternative. If you resisted you stayed in jail longer. So I just signed it." It was a dark time: "When I was in jail I was thinking, I'll never be able to come back." He was wrong. He was taken to the airport in handcuffs and placed on a plane to Miami, with a connection to San Salvador. But staying home for a month was so frustrating that he was determined to return "*muy rapido*," very quickly. He retraced his route to Tijuana, called another coyote, crossed the border again, and returned to Washington. Nothing had changed. His old job was waiting for him, plus a check for back wages he had not collected. So was his old apartment: "I had just paid rent for the month of September, so the landlord gave me credit for that. I still had the key, and I just walked right in to my apartment again."

He lived in Washington as a fugitive for another twelve years and never got caught again. "I've always been very careful and I'm still very careful," says Jose, who finally got his papers in 1986, after his marriage to Beti. "You can't go places where you could have problems, like the airport. They catch you at the airport." His closest call came one day when he was working as a busboy at the Hamburger Hamlet, a restaurant near the Maryland line. Word spread among the staff that immigration authorities had arrived, hunting for illegals. With great glee he tells the story: "I went to the locker room, took off my uniform, changed into normal clothes, brushed my hair in the bathroom, and walked right past the immigration authorities. All my other friends went running. I was just calm and composed, *tranquilo*. The people who ran, the authorities followed them. I wasn't running,

I wasn't wearing my uniform, they looked at me but they didn't stop me. I just went to the bus stop and went home." While he was waiting for the bus, he saw the cars of the agents parked at a gas station. "That was the only time I came close," he says.

He lived a quiet life: working hard, saving money, learning the restaurant business. He attended church regularly at the Shrine of the Sacred Heart, an old stone edifice on the edge of Mount Pleasant that catered to the neighborhood's changing population by holding masses in Spanish, Vietnamese, and Haitian Creole. He played soccer on Sundays with other Salvadorans, attended cookouts in city parks, took literacy classes at a local community center, picked up the guitar. But he had no papers and no family. A friend at work kept telling him about Beti, and convinced him to attend a party at her house. The day after the gathering, he showed up to give her a driving lesson. "She liked me," he says with a laugh, "because she opened the door for me and let me go through into the house." Beti's English is not perfect, but good enough to carry on a conversation, and she offered this version of their courtship: "He used to work with my cousin's husband and I'm very close with my cousin. She come to me and say, 'Beti, you have to know Jose. Jose like this, Jose like that.' And she put us together, yes. He came to my house and say, 'You want to learn to drive?' and he teach me to drive. And after that . . ." Her voice trails off in girlish giggles. They were married less than a year later.

Beti was born in the village of Intipuca, a major source of migrants to America that survives largely on remittances. (A *Financial Times* story in 2004 described it as a place "where no one works but everyone has a pick-up truck.") Her mother died when she was five, leaving her largely in the care of her tamale-making grandmother. Her father, who worked spreading pesticides on local farms, died when she was twelve, and she's convinced his job killed him. At that point she moved in with her aunt and uncle in the provincial capital of La Union. Living in a city enabled her to finish eighth grade, but she still had to work constantly: sweeping floors in the family's small grocery store, taking care of her younger cousins. "It's never the same," Beti says, "when you don't have your father or mother." She came to resent her uncle: "I'm not happy. All I do is work with him. In my mind I say, if I'm going to stay all my life like this, just work with him, where am I going to go? What am I going to do?" And like Jose and so many others, she was drawn to the United States by economic opportunity: "In Salvador it's hard, very, very hard. If you come from a poor family there's no way you can make the money for living, or to buy a house or something like that. The only way is to come to the United States, to work and save your money." She already had a cousin in America who agreed to help. So she borrowed money from other relatives and, at age sixteen, left home.

From Tijuana she crossed the border with forged papers and a coyote moved her north: "They put five people in the trunk of one car and they tried to cross from San Diego to Los Angeles. I felt the car running like crazy, I felt that something was happening, and then I hear a knock. It's Immigration. They opened the trunk, we were all stuffed together, and they kept me for three months in jail." It was a horrifying experience. The food was strange ("we not used to eat sandwich everyday") and she felt constantly threatened by other female prisoners: "I never see something like that. I was only sixteen. In our country, in those years, you were not used to seeing a woman with another woman." An older inmate from Ecuador saw what was going on and protected her from the predators: "She took care of me like her baby, thank God. Yes, God put with me that lady over there." (Ana has heard these stories countless times and says of her parents: "I think it's kind of funny they've both been in jail. To me it sounds like a movie.")

After her release and deportation, Beti immediately started planning and saving for another attempt. Using a fake ID she crossed the border again two years later, and instead of being stuffed in the trunk of a car, she and five other fugitives rode on the floor of a VW bus with no seats. This time they arrived safely in Los Angeles and she flew to Washington, where she already had family connections, and started work the next day at a Spanish restaurant: "I laugh every time I remember that. They put me to washing dishes, and I never finish. Dishwashing is hard work, especially for a woman. I was only eighteen. The cook and the waiters, they came and helped me out." She spoke no English and found that frustrating: "I don't understand nothing, nothing, nothing. People ask you for money on the street and try to press you." She lasted two weeks at the restaurant before taking a job as a live-in housekeeper and babysitter with a family in Maryland for fifty dollars a week. But her business instincts kicked in and she figured out that she could make more money living on her own and cleaning house for several families. Then her cousin found her a job running an elevator for a federal agency downtown. Was she worried about the immigration authorities? "Yes, especially in those times, they can catch you at the bus stop, or they go to the restaurant and get you." But her faith, she believes, kept her safe: "What I do, all my life, before I get out of my house I pray to God. Every day, especially in those days because of the immigration. I thank God, after I crossed the border, I was never caught." Before meeting Jose she had had two children, Erick and Evelyn, with another man. Since they were born here they were automatically American citizens, and under the rules at the time, that entitled her to become a citizen as well. And Jose, in turn, was able to legalize his own status by marrying Beti. She brought her two children with her, they quickly had two more together, and with four little ones to raise, they decided to start their own business. "I always had the goal of being independent," Jose recalls. "I didn't know exactly what I wanted to do, but since I worked in a Mexican restaurant, that's what I learned."

Their first venture was a billiard hall. Beti would make her tamales at home, and Jose would sell them to the players along with coffee, hot chocolate, and doughnuts. When a retail space opened up nearby, she pushed Jose to expand: "I say to my husband, why don't we rent that place and open a restaurant. Instead of making my tamales in the apartment, I can make the tamales over there, and I can make more food and sell to the people. That's my idea, to open a restaurant. But I don't have any idea in how to run a restaurant."

The place did well at first but soon their inexperience showed. One day Beti was working the floor with one other waitress, who spoke no English. "They started getting busy and they were freaking out," says Ana. "The other woman told Mom, 'You take the gringos and I'll take the Latin people.' From what I hear it was insanity." Staffing was a big problem, Beti recalls: "One day the cook don't want to come, we don't pay enough, but we don't make enough [to pay more]. And the business go down, down, down." Beti tried her own hand in the kitchen, and while her tamales were fine, her other cooking skills fell short. Take *pupusas*, the stuffed tortillas. "To make them perfectly round you have to practice and practice, and she didn't know how to make them," says Ana. One time a customer ordered sixty *pupusas* to go and it took Beti three hours; an expert would have filled the order in less than an hour. Budgets were an even bigger problem. "Sometimes handling money is not easy, you do so many things wrong," says Beti. "We'd have a band, people would come and dance, we sell a lot of beer and make a lot of money. But the money would all go to the music and the publicity." Not long ago, an old customer dropped by El Tamarindo for the first time in more than twenty years. The woman was "shocked" to learn that the same owners still ran the place and told Ana: "When these people opened they had no idea how to run a restaurant. The food was fantastic, but the way they ran it was horrible. I thought there's no way they would survive."

The issues went deeper than finding a cook or paying a band. Jose had grown up very poor, an illiterate farmboy plowing fields with a team of oxen. Now he had money for the first time in his life and it went to his head. A hint of what happened shows up in his music videos. In one he seems to be wearing a wig, giving himself a fuller head of darker hair and longer sideburns; in others his own hair is clearly dyed. The dancing girls in the song "El Tamarindo" are much younger, and in several scenes he awkwardly looks into their eyes, holds their hands or touches their shoulders. The man in that video would probably not be content peddling *pupusas* till 5 A.M. Jose and Beti grew apart, she recalls: "When we have a good business, our relationship is no good, because money changes your mind sometimes. This is what was happening in our case. You feel like you're rich; you're going to spend more money on this and this and this. But you're not rich."

Finally they decided to sell out. They owed a lot of money and couldn't meet their payroll. They made a deal with a buyer and had their lawyer draw up papers, but the lawyer warned against going through with the sale. Any money they were paid would go to creditors, and they would end up with nothing. So what should we do? they asked the lawyer. Just don't sign the papers, he replied. Beti remembers the scene with the buyer: "He say don't sign so we don't sign. That man was very angry, very angry." But that moment, leaving the sale papers unsigned on the table, was a turning point. Says Beti, "I feel like we go through one experience God put to us. If you don't change those things it's not going to go right. But something changed, and after that things got better and better." Mainly, Jose started paying attention to his wife, the businesswoman: "After that he listened a little bit more to me, and when he listened, I started putting more and more of my own ideas and effort in. And his, too. He worked more than me, in some ways. He's a very working hard man."

When I asked why the restaurant had survived and prospered, Beti groped for the right English word. "Constancy," she said, meaning "consistency." The key was always being there. "You have to make sure the food is the same—everything, everything," she said. "It's nice when a customer says something is not good, they not happy, we take care of that. If we not here, sometimes the employees, they don't do too much." A lot of their customers are regulars from the neighborhood, including two men who have come in every day for twenty years and placed exactly the same order: chiles rellenos with salad. The busboys and kitchen staff from other restaurants in the area often descend, for drinks and *pupusas*, when their own places close. No one stays open later than El Tamarindo. The reviews in local papers and websites stress the large portions, reasonable prices, and "low-key casual atmosphere." One woman describes it as "definitely a good place to take a date to actually get to converse with him/her and to relax." But, she warns guys, it's a little too downscale for a first or second date, when "most chicks . . . want a little wining and dining. Maybe a fourth date and definitely after you've coupled up and just want to go out for some vittles."

When times were tough, the salesmanship Beti learned as an eight-year-old, selling tamales door-to-door, served the family well. "I think my mother is an amazing businesswoman by nature," says Ana. "She can sell you this napkin rack for four times the price and you would have no idea." On trips home to El Salvador she would pay for her plane ticket by purchasing goods cheaply—women's underwear and local cheese were favorites—and reselling them to customers at El Tamarindo. Ana still laughs about the time Beti had a pair of small women's panties left unsold and "somehow convinced this very large lady to purchase them." The woman was skeptical but Beti kept saying the fabric "is durable, it stretches." When the customer returned a few days later and complained the garment was "the most uncomfortable thing she'd ever worn," Beti relented and returned her money. Ana is also surprised at the market for *queso seco*, a hard, salty cheese her mother would bring back in her luggage: "I guess you have to be Salvadoran to miss it, because it's not that great. [But] it's part of home."

Like many Salvadorans, the Reyeses regularly sent money, and dreams, back home. As a young man Jose had fathered a child and he never lost touch with the mother, sending her four hundred dollars every month. (His own children did not know about their half sister, and when Jose finally brought her to America they were quite surprised. "She came when she was thirteen; that's the first time we met her," recalls Ana. "We didn't have any communication with her before." The woman still lives in the area and has three children of her own.) Beti still has a brother back in Intipuca, but over the years they have helped virtually every other family member on both sides to come to Washington (where 28 percent of the foreign-born population is from Central America). Most run restaurants or own stores; one drives a taxi. Beti's son Erick is also a photographer, and on his website he lists seven businesses as clients. At least three are owned by relatives and he uses the walls of El Tamarindo to display and sell his pictures. All the relatives originally arrived without papers but have managed, one way or another, to legalize their status.

It's also common for Salvadorans to raise money for charities back home, and over the years Jose has worked with Radio Borinquen, a Spanish-language outlet that regularly sponsors fund-raising drives for an orphanage, say, or a school: "People sometimes come in here and give me a dollar, two dollars, whatever they want." Sometimes he goes to places where Salvadorans gather—soccer games, nightclubs— "to collect money for the people." The library he helped support was built through Empresarios Unidos, an organization of Hispanic business owners.

This is all part of the legacy Ana embraced when she took over the management of El Tamarindo. She wasn't just acquiring a business, she was joining a community. In one sense she didn't have a choice. "We almost forced Ana to come here, because I don't want to do it anymore," says Beti. And Ana admits there was plenty of pressure: "My mother is tired. She's like, 'I'll collect some money and you take

care of this.'" When I asked Ana if her decision was an opportunity
or an obligation she answered, "A little bit of both. But I kind of see it
as an obligation that will pay off. It's not like an obligation that won't
have any fruit." Ana has absorbed the strong impulse from her parents to be independent, her own boss. After she graduated and took
a job managing a men's spa owned by someone else, her father kept
badgering her: "You can't do this for long." She has also absorbed her
parents' work ethic: "They worked day and night, for I don't know
how many years, and you see how far hard work can take you." El
Tamarindo opened in 1982, the year she was born, and as she sits at a
back table, next to the one her parents have manned for her entire life,
she smiles and says, "It kind of feels like home.".

For good reason. When the kids were small, Beti would pick them
up at school most days and bring them to the restaurant. "I remember
one waitress who still works here, named Gladys," says Ana. "She
was always yelling at us because we would throw spitballs. There are
four of us and we would completely tear the place apart and she would
be sweeping up around us." One time when the place was busy, young
Ana decided to help out: "I walked into the kitchen with a tray that
had one cup on it and they all started laughing at me. Wow, you're
such a big help!" By age eight she could serve as a hostess, showing
people to their table and handing them menus: "When we were small,
we were pretty much always here." But there was a downside as well.
Three of the kids (with the exception of Evelyn) were "all very fat,"
says Ana, and she blames the restaurant. Many nights, "We'd be waiting in the car to go home, and Mom would say, just wait for me, I'll
be right out. But if it was busy you can't leave, it just pulls you in."
When she finally could break away Beti felt guilty: "Mom wanted
to spend a little bit of time with us, so she'd take us out to eat like at
three o'clock in the morning." That's not a healthy time for kids to eat,
and the food you can find at that hour is not great for the diet, either.

Often the kids would spend entire weekends, the busiest time at the restaurant, without seeing their parents while an aunt or godmother watched out for them.

Coming home has been an education for Ana. The college graduate finds it "pretty shocking" that her father, who was illiterate into his twenties, "has pretty much the same knowledge I have" when it comes to running a business. "Things I would read in a textbook, he's giving me advice on. He just figured it out." Jose is particularly deft at managing people, but dense when it comes to technology. Regularizing records has been a nightmare: "They didn't even have a file cabinet before; all the papers were spread out everywhere." Installing a computer—to buy supplies, track inventory, pay bills—has been even more daunting. Beti simply refuses to learn anything. Jose can place an order on a touch screen, "but as for reading reports or anything like that, it's like trying to teach him Chinese." At times Ana gets frustrated with the slow pace of modernization: "It's hard to do it by yourself, if your business partner has certain limitations." Especially if that partner is also your father. But when it comes to dedication she is clearly her parents' daughter. One Sunday she was determined to take the day off. She was still at home, lounging in her pajamas and watching a movie with her boyfriend (an immigrant from Peru), when the phone rang. The restaurant had run out of sour cream. "I'm like, 'I knew it, I knew it,' so I had to run out and buy sour cream," Ana recalls. "So you can't really get a full day off." While she was trekking out to Costco in Virginia for the sour cream, she bought some other supplies as well—honey, soda—and wound up spending four hours. No wonder that her boyfriend, who idles away hours waiting for her to finish work, recently had a bad dream. "It's this weird thing," she says, gesturing toward the walls of El Tamarindo: "He's sitting somewhere, staring at a brick wall, and it was these brick walls."

Since most of her family has come to America, Ana does not feel particularly close to her parents' homeland: "I don't go to El Salvador and say I'm home." She tells the story of a recent trip there, when she was taking a niece for ice cream: "I couldn't get across the right word for sprinkles; I had a hard time communicating." But she does feel attached to the Latin culture, and despite being totally bilingual, she prefers to read favorite authors, like the Brazilian novelist Paulo Coelho, in Spanish (he writes in Portuguese but is widely translated): "I think the Spanish language is more romantic, more passionate; the tone is stronger." When we talked, she was pregnant with her first child, and she's determined to teach the baby Spanish first, then English: "Your culture plays a big part in who you are. If you don't speak the language, you're losing a big part of your culture and your background. It's something to be proud of."

Beti is increasingly detached from El Tamarindo, happy to let Ana take over while she spends more time with her grandchildren, Evelyn's three daughters. Jose is having a harder time letting go, but Ana is grateful he still works the night shift. "He sits in the little back room and plays the guitar sometimes," says his daughter. "He's here all the time. I don't think he knows how to stay home and watch a movie; he doesn't know how to live any other way. He has to be here, even if he's sitting outside in the parking lot, talking on the phone. He has to be here; he's just too used to it." As for her brothers, Ana does not resent their decision to abandon the family business: "One child does one thing, another does another." But she slyly points out that food and music are not far apart: "That's how we can have a complete party."

Part IV

———————— ❧ ————————

T H E

PROFESSIONALS

It's a common perception that immigrants often lack skills and education, but that's only true for the twelve million foreigners now here illegally—many of them poor peasants from Latin America. Of the foreigners who have acquired citizenship, 12.8 percent hold graduate degrees, compared to 9.9 percent of the native-born workforce. Other statistics are even more startling: in 2007, foreigners earned two-thirds of the doctorates in computer science awarded by American universities. In physics the figure was 58 percent, and chemistry 53 percent.

The economic downturn that started in 2008 triggered a fierce debate over whether these foreigners were taking jobs away from Americans. One amendment to the federal stimulus package actually made it harder for firms receiving government help to hire outsiders holding H-1B work visas, and foreign-born graduates started losing job offers they thought were secure. But every fair-minded study has shown conclusively that these restrictive policies are self-defeating and counterproductive. As journalist Blake Fleetwood wrote in the Huffington Post, "Damming up the river of talented foreigners will cost American jobs, not save them." Brad Smith, Microsoft's general counsel, notes that 35 percent of the company's patents are generated by these "talented foreigners" and adds: "The future success of Microsoft and every other U.S. technology company depends on our ability to recruit the world's best talent." A recent editorial in the *Cleveland Plain Dealer* said the city "needs to re-establish itself as a magnet for new Americans. We need their fresh ideas, entrepreneurial zeal and optimism." I saw this from another perspective when my mother spent a week in the hospital after a bad fall. A procession of good-hearted, dark-skinned women from Ethiopia, Jamaica, Trinidad, and the Philippines performed most of her tests and treatments. Few homegrown Americans were in sight.

Some foreign-trained professionals cannot find work in America because they lack the right credentials. More than one cabdriver has told me about the degrees he earned back in Pakistan or Russia that are useless here. Nicholas and Sarah Stern both trained as engineers in Ukraine because Jews were banned from virtually every other profession. When they settled in St. Louis, Sarah found work as a computer operator (she had to tape Russian commands on the keys at first) and eventually earned a real estate license and sold houses to other Russian émigrés. Nick was determined to practice his profession and got lucky in his first job. Many of the engineers he worked with were also foreign-born and less than fluent in their new language: "We were all using our hands and drawing diagrams." Only the state of Kentucky, however, would accept his Russian degree and allow him to take a licensing exam. He would study every night, carrying his newborn son under one arm and a textbook in the other. After he finished second in the state test his career took off, and he eventually became a highly successful investor, building power plants that "cogenerate" heat.

Like the Sterns, Munr Kazmir received his professional training abroad, earning a medical degree in his native Pakistan. He was already enrolled in a postgraduate program in London and on vacation in America when he heard about an internship at a hospital outside New York City. On a "whim" he took the unpaid post and he's never left. By his own account he was a "lousy doctor" but a keen businessman, and he created several prosperous enterprises in northern New

Jersey that provide technicians to hospitals and drugs to patients. Immigrants, however, do not always get along with each other. He lost a lot of business, he says, because "big Muslim doctors" stopped using his companies when they learned he had a Jewish mother.

Pablo Romero represents a different version of this story: he dropped out of school at age eleven in his rural Mexican village and came to California two years later as a farmworker. But he had to leave America to find his full potential. When the U.S. Army demanded his services and sent him to Germany, he read every book in the post library and passed his high school equivalency test. College scholarships followed but he didn't focus on medicine until a professor asked him how many Hispanic doctors were practicing in his hometown of Salinas. The answer—none—pushed him toward medical school, and while he dreamed about opening a high-priced surgery practice in San Francisco or Beverly Hills, an internship in Salinas taught him where he belonged. Back home. Today he runs a neighborhood clinic where most of his clients are farmworkers.

8.

Sarah and Nicholas Stern

UKRAINE

It was great. It was warm but it was great.
It was very carbonated. It tasted like freedom.

In 1978, Sarah and Nick Stern left Ukraine with $120 apiece. Today they live in a penthouse overlooking New York's Central Park and vacation in a Florida condo where Sarah's closet, jokes Nick, is bigger than the entire apartment she grew up in. An electrical engineer by training, Stern shoveled snow and raked leaves when he first came to America. Eventually he made a fortune building and financing power plants and he attributes much of his success to his immigrant origins. "The fact that we came from the Soviet Union made us very disciplined," says Nick, a gentle man with a full beard and a soft voice that still reflects his Russian past. "It also made us very optimistic. So when an opportunity came along I plunged into it, but I never did it in a way that I could lose money. I was very cautious. When we came here we had no money whatsoever, so when we made some money the first focus was on not losing it. It was as simple as that. It got ingrained in us pretty fast."

One of Stern's investors is a British shopping-center tycoon, and after the man's business adviser checked out Nick's company he remarked: "What you guys did is quite amazing." And, he added with emphasis, "It would never have happened in Europe." Nick agrees: "There are much more barriers, much less meritocracy, than here. When we look at business propositions over there, they're so convoluted. You've got to have a local, well-established organization to do anything. Whereas here, you can start from scratch." That's what Nick Stern did. He started from scratch. He was able to succeed because he brought valuable traits with him to his new country: drive, ambition, tenacity. But he thinks the most important quality immigrants contribute is optimism: "They come because they feel optimistic about their future. Otherwise people would not be coming here. The optimism drives everything."

The Sterns never felt optimistic about life back home, and for good reason. Says Nick: "The Soviet Union was a land of no opportunity no matter who you were, but especially if you were Jewish." At seventeen Sarah's mother had fled to Kharkov, an industrial city in northeastern Ukraine, searching for food. It was the early 1930s and like many rural areas, her hometown of Uman was gripped by "a total famine." But it was a famine caused by politics, says Nick, not weather: "Stalin was consolidating his power and starving areas of the country that showed potential opposition to the regime." Adds Sarah: "It was a horrible, horrible time. My mother would say, 'They just died: aunts, cousins, sisters.' That's what happened." When Sarah's uncle was thirteen, he lived as a "street child" in Kharkov, with no real home (although he eventually went to school and became a chef). Two years after arriving in Kharkov, Sarah's mother married a man nine years older: "I guess she didn't have any choice. He was an okay guy, and he had a room of his own."

Sarah's father worked at one of Kharkov's biggest factories, which made train locomotives. As war approached it switched to building tanks, and that probably saved his life. The entire factory was moved eastward, to the Ural Mountains, to keep it out of Nazi hands; key workers were exempt from military service and evacuated to run the machinery. So her parents were far away from Kharkov when the Nazis invaded, destroying 70 percent of the city and causing tens of thousands of casualties.

In 1946, when Sarah Rubin was born, the city was still recovering from the devastation. Her entire family (including her parents and a sister) crammed into one room barely 250 square feet in size. Nine families on their floor, twenty-eight people in all, shared a single toilet. "You can imagine how clean that was," remembers Sarah, a small woman with a sly grin. "Some old people would miss, you know," soiling the floor. One resident left regularly without flushing and "twenty-seven people would complain; he was a hated man." Another took his time in the toilet, while smoking up a storm, "so you'd get in there and it was like, totally awful." But Sarah's mother was clever; she converted a small closet into a makeshift kitchen. "That we had our own sink and stove was a luxury," she recalls. The Rubins were able to take regular sponge baths, and once a week they would all go down to the local bathhouse, but not all of their neighbors were so concerned about hygiene: "I don't know what they would do. And besides, there was no deodorant."

As a child, Sarah thought her life was wonderful: "I was reading early and in first grade I read these children's books and I thought, How lucky I am that I was born in this country, where this great revolution happened. You know how they brainwash you." Despite the severe overcrowding, life in the apartment building provided some "nice moments" for a child whose curious mind earned her the nickname "Old Nose." There were "some very wise women there," says Sarah, and during summer days, when her mother was at work, she would "hang out with them," washing and sewing and ironing, cooking borscht and serving tea: "I learned a lot from those people."

Anti-Semitism, however, was never far below the surface. Sarah would hear muttering behind her back: "that one is a *jid*," the term being a corruption of *yid*. To Jews it was an insult, but non-Jews used it casually, as in, "Go to the *jid* and buy something." Adds Nick: "You're looked at differently. I had plenty of friends, Jews and non-Jews, but nevertheless, you get into a little fight, and suddenly you're a kike. It comes out so naturally and easily."

As Sarah grew older, anti-Semitism became more corrosive. In an earlier generation, many Jews had earned professional degrees, especially in medicine (Nick's mother was a doctor). But in 1947, Stalin started denouncing Jews as "rootless cosmopolitans" with no loyalty to the state, and that campaign culminated in 1952 with his denunciation of a "doctors' plot," aimed—or so he claimed—at destroying the Soviet leadership. At a Politburo meeting in December of that year Stalin declared: "Every Jewish nationalist is the agent of the American intelligence service. . . . They think they're indebted to the Americans. Among doctors, there are many Jewish nationalists."

Many Jewish doctors were arrested or dismissed, and the doors to a medical career—and many other professions—slammed shut for Jewish applicants. As she approached college age, Sarah wanted to study law or foreign languages, but even though she was a top student, she had a hard time getting into any university. As she tells the story: "We had a family friend, a neighbor, who became the dean of a technical school. My mother went to him for advice and he said, 'Let her try. The first year she will not be accepted, the second year she will not be accepted, and by the third year she will lose her confidence and that will be it.' My mother said, 'But she graduated first in her class,' and he said, 'So what?' He would not say it was because I was Jewish, but he said she will not be accepted. I remember how I cried. I felt awful, really. I realized what was happening in this country." Nick breaks in: "Your mother was a very plainspoken, strong woman; she probably cursed the guy." Adds Sarah: "She could not believe he said such a thing. He really wanted to hurt her. For what? Because we were Jewish? That was the only reason." With a great deal of trouble, Sarah finally got accepted to engineering school, the one profession still open to Jews, and after graduating was hired by a government ministry that designed electric power systems.

Nick grew up in slightly better circumstances. His father came from a poor farming family of many children, but he wound up in military school, where he received a good education and a ticket to the front lines during World War II. The elder Stern was seriously wounded near the Polish-German border, but managed to return to Kharkov a decorated veteran, and found work as a bookkeeper for the military. On Nick's mother's side, the family had immigrated to Ukraine from Lithuania during World War I. His maternal grandfather, who worked in the same factory as Sarah's father, came from a long line of rabbis. Nick's mother had made it through medical school before Jews were excluded. In the Soviet Union, there was no private medicine—doctors were civil servants working for the state—but the family qualified for a two-room apartment. "By Russian standards it was quite decent," says Nick: his grandmother in one tiny room, two parents and two sons in the other. To supplement her salary, his mother would sometimes receive gifts from grateful patients: "My mother was one of the best diagnosticians, and as a typical sign of gratitude, people would bring her a box of candies. So we always had candies, thanks to her."

Like his future bride, Nick quickly became disillusioned with the Soviet system: "I grew up in a family where both of my parents drilled it into us, you have to study hard, you have to learn, and then, as a result of that, you'll have an interesting and rewarding and challenging life. But as we were growing up it became clear that the system did not encourage you to do that. In fact it discouraged you from doing

that. For ninety percent of the population, whether they were smart
or whether they were dumb, the incentive was to stay in the main
channel of mediocrity. Because if you were not mediocre, you could
become a target; something bad could happen to you. In our case it
was compounded by the fact that we were Jewish. Even what was
available to non-Jews was not available to us."

Nick's parents had lived through the worst of the Stalin years,
"pretty tough times when the gulags, the labor camps, were the price
you paid if you talked too much." By the time he got to college in the
late 1960s, the gulags were gone, but the thought police were not. He
remembers 1968, when the Soviets invaded Czechoslovakia and the
press was filled with justifications for crushing democracy. What he
read was "inconsistent bullshit," and he couldn't stand it: "I was fool-
ish enough to write down, 'Okay, here's what they say here and here's
what they say there.' It looked real silly. I showed it to a few friends
of mine, and then I got a call from a department of the college, human
resources, but it was really the KGB. If it happens in Stalin's time
I would probably disappear. But then they just said, 'Everything's
going good for you here: you're doing well, your parents are doing
well, don't be an idiot.'" Nick was also frustrated by his professional
choices. Medicine, law, and advanced sciences were out. History and
philosophy offered intellectual rewards but not financial ones. So like
Sarah he became an engineer by default. In those years, he explained,
"Russia produced an enormous amount of talented engineering grads
because everything else was closed to Jews."

After finishing school, Nick was hired by the same ministry where
Sarah (four years older) already worked. It was run by a "good old
Jewish guy," as Nick put it, whose "claim to fame was that he would
hire the best Jewish graduates and stuff them in his department. His
department was always the first in all the projects. The work was
done phenomenally well, but the only reason he was able to do it was
because there were not too many places you were able to go. Supply

was huge and demand was limited, so he was able to pick and choose."
On Nick's first day, he was assigned a desk in a large room near a
telephone, and Sarah came in to make a call. "She was the cutest of
the girls," Nick remembers. "I thought she was a secretary; she looked
very young. I hit on her right away. She rejected me at first but the
power of persuasion was big, so I won her over."

Nick and Sarah were both living at home, three blocks apart, with
no privacy of any kind. But love, like water, finds its way through the
cracks. "You get inventive," recalls Nick. "You want to be alone with
each other. One of your friend's parents goes away, so you visit your
friend and they conveniently leave you alone." But as their romance
blossomed so did their resentment. They started to feel trapped, in
dead-end jobs in a dead-end city in a dead-end country. When she
complained to her boss, says Sarah, "he would say, 'You can't leave—
where are you going to go?' and I knew he was right." She had started
working at twenty-two, and as she watched other women preparing
to retire at fifty-five she said to herself, "Oh my God, I just don't want
to end up retiring here." The Sterns were hardly alone in their frustration, and that's why, Sarah says mordantly, there were always "incredible lines to buy vodka." But under the Soviet system, moving to
another town was almost impossible. Every citizen needed a *propiska*,
or residence permit. Without one you couldn't get a job, an apartment, a place in school. About the only area issuing new *propiska*s was
Siberia. In fact, Sarah's sister got so stir crazy ("she wanted to escape
our room") that she did move to that remote Asian region for a year.
When she wanted to return home, her parents had to use connections
and pay bribes to renew her permit to live in Kharkov.

Since moving within the Soviet empire was out, leaving entirely
was the only other option. When I asked the Sterns how and why
they decided to emigrate, Nick answered: "It wasn't any particular single event, it was the cumulative effect of everything that was
going on." Part of that "cumulative effect" were the "little bits and

pieces of information" about the outside world that had started to filter through the Iron Curtain. After Stalin's death in 1953, the rise of Nikita Khrushchev had led to a gradual "thaw" in the Cold War. By the early 1960s people were feeling bold enough to buy shortwave radios and listen secretly to the Voice of America (VOA) and the BBC. The broadcasts were still jammed periodically but as Nick recalls, "The technology improved. You couldn't jam everything. The VOA was phenomenally inventive at changing the frequency every other day. I probably started listening when I was thirteen [in 1963]. The good thing about the VOA was that they stuffed those programs with a lot of Beatles. The Beatles' music was great.

"We knew everything we were getting in the official media was all propaganda," adds Nick, and the foreign radio broadcasts offered an "alternative version" of reality. "We could see, more and more, that the alternative version feels and smells like a much more truthful description of events than in the native newspapers and broadcasts." Even a few Russian journalists were getting bolder: "People who were correspondents, publishing in the newspapers, they still followed the party line, but they would slip in a little line here and a little line there. It was great entertainment for all of us to find those lines and say, 'See what he says, isn't that funny, look how inconsistent that is with the official description of say, America being a place of horror.'"

Some American films were shown, mainly Westerns such as *The Magnificent Seven*. "Italian movies were incredibly popular, mainly comedies," says Nick, and while government censors "were very selective about foreign movies you were allowed to see," they were more tolerant of directors and producers who "had socialist leanings," such as Federico Fellini and Carlo Ponti. And even their nonpolitical films had an impact: "A little bit here and a little bit there, you formed a picture, which is very inaccurate but nevertheless, it's something different, a different view of the outside world." Adds Sarah wistfully, "You could see some apartments." And when you were living in one crowded room in Kharkov, a terrace in Rome seemed pretty appealing. Listening to the Sterns, I thought of my own grandfather, Abe Rogow, who immigrated to America from Russia as a young man in 1914. Fifty years later, after visiting his sister who was still living in Moscow, he decided that the great flaw in the Soviet empire was plumbing. If Russians could see how Americans lived, he was convinced, they would rise in revolt, so he started sending back to Moscow every magazine he could find with a picture of a bathroom. Crazy, yes. But was he essentially right? Absolutely.

The thaw also produced a trickle of immigration, and settlers started sending letters back home, detailing life abroad. Sarah's mother had a friend with relatives who had moved to Israel from Kiev, Ukraine's largest city. And while things were hardly perfect, they wrote, if you studied Hebrew and worked hard, you could find a job and an apartment of your own. One letter contained a vivid line Sarah has never forgotten: "We eat oranges here like you eat potatoes." Sarah's mother was entranced by the letters, and while she was a homebody who "wouldn't travel two blocks," she would say to her daughter, "When I'm gone, you should go."

Russian writers were emboldened as well. In 1962, Aleksandr Solzhenitsyn was allowed to publish his groundbreaking novel, *One Day in the Life of Ivan Denisovich*, detailing the horrors of Soviet labor camps under Stalin. In the late 1960s, dissident writings by the famous scientist Andrei Sakharov started to circulate in underground versions and they were eagerly consumed by young intellectuals like the Sterns. "Sakharov was an incredible writer," recalls Nick. "Initially, he was very mildly critical of the system, but coming from a guy who was worshipped by much of the country, it had a big effect on guys our age."

Solzhenitsyn and Sakharov are famous, and revered, figures in the West, but to young people like the Sterns, no one had a bigger impact on their outlook than the "bards," an informal movement of Russian poets and songwriters that flourished from the late 1960s through the mid '70s. New technologies that made reel-to-reel tape recorders (and later cassettes) widely available allowed the bards to reach vast audiences without official approval. "It was a way," says Nick, "for the entire population, who was fed up with the life, to sing their songs, to listen to them, to laugh out loud." Even Leonid Brezhnev, who had succeeded Khruschchev in 1964, was a fan of the bards: "It was known that he enjoyed them immensely, although they made fun of him."

The Sterns' favorite bard was Vladimir Vysotsky, a prominent stage actor who married a famous French actress and drank himself to death in 1980 at age forty-two. During his brief but intense career he wrote songs that captured the feelings of restless young Russians longing for a different life. Often he sent his messages through allusion and metaphor, but his eager listeners received them loud and clear. A good example is this verse from "Ballad of the Free Archers" written in 1975:

> All misfits and lonely paupers,
> Scornful of servant's lot,
> All unlucky homeless loafers,
> So that debt is all they've got,
> Every flotsam, every jetsam
> Flee to freedom in this wood,
> 'Cause its master is a handsome
> Good old fellow—Robin Hood!

Each of these influences—movies and letters, songs and novels, radio broadcasts and journalistic reports—contributed to the Sterns' decision to leave. "History teachers know," says Nick, "that once you liberate a little it's very difficult to put the genie back." They were married in 1974 and were ready, in Vysotsky's words, to "flee to freedom," but still, they held back. Nick's mother, who was responsible for several aged relatives, felt she could not abandon them. And yet she did not want her son to leave without her. The young couple was gripped by a "fear of the unknown." What would happen if they applied for visas and were turned down? Their lives would be over in Kharkov, forever branded as traitors. And what if they were accepted? Could they learn a new language? A new way of living? Sarah remembers that troubled time: "You think, oh my God, I don't know English. I will never be able to express myself the way I can in Russian. I was very proud of my knowledge of the Russian language. I loved the language, and I knew some of this would not be the same in English."

"It was an interesting subject to talk about," Nick recalls, "but actually crossing the line is a big step. So you have to let it all build up, and then you always need a little trigger event." Or two, in the Sterns' case. The first was the arrival of their son, Saul. The second was the arrival of Nick's draft notice. Suddenly they were out of options. Serving in the Soviet army was a long and harsh sentence. Nick went to the authorities and pleaded his case as a young father: "I sweet-talked my way out of it and they gave me an extension and I came home to Sarah and I said, 'We've got to go. We've got to go.'"

Opportunities to flee to freedom had expanded a bit. The Jackson-Vanik amendment, passed by the U.S. Congress in 1974, had threatened to withdraw trade benefits unless Soviet authorities agreed to let more Jews emigrate. "The Western media was extremely helpful," added Nick, with reporters from papers like the *New York Times* and the *Washington Post* "running around looking for stories of people being abused." And Soviet leaders "started getting more sensitive to world opinion. Before that they didn't give a damn."

So a grand fiction was created. To save face, Soviet authorities agreed to let people out for reasons of "family reunification." In theory, visas would only be granted to applicants with relatives outside the country who were willing to sponsor them. So the Hebrew Immigrant Aid Society (HIAS) office in Vienna set up a process: Russian Jews would smuggle out information about themselves; HIAS would match that information with people in Israel who would then agree to vouch for their phony "relatives." In almost every case no relationship actually existed, but every interested party was served by the deceit: the Jews got out, Israel got new blood, and the Soviets forestalled a propaganda nightmare.

For the Sterns, the first step was getting their vital data—names, addresses, birthdays—to HIAS in Vienna. The mail was useless. Soviet border guards and customs officials often confiscated documents carried by departing Jews. Deception was essential, and Sarah used a trick passed on by others: She would take Nick's boxer shorts, cut off the waistband, write all of the key information on the elastic, then sew the pieces back together. "Whenever somebody would get permission to leave I would give them some of my boxers," laughs Nick. "I figure by the time I actually got an invitation back, half of Vienna had walked around in my underwear." It took many months. The trick had to be repeated dozens of times. Even if HIAS received the information, "the Soviet postal service had an uncanny ability of losing the invitations in the mail." Finally several offers of support from ersatz "relatives" got through, and the Sterns faced the final decision: Would they accept one? Could they really make the break?

They hand-carried their visa requests to the local KGB office, a "dirty and dingy" place filled with rude and officious bureaucrats. The process required countless visits and "every time they'd give you a dirty look," Nick says. "But you get adjusted to it, you accept it, you keep going." The next task was to raise enough money to pay the exit tax, seven hundred rubles apiece, the equivalent of seven months' salary. "For us it was a huge amount of money," says Sarah, "so you sell everything you have, even your clothes, I'm not kidding, to get that money. Otherwise they won't let you go."

Most Russians quit work after filing visa requests because the abuse got so bad, and that's what Sarah did, but Nick stayed on. The family needed the money and he had a "thick skin," so every morning the office would assemble to denounce him: "People, including my friends, would have to tell me what they think about me being a traitor and all that stuff. I would stand there, and the main challenge was not to speak, not to talk back. It was very easy because I was always a disciplined dude. So they'd say all these terrible things about how ungrateful you are, how you always had a corrupt soul. It would take about thirty to forty-five minutes. You'd also get the worst assignments. But then you'd go home and spend time with family and friends and you were okay."

In January 1978, word came down from the authorities: Sarah; their son, Saul; her father; and Nick's brother could all leave. But Nick could not. It was one final attempt to shatter the Sterns' resolve, and it failed. The family refused the offer, and every week for the next four months Nick went to the KGB office, fruitlessly asking for news. Finally, on April 26, the head of the office threw a paper in Nick's face and said, "Here's your visa. Now get the hell out of here." Nick could barely believe the words: "Despite all the crap I had gotten from him before I was ready to kiss the guy." Outside, on the street, he ran into a schoolmate of his younger brother. "He looked at me and he said, 'What's going on? You look so happy.' I told him and we went and bought a bottle of vodka and finished it on the bench in a little park. I was elated."

Elated and frantic. They had decided to go to America. Sarah's sister had recently moved to the United States, and they were uneasy about stories drifting out of Israel: the influence of ultra-Orthodox Jews, the threat from Arab armies. They wanted to go where they would "feel most free." The first thing the Sterns did was file an application for Nick's parents to join them. The second was to focus on money. Other émigrés had told them that in America, they would need a car to find work, but the $120 in cash they could take out of the Soviet Union would barely buy a bicycle. Well, the couple that had contrived the Great Boxer Short Scam was not about to be thwarted this time. Jews who arrived in Vienna and decided to head for America had to spend several months in Italy before their paperwork cleared, and word was out that Russian immigrants could make money at flea markets in Rome selling items such as vinyl records, linen sheets, cameras, and coral jewelry. During those last days, the Sterns sold everything they could not take with them—clothes, furniture, appliances—and bought things that could be turned back into cash in the West. But that was not always easy. Since earlier immigrants had already cleaned out Kharkov's supply of marketable goods, they had to visit rural villages to stock up on coral beads. The border guards knew the game, of course, and would confiscate any valuables they found. So Sarah hid some beads by sewing them into the yarn-covered buttons on the sweater she planned to wear on the journey. Other gems were attached to her skirt.

By June they were ready to go, "but leaving family and friends was very hard. I was very, very upset," Sarah recalls. "Some people were afraid to come to our good-bye party because the government considered us traitors. One of my best friends barely came to say good-bye to me because she was afraid that if someone saw her, they would think she was supporting me, a traitor." Nick has a happier memory of their last days in Kharkov: "There was so much vodka consumed at our good-bye party that everybody there was drunk."

The entire family traveled with the Sterns to the Belarusan city of Brest, a key border crossing between the Soviet Union and Western Europe. As the departing immigrants went through customs, officials searched them for contraband. Sarah was wearing the sweater with the coral beads attached. But it was a sweltering summer day. Saul, then age three, started "crying like crazy," and Sarah made a mistake. She took the sweater off to deal with her child. "They went for my buttons right away and cut them off," she remembers. "If it was on me,

maybe it gets through, but I had to take it off and put it on the table."
As the young family headed for the train, Nick watched his parents,
standing behind a glass partition and waving good-bye: "My mom
was crying and my dad was biting his lip. You don't know if you'll
ever see them again. So that was bad. In terms of losing this stuff [like
the coral beads] I really didn't care." (The elder Sterns did receive
visas a few months later, and are alive today and living in Chicago.)

The Sterns struggled onto the train. The border guards "just threw
suitcases at you; many families shared one little compartment and
there was like mountains of junk." The train finally started and
Nick remembers: "The first thing we did was cross the border [into
Poland]. That's good. Wow. The second thing we did, in good Russian fashion, we opened a bottle of vodka and finished it real fast.
The third thing we did, we sorted out all the goods. After they had
confiscated so much we didn't need all the suitcases, so we repacked
them." After a few hours the train made its first stop. There was no
water on board, and the whole family was thirsty, so Nick got off and
used Russian money to buy two bottles of Coca-Cola, a drink they
hadn't tasted before. I asked his reaction: "It was great. It was warm
but it was great. It was very carbonated. It tasted like freedom. And
the next morning we hit Vienna."

Families headed for Israel were sent off immediately. The Sterns,
like others bound for Canada or America, spent a week or so in Vienna
before boarding a train for Italy. It was late afternoon when they pulled
out, and Nick recalls gazing out the window: "As we crossed the Alps
the moon was full; it was a beautiful sight." Italy was not so beautiful. Afraid of terrorist attacks, officials hustled the immigrants off the
train "in the middle of nowhere" and settled them in the seaside town
of Ostia, outside Rome. The living allowance provided by HIAS was
meager, barely enough to rent a dirty, crowded apartment, and at that
point Sarah put her foot down. After thirty-two years living in one

room, sharing a toilet with twenty-seven other tenants, she told Nick to spend everything they had on a nicer place. "It's a new life," she insisted. "We're going to live like people."

The entrepreneurial instinct that would make Nick a rich man in America first flourished in Italy. The flea market in Rome (known as the "Americana" because of the tourists who shopped there) was open on Sundays. Nick and his brother were up at 3 A.M. They lugged suitcases filled with seventy pounds of trade goods several miles to the Ostia train station. Sarah remembers seeing them off: "If only luggage back then had wheels like it does now, life would have been so much easier." But if a bottle of Coke represented freedom to Nick, so did the flea market, the first chance in his life to use all of his enormous energy and talent. "Showing up early was one of the keys to selling a lot," he remembers. "We always tried to get there first and buy the booth in the best spot, where most of the tourists would walk past. I carried those heavy suitcases to the market and I sure didn't want to carry them home at the end of the day." Not only was Nick the earliest salesman at the market, he was the cheeriest. Most of his fellow Russians were too tired, or grouchy, to make an effective pitch. "I would speak what few words of Italian or English I knew, but always with a smile," he recalls. "I would shout 'Signora, regalo per bambino' [Madam, gift for baby] or 'Very cheap!' But unlike most of the Russians, I was smiling." It worked. The Sterns sold out within a few weeks, earning about one thousand dollars. When they weren't traveling to Rome they were taking English classes. After three months their visas came through and HIAS flew them to America.

The first night in their new land was not exactly wonderful. In fact, says Sarah, "It was horrible." They were taken to a motel near New York's Kennedy Airport: "There were no windows in our room and we had never heard of air-conditioning so we didn't turn it on. It was ninety-five degrees, extremely hot for September. Then, we didn't know how to flush the toilet. In Russia, when you flush the toilet, the water goes down all the way. In America the water stays high in the bowl. So we worried that the toilet was broken." Nick: "I kept flushing. The water kept returning. It was killing me." Sarah: "We couldn't wait for the night to end."

Many Russians settled in New York, often in the Brighton Beach section of Brooklyn, but the Sterns headed for St. Louis, where Sarah's sister had located. They wanted a "clean cut from the past," not a place where immigrants "lived like they'd never left Russia." On the flight west the next morning, Sarah's father was taken with the little plastic cups of cream served with the coffee: "He grabbed a whole bunch of them; he was drinking them like shots. He turned to me and said, 'Oh, it's so good!' We didn't understand what they were giving us."

They spent the night with Sarah's sister, and got their first taste, or whiff, of a midwestern heat wave. "The air, the humidity, I'd never smelled anything like this," Sarah recalls. The next morning, the young couple decided "to go for a walk, to see America." The sister lived in a converted army barracks, in a run-down part of town, filled with small dwellings that "looked a little crummy," says Nick. "It didn't impress us." They expected America to look like all the pictures and movies they'd seen—big buildings, bright lights, bustling streets. "We just looked at each other," says Sarah, "and said, 'What is this?'" But a day or two later they moved into their own apartment (provided by HIAS, which paid the rent for three months). The neighborhood was marginal but the rooms were spacious and freshly painted. "I had my own place for the first time in my entire life," says Sarah. "I was the master of my domain." Adds Nick: "She started nesting. It was a great feeling."

Buying a car was not such a great feeling. They spent $950, almost all of their cash, on a 1973 black Chevrolet Impala, and before Nick got it home the muffler fell off. "I had to tie it up with a shoestring— literally," he says. "I pushed that car far more than I drove it." Adds Sarah: "I knew that every night when I was working, that whatever money I made, the next day that car would eat it. Either it would break or I would have to fill up the tank because it got eight miles per gallon." With both parents studying English and looking for work, Saul was sent to a local preschool and had a very hard time adjusting. "That was very painful. I felt very sorry for him," recalls Sarah. "He was in a state of total shock at first because he couldn't understand what was happening. He didn't even know how to tell people that he wanted to go to the bathroom. He didn't speak there for a month or so. He was totally mute."

Gradually, each of the Sterns found a voice. Saul quickly picked up the language from his classmates. His parents honed their English by watching TV (Sarah liked *General Hospital* and *M*A*S*H*, while Nick preferred *Hogan's Heroes* and *The Three Stooges*). But scientific concepts are the same in any language. As engineers, they were better equipped than, say, teachers or journalists to use their professional skills in a new culture. Sarah found part-time work as a computer operator (but had to tape little notes to her machine, identifying the keys and functions in Russian). She also studied for a real estate license, and for the first time in her life, found academics difficult: "I had to translate every work in the book in order to study. The dictionary was next to me at all times." She failed the exam the first time around, in part because her eyesight was poor. But Sarah was not about to give up. So she got glasses, passed on her second try, and started selling houses to other Russian émigrés.

Nick raked and shoveled to bring in some cash while scouring the papers for job openings. An electrical manufacturing company offered him $7.50 an hour. An engineering company paid a dollar less, but Nick's entrepreneurial flair, which had surfaced in the flea markets of Rome, kicked in again. The engineering firm, he felt, was growing fast and offered more opportunity, so he took the lower-paying job, and less than two weeks later his instincts proved correct. His boss "drank like a healthy horse" and most days, was dysfunctional by midafternoon.

So when a big meeting with an important client suddenly came up in Kansas City, the company sent Nick to do the briefing. His English was still shaky, but "one of the good things about America" is that many of the engineers at the meeting were also foreign-born and less than fluent in their new language. "We were all using our hands and drawing diagrams," he remembers. The meeting was a success: the contract was renewed. Nick received a promotion and a 30 percent raise. He was on his way, but he still needed to pass an exam to become a full-fledged engineer, and the only state in the region to accept his Russian degree was Kentucky. By this time a second son, Ben, had arrived, and Nick would study at night, carrying the infant around in one arm and a book in the other. For the exam he followed the tradition of Old World formality, dressing up in "a three-piece suit, Italian, very nice cut." Everyone else wore shorts and T-shirts. "I was over-dressed," Nick recalls sheepishly, "so I took off the tie and two pieces, but I kept my pants." And his cool. He finished second in the state.

The Sterns are deeply grateful for their time in St. Louis. Many Russians who never leave New York "live in a ghetto" and never adapt to their new country. But the Sterns made American friends and sampled American customs. Sarah remembers her first taste of American food, particularly the salads: "That was very different from the way we used to eat." But the biggest shock was cream cheese, smooth, white Philadelphia brand cream cheese. "It was like food from heaven," Nick recalls, "and Sarah wrote it down, 'Philadelphia cream cheese.' We both thought, What is this wonderful food?" Sarah preferred shopping at small neighborhood stores, and grew particularly fond of corned beef ("very impressive, I really liked that"). But the Sterns hated big supermarkets and still do. "They make me dizzy," says Nick. "I can't shop for more than ten minutes. They're too big, there's too much stuff to choose from."

Work did not make Nick dizzy. He kept getting promoted and after two years, the Sterns saved enough to buy a small house, a new car, a better refrigerator. And while he was saving, Nick was also learning: "I stumbled on an idea that I didn't know existed before." That idea was embodied in a law, passed in 1978, during the height of the oil crisis, to promote energy conservation. The statute required utilities to buy energy from independent producers who could supply less expensive power from renewable sources. The result was a boom market for "cogeneration" plants that produce electric power and steam at the same time, holding down energy costs. In 1987, Nick quit his company and started his own business as an independent power producer: The key, he figured out, was to obtain a contract to supply a utility. "Once you have it, you have your revenues," he concluded, and banks would lend money based on that revenue stream. Nick found a small "mom-and-pop" company in upstate New York that had a contract with a utility but lacked the financing to finish the project. He bought up the contract, went to Wall Street, and borrowed "pretty much one hundred percent of the capital that we needed" to build the plant. A few years later he sold the plant at a large profit. More projects followed. Eventually he moved from the role of developer to investor and financier. Nick had come to America virtually penniless, but through "a lot of work and a lot of luck" he had figured out a way to "create a significant amount of capital out of a pile of papers."

Sitting in their New York penthouse, gazing out at the sun-splashed park and the city beyond, Nick and Sarah muse about their journey. "I enjoy being comfortable but I don't care about luxury," he says. "We come from a very humble background." But he is pleased that he's created an investment company that can "last for a long time." Saul has joined the business, produced their first grandchild, and settled down a few blocks away. Ben spent several years learning the business as well before entering law school. Both are hardworking, levelheaded young men, but Nick worries about the impact that wealth can have: "We've seen so many people who get spoiled by all this crap, to be honest with you. That's a big concern." The Sterns are charitable people who avoid the limelight ("we frequently appear as anonymous donors," usually to Jewish or artistic causes). They have no desire the return to Russia ("There's nothing there that attracts me. It is an anti-Semitic, xenophobic, disgusting place"). But they have returned to their Jewish heritage, a heritage that their families had largely abandoned back in Kharkov. While Nick is hardly devout, he finds that reading the Torah and occasionally attending services creates "a strange sense of belonging." When Ben was bar-mitzvahed at age thirteen, Saul, six years older, decided to join him, telling his parents, "Why don't we just close the loop." But they can't fully leave the Old Country behind. Nick's parents came to America but Sarah's mother never made the journey and the brightness of the day stirs memories: "In our apartment in Russia, we only had one window, which looked north, and my mother would always dream about sun. Sun would never shine in our room. I feel sorry for my mom that she never had the sun."

9.

Munr Kazmir
(Munir Kazmi, Meir Kazmir)

SYRIA, PAKISTAN

If there is a poor man with you, one of your brothers, in any of your towns in your land which the Lord your God is giving you, you shall not harden your heart, nor close your hand from your poor brother; but you shall freely open your hand to him, and shall generously lend him sufficient for his need in whatever he lacks.

DEUTERONOMY 15:7–8

Every Monday morning at ten, Munr Kazmir meets with a rabbi to study and pray. They put on their tefillin, sets of leather straps and boxes that devout Jews wear when they worship, and read and discuss a portion from the Torah, the first five books of the Old Testament. These sessions take place in northern New Jersey, but the language is Farsi, a tongue Kazmir used in his native Pakistan when he first learned about Judaism from his grandfather. (While Urdu is the national language of Pakistan, Farsi, or Persian, the principal literary language, is frequently spoken by the educated elite.) "It's something I believe in," Kazmir says of his Monday morning ritual. "Somehow I feel comfortable. That's how I want to conduct my entire week. I want to be good. I'm not good, but I'm improving myself every year. Every day is a new chapter in the life, and the Torah tells you every part of the life."

No passage in the Torah means more to Kazmir than the verses from Deuteronomy that encourage Jews to "freely open your hand to . . . your poor brother." They are often cited as the origin of the Hebrew concept of *tzedakah*, usually and inaccurately translated as "charity." *Tzedakah* actually derives from the word for justice and means "righteous action," says one rabbinical sage. It is "not voluntary philanthropy" but "a matter of duty." And that's how Munr Kazmir lives his life, distributing his sizable wealth to a wide variety of causes he deems "righteous," from handicapped children in Israel to Republican candidates in New Jersey. "I do not remember what charity I supported yesterday," he says. "I want to remember what I want to do tomorrow."

Deuteronomy speaks of "your land" but to Kazmir, that phrase has many meanings. One is America, his adopted country, which took him in as a young medical student in 1984. A second is Israel, which provided refuge for persecuted Jews from around the world, including Syria, his mother's homeland. A third is Pakistan, his father's native nation, where Kazmir spent his childhood. Pakistan might be an unlikely target for *tzedakah*, since it is a largely Muslim country that harbors many religious extremists. Osama bin Laden, for one, has long found a safe haven in the remote mountains along the Pakistan-Afghanistan border. But that's precisely why Kazmir has gone back to his hometown of Lahore and financed an elementary school based on Western traditions and teaching techniques. He hopes his school will directly counter the influence of the "jihadis," as he calls the Muslim clerics who have built madrassas, or religious schools, throughout Pakistan. "They teach their children hateism, but we teach our children tolerance," he maintains, "and it's important to show what America is all about. I'm a private citizen but I really want to help the U.S. This is how I see it. There is no self-interest. I'm doing it for the country."

Like many new Americans, Munr Kazmir has refashioned his identity and reinvented himself. His father was a Pakistani Muslim; he's an American Jew. He's even chosen his own name. It was originally Munir Kazmi, but he changed the spelling after he became an American citizen in 1991, and he's offered several explanations for that decision. The new version "had a more Jewish-sounding appeal," he once told a reporter. In our conversations he said, "I never liked the name; it was given to me by my father. My father's name is something I don't want to be associated with it, or think of it. It's just too painful." In fact, his identification with Judaism has grown stronger over the years and his choice of names reflects that. In 2008, when he gave $2.5 million for a chair in Judaic studies to George Washington University (which one of his twin daughters attends) he specifically called it the Meir Kazmir, M.D., Professorship in Hebrew Bible. "Meir," his Hebrew name, means "light."

Kazmir's resentment about his name is rooted in the story of his parents' courtship. His father, Yusef, came from a wealthy family that owned "a lot of properties, a lot of farms" outside of Lahore. They also owned factories, including one that made uniforms for the Pakistani military. His father's brothers worked for the family business but Yusef studied law in London and joined the Pakistani diplomatic corps. He was serving as first secretary in the embassy in Syria when he met Sheila Hakim, the daughter of a prominent Jewish family in Aleppo that had prospered in the jewelry business. Aleppo was one of the oldest Jewish communities in the biblical world. According to legend Abraham lived there for a period and milked his herd of cows in the area. The Arabic name for the city, Halab, derives from the word for "milked." Another legend says that the foundation for its first synagogue was built by one of David's generals after he captured the city in about 950 B.C. In the modern era, Aleppo became a haven for Sephardic Jews driven out of Spain in the fifteenth century and one historian calls the city "the crown of Jewish splendor in the Sephardic world." But by the 1950s, life for Jews throughout the Muslim world had deteriorated drastically, and Syria was no exception. In 1947 pogroms torched Jewish businesses and sanctuaries. After Israel was founded a year later, Syrian Jews were barred from owning property, traveling abroad, or practicing their professions. So when Yusef Kazmi showed up in Sheila Hakim's life, wealthy and well traveled and twenty years older, she was swept off her feet. "I think my mother was impressed, and nervous over what was happening in Syria," says her son. "It was a bad time for the Jews of Syria. A lot of young ladies were wondering if I have a future. He was sending her a lot of gifts, so finally they decided to marry. I think it was a love story; they fall in love." The Hakims were "very upset" with their daughter's decision to marry a Muslim, and years later, after the marriage fell apart, Munr asked his mother why she had agreed to the match. "If you're not a woman you don't understand," she told him. "He was very smart looking, very well dressed. He was charming me."

They had a small wedding, a "Muslim ceremony" with "just a few witnesses," and "within a few weeks" the couple returned to Pakistan. Once there, however, Sheila learned a stunning secret that reverberates to this day. His father, says Kazmir, "tell a lie to my mother. He say he never married." But soon she learned the truth: "When she moved in Pakistan she find out. He put her in a beautiful house, but some of his friends say, 'You know, he's married, he has another wife.' She's shocked, and she's pregnant. She pregnant when she find out he have another wife." A wife and five children, actually. To her son, Sheila never really recovered from the news: "She always crying. I remember her being very nervous, always going into the other room and crying. My father drank and maybe he go to his other wife. It made her very upset." Kazmir has never forgotten those days: "Syrian Jews have very strong character. When I look back I think, Why this happen in my life? I think her suffering made me a strong person. She sacrifices her parents for somebody and then you find out . . ." As he tells the story he starts to weep and cannot continue.

In 1959, when Munr was three, his mother took him to Syria for a visit. "A lot of the Jewish community in Syria did not know my mother married to a Muslim guy," he says. "The family was well-to-do, respected." Sheila seemed ready to stay in Syria with her son. Her parents were very lonely without her, but her husband arrived after several months and demanded that she return with him to Pakistan. She did, but she left her son behind, and that decision changed Munr's life. He bonded deeply with his grandparents in Aleppo: "They fall in love; my mother got them addicted to me." And eighteen months later, when Sheila took her son back home, her parents decided to leave Syria and join their daughter and grandson in Lahore.

There was a small but wealthy Jewish community in the city. The Hakims settled in the Anarkali section, a "very busy" area where they opened a jewelry store, selling Syrian-made items. "It was hand-made, handcrafted, much better than Pakistani jewelry," recalls Munr. "My grandfather provide jewelry to a lot of VIPs; a lot of ministers came to buy jewelry from him." The Hakims also bought a large house, with commercial shops on the ground floor, within walking distance of their business. But to young Munr the most distinguishing feature was a Star of David set into the wall of the house. The previous owners were a Jewish family who had moved to India, and that sign of their religious identity had a strong symbolic meaning for the young boy. His parents' house had "a beautiful garden, five acres of land," but it was a house marked by betrayal and sadness. At his grandparents' house he felt comfort and love: "That house I enjoyed much more. My grandfather would pick me up at school and take me to his house. I was more enjoying that house. The other house was not very satisfying to me as a child. There was no peace."

One story conveys the discomfort young Munr felt in his parents' home. His father's mother was often there, dressed in traditional, loose-fitting Pakistani clothes. She carried a "very special, hand-made" walking stick—and a deep grudge against her Jewish daughter-in-law. "She had some good qualities," Munr says of his Kazmi grandmother, "but if I balance it out, she had more bad qualities." Instead of traditional dress, Munr's mother favored pants and short-sleeved shirts and her mother-in-law was scandalized. Munr recalls his grandmother's reaction to his mother's outfits: "Oh my God, this is so bad, this is disrespectful of the family. People coming here can see her body. She's creating prostitution in our home, destroying the family name." At one point the three of them were sitting in a room together. Munr's mother got up to leave, and he heard his grandmother mutter after her: "I hate her so bad. She's *kafir*," using an Urdu word for infidel. Munr knew the word because his Jewish grandparents had neighbors who were Sikhs, members of a religious sect from the Indian state of Punjab who are commonly called *kafir*s in Pakistan. "So after a couple of days," recalls Munr, "I talk to my mother and I say, 'Why does my grandmother not like you? Why she call you *kafir*? You're not *kafir*; you're my mother.' That word just bothered me at the time." Munr's mother admonished her son to "respect your grandmother," and on some level, perhaps he did. But he clearly had no respect for his father. The family was trapped in a web of lies they could never untangle or ignore: "He tell my mother, 'I'm going out of town,' but actually he was going to see his other wife." At other times Munr noticed a swelling in his mother's neck: "I think he beated her."

His mother's parents provided the peace that young Munr never felt at home. He would arrive at their house after school let out at three and stay until six or seven. Siestas, or afternoon naps, were a common practice and often the child would fall asleep on his grandfather's chest. As he got older, and napped less frequently, he would play with the children of the Sikh family next door. Munr's mother was nervous about these visits: "Anarkali was a very busy area and she always worry because somebody could take me for ransom." But she also knew Munr was absorbing something important in her parents' home, something that went beyond security and affection. He was becoming Jewish.

It wasn't just the Star of David on the wall of their house. His grandfather, whom Munr addressed as "abba," an Arabic term of endearment, read him endless tales from the Bible about Jewish heroes: "I learned about Moses and David; he read me all the stories. They teach me about everything. My grandparents played a big role in my Judaism." His favorite story was about Queen Esther, who saved the Jews of the Persian Empire from a murderous plot hatched by Haman, an evil adviser to the king. "She sacrificed, making a difference," he recalls. The Jewish festival inspired by Esther's story is called Purim, and every year Jewish families from all over Pakistan would gather at the mountain retreat of Murre, near Rawalpindi, to celebrate the holiday together. As a tiny and often persecuted minority, they had to be very careful not to attract attention. The families traveled separately and in secret. They brought their own servants, so hotel employees could not overhear their rituals or spy on them for Pakistan's powerful intelligence services. "You have to worry for the life," says Munr. "This is a Muslim country. You can't tell the outside world you are Jewish." The Jews of Pakistan had a "royal life, a luxury life" in terms of material wealth, but "you cannot express yourself and that's a problem. Safety is very important."

There was no rabbi at Murre, but the families conducted services among themselves. The Book of Esther, called the *megillah* in Hebrew, is overly detailed and takes an hour to read, but the Jews gathered in their mountain hideaway recounted it from beginning to end—in Farsi. (The phrase "the whole megillah" has made its way into American slang and means a long and tedious tale.) Munr's mother wanted him to feel a connection to other Jews ("she involved me with this group"), and even sent him to stay for a time with a prominent Jewish family in Karachi. While there he remembers meeting a rabbi from the Chabad-Lubavitch movement, a branch of Orthodox Judaism centered in Brooklyn that maintains outposts around the world. (It was a Chabad-run center in Mumbai, India, that was attacked by terrorist gunmen during their siege of that city in late 2008.) His mother and grandparents even arranged for him to travel to England, where they had many relatives, for a bar mitzvah, the Jewish coming-of-age ritual that boys celebrate at age thirteen. "It's giving me something I needed," he says of his Judaism. "It give me more strength in my life." Munr's father did not attend his bar mitzvah; in fact, he didn't even know about it. Some years later, when Munr was in college, he recalls, there was a heated argument between his parents: "My mother says, 'I want to tell you something: your son have a bar mitzvah done in England.' He got angry and said, 'How can you do that without my permission?' And she said. 'You're married to somebody else and you never told me. So don't talk to me about it.'" There were many things the Kazmis did not tell each other. Sheila did a lot of work in Lahore with Christian missionaries, dipping into the family's fortune to provide dowries for poor girls. "She spent a lot of my father's money," Munr recalls with considerable satisfaction. She also counseled the young women whom she helped: "Whatever you do, don't allow your husband to have three wives. He should have only one wife. Christian people don't marry three wives." (After Munr left for college his father married a third wife.)

Munr's formal schooling began at the Cathedral School, an old and proud institution founded by Christian missionaries in the 1850s. He went on to the University of Punjab and King Edward Medical School, and he thinks his grandparents influenced his career path as well as his religious identity. They gave him toys to play doctor with and told him that physicians "have a status." And he recalls fondly giving his grandfather "five or six spoons of cough syrup so he can sleep all night." But years later he told me, "I'm more a businessman than a doctor. I was probably a lousy doctor. My heart was not in medicine. In Pakistan I don't have another choice. I always wanted to do a different thing. I never had a medical practice." During his school days Munr made a close and important friend, Chaudhry Pervez Elahi. "The Chaudhry," as Kazmir refers to him, belongs to a very wealthy and well connected Muslim family and often served as a protector, a sort of Pakistani godfather, for his younger Jewish friend. As the chief minister of the state of Punjab, "the Chaudhry" was instrumental in helping Kazmir start his school in Lahore and spoke at the opening in 2007, praising its "missionary spirit."

In Kazmir's telling, his youth was full of rebellious acts against established authority in general and fundamentalist Muslims in particular. In one story local jihadis were stoning a Christian church in Lahore, and Munr organized a demonstration against them that landed him in jail for several days: "I got beated by police so badly in my back." In another tale, Munr and a Jewish friend were traveling to a beach outside Lahore and decided to stop at a mosque that offered free food to worshippers. The two boys listened to the imam preach "ten or fifteen minutes of nonsense," saying that the movement of the earth would eventually bring all devout Muslims to the holy cities of Mecca and Medina. "I stand up and say, 'No, imam sir, that's not true, according to science.' And the imam pointed at me and said, 'Look, we have a infidel with us.'" Munr's decision to interrupt the service and taunt the preacher reveals a growing determination to confront the religion of his father, a religion he blames for his mother's unhappiness. "Out of the audience of five hundred people, no one have the courage to say, 'Imam, you are wrong,'" he says. "Technically I was an infidel, but listen, the question is, what was the right? That goes back to the heart of education. So can you change people's minds? It's very difficult work." In 1979, when Iran's secular regime was replaced by an Islamic dictatorship, many of that country's Jews fled in terror. Munr says he obtained "lots of money" from wealthy friends to help smuggle some of those Jews across the border that Pakistan shares with Iran. He particularly remembers one family of four siblings, three girls and a boy, who had been sent to safety by their mother. When he met them in the border town of Quetta they had lost their luggage and Munr gave the boy his underwear: "You know what? It made me feel good." Eventually, he says, he escorted the four young people to Karachi, where they were able to get a flight to Paris. At the time, about 80,000 Jews lived in Iran and Munr estimates that 3,000 to 4,000 escaped through Pakistan.

Using his father's money, Munr traveled frequently as a young man—London, Paris, New York. Many Syrian Jews had settled in Brooklyn or on the Jersey shore and his mother had relatives in America. In 1984 he had completed his medical residency at a hospital in Rawalpindi and was planning to go to London for advanced training: "I always have a dream to settle in London. I thought I would study in England. I had already enrolled and paid my tuition." Before his course began in the fall, he took a summer vacation in America. He never made it back to London. He was staying in Brooklyn with family friends and because of his father's religion "I was not looked on very kindly." His complexion is the color of dark olives and "people would say, 'You look Muslim to me,' and I'd say, 'I hate that word. I can't change my look.'" Still, America was considerably more hospitable to Jews than his home country, and as a political person, Kazmir loved the clash and clamor of the election campaign that was in full swing that summer. The fact that Geraldine Ferraro, a woman from Queens, right next door, was running for vice president on the Democratic ticket intensified the interest in the streets and synagogues of Brooklyn. Kazmir remembers watching the debate in late August between President Ronald Reagan and Walter Mondale, the Democratic nominee: "I say, 'My gut feeling is, Mondale's going to win.' And my friends say, 'Hey, what do you know about American politics?'" (Not much, obviously, but he would learn quickly, becoming a major contributor to the Republican Party and George W. Bush.)

The day after the debate his life took a sharp and unexpected turn. A family friend told him that an internship had suddenly opened up at a hospital in White Plains, in Westchester County, just north of New York City. On a whim he decided to apply for the job but needed a suit for the interview. "Somebody took me to JCPenney and got me a suit for a hundred and ninety-nine dollars," he recalls. "I was very handsome in that suit, a striped suit and a white shirt. Maybe he knew somebody; we got a good discount, a very good price. I also applied for a credit card, my first credit card in America." The next day he went for the interview with a hospital official, a Dr. Ross: "He asked me a few questions. After that he said, 'I will perhaps give you an internship but it will be unpaid.' I said, 'Okay, I will have a crack at it, I'll just take a shot, let's do that,' and he said, 'Come in tomorrow.' I had ten thousand dollars. I don't even care if I get paid. I can use my own money. I liked the hospital. I liked Dr. Ross, who became a mentor. I liked Brooklyn." One of the appeals of Brooklyn was the Chabad-Lubavitch movement, which made its headquarters in the Crown Heights neighborhood. Kazmir had met a Chabad rabbi back in Karachi, and his family connections gained him an audience with Rebbe Menachem Mendel Schneerson, the spiritual leader of the movement. Today, his Monday morning prayer meetings are with a Chabad rabbi and he contributes heavily to Chabad's worldwide operations.

After Munr started at the White Plains hospital he moved to Yonkers, a neighboring town, "rented a basement apartment from an Indian guy," and bought a car, a "silly thing" to do because he didn't have a license, only a learner's permit: "I drove that car on a permit for six months; it makes me feel guilty." As that story reveals, Munr can be a stubborn character who plays by his own rules. And he can be quick to feel slights and insults. He fought bitterly with his landlord because "he not give me heat, it was so bad." In retaliation he sublet the apartment "illegally [and] made a profit. I kind of cheated them." (Years later, to appease his guilt, he made a donation to the Yonkers school district.) At the hospital he felt that some of the staff "treat me very bad" because "when you're unpaid, everyone dump their work on you." At times he would use his personal funds to "pay some other interns" to finish the tasks he'd been assigned. He liked to study with a Chabad rabbi but he resented the Orthodox custom of separating men and women at public services. So on Friday nights he usually attended a more liberal congregation: "I like to sit with the ladies, and Orthodox services are too long."

"The ladies" caused him his first big problem in America. A rabbi he knew in Brooklyn "tried to introduce me to Iranian girls" but he resisted that matchmaking. Instead he proposed to a woman who worked in a dentist's office in White Plains, where he went for treatment of a toothache: "I thought I was in love. [But] the marriage was on the rocks within a month. I was very shocked; she ended up filing for divorce." His wife's smoking "was a really big issue." So was her wandering eye. Munr worked late hours "and she was lonely at home, so she was dating other guys." In retrospect, he says, "she was a good woman, she cooked a lot of good food, but she was not Jewish. Actually when I was married I was very faithful. I thought she would convert. It's my fault. I didn't listen to the rabbi. I think I made a bad choice. But I wanted to be settled myself; I wanted to be successful myself."

After his marriage crumbled Kazmir was "disappointed in New York" and contemplated leaving the country: "My heart was not in America. I still thought I'd go back to London." Instead he applied for medical positions around the country, including several in Texas. After an interview in Austin, he was leaving the hospital and "there's a lady sitting in the lobby, a gorgeous skinny lady." So he devised an excuse to approach her: "I just ask her which way to go out, and we start a conversation. I was wearing a suit, a nice suit actually, a striped suit. I turn back and I saw she's watching so I walked back again. I waited outside, she came out, and I said, 'Listen, I'm here for an interview,' and I asked for recommendation about where to eat. She was a very sharp woman; she had a beautiful dress and was very sophisticated, so she had me totally. I can't think." Her name was Aisha Farhad. She was a Muslim who grew up in Pakistan but combined several Asian bloodlines—Iranian, Indian, Bangladeshi—and was visiting a brother in America. Munr had to leave for San Antonio, where he had another interview, but he obtained her phone number and gave her a call: "Her sister-in-law answered the phone, so I hung up and called again and she answered the phone. She said, 'You're the one who called before' and I said, 'Yes I did.' I came back to New York and we started talking for hours and hours on the phone." Munr was in love again: "I was offered an unpaid job in Houston and I accepted, because I really wanted to be close to her. The feeling was so powerful. Short story—we got married in six or seven months and moved into an apartment in Houston. I didn't know she was a very wealthy woman. She bought me a beautiful car after we got married."

In his own marriage, Munr repeated the pattern of deceit he had always resented in his father: "She asked about my background and I said I was half Pakistani, half Syrian, but I did not discuss my religion, what I am practicing. There was totally no discussion. She said, 'I am a Muslim' and I said it didn't make any difference." But it did make a difference. Three days into their honeymoon he revealed the truth: "I tell her I'm Jewish and she said, 'Excuse me, I don't believe you,' and I said, 'Yes, I am. I was going to tell you.'" Moreover, he added, "we cannot have babies" because under rabbinic law, religion comes through the mother and their children would not be Jewish. "That week the tension was horrible," he remembers. His bride told her mother, who replied: "'Whatever happens just accept it; it's all right if you love each other.' She was a very wise woman." But the tension only increased when Aisha turned up pregnant. Munr consulted a rabbi, who made matters worse by telling him: your child won't be Jewish and your wife can't convert now because she's already pregnant. "So I started giving her a hard time when she's pregnant. I feel guilty about that. She had a miscarriage from the stress. We are fighting, she said, 'You never told me.' I look back and I think I hurt her feelings. It makes me feel bad what I did. I wasn't cursing but I say, 'You are bad.' I make a remark about what your country did to my mother. But it was not her fault."

After the miscarriage their relationship did not improve, in part because Aisha wanted to return to London, where she had family. "I hate it here," she told her husband. "I have to get up early in the morning. I have to cook. I grew up all my life with servants. I just don't want to stay in America." Then Aisha got pregnant again. "We had a fight when we went to the doctor," Munr recalls. "She got so angry. She said, 'I cannot take this nonsense anymore. I can't tell my brother, I can't tell my father, you misleaded us, you didn't tell us you were a practicing Jew.' " Munr pleaded with his wife, "Just keep it between you and I; don't tell anything to anybody," but he failed to appease her. "There was a time when it was so hard," he recalls. "I mean I never raised hands but I said a lot of words. She wanted to open the door and jump the window and I said, 'No, please don't do that.' She so angry. All of a sudden we are going to this doctor, the doctor examine her, and she said 'Yes, you are pregnant. You have twins coming.' "

The girls were born in January 1989. Munr asked his wife to consult a rabbi and convert to Judaism but she refused. The children were born prematurely and had to spend their first few weeks in the hospital, but when they came home Munr confronted a wife who had experienced "a complete turnaround," from docile to determined. "She changed," he says. "She was tough, so tough, I had never seen that side of her. After the kids came home she said, 'You did something. It's your time to pay. I will teach you a lesson.'" When the twins were one month old Munr came home one day to find his family gone. "I have no idea where she is," he says. "I'm calling her parents, her family. I was angry and disappointed. My first wife has an affair, my second wife leaves, I think I have something wrong with me." He wouldn't see his wife or children for two years. But his career as an entrepreneur was about to begin.

Munr moved back east and kept his family a secret: "I cannot tell a lot of people I married a woman and she not Jewish." He finished his training at Beekman Hospital in Manhattan and got a job at a nursing home in New Jersey, taking care of patients during the night shift: "It was just coverage, mainly a sleep job." One night he was summoned to a patient's room: "I see this beautiful Polish nurse; she's from Bayonne. I said, 'Hey, good-lookin', I never seen you here before.' She says, 'I work for an agency,' and I say, 'What agency?'" He did not understand the concept so she explained it to him: she worked for an independent contractor, not directly for the nursing home. It was a good deal, she told him: "I make thirty-two dollars an hour, I can have my own schedule, I have fun, I hang around, I go out with my girlfriends, I travel on vacation." For a man who was a "lousy doctor" by his own admission, but a keen businessman, the idea was intriguing. The next day he did some research and decided to open his own agency. "You make a decision by your gut feeling," he says.

He had little capital, so he took a five-thousand-dollar advance on his Visa card to get started. He went all over northern New Jersey signing up staffers and then approached hospitals asking for contracts. His first one was in Bayonne, the hometown of the pretty Polish nurse (and mine as well), and soon he was growing fast: "All the big agencies, I took their contracts away." When I asked how, he replied: "Competition. I reduce my prices." But the hospitals were often slow in paying their bills and from the beginning he was strapped for cash to pay his employees. He sought out "factors," money brokers who would buy his accounts receivable, the obligations owed by the hospitals, at a discount. The arrangement cut his profit margin but enabled him to stay in business and he figures his company was soon "worth about seven or eight million dollars." He moved to a "nice apartment" in Fort Lee, an upscale town right across the Hudson River from New York. But one day, "early in the morning, the sheriff was coming and knocking at my door." His wife had read a story about his success: "I don't know which newspaper but somehow she find out." And now she wanted a share of his new fortune. Munr consulted a lawyer, who said he had two options: 1) get divorced, pay his wife half of his wealth, and keep paying "for the rest of your life," or 2) the "best option: bring her back and forget everything." He took the second course: "I charm her. I hadn't seen the girls, so I went back to her." The reunion was frosty at first, but a year later the twins, Husna and Sundes, were joined by a sister, Sima: "Sima brought us together. Somehow she was the most brightful child."

Now there is also a son, Abraham, and while Munr is secure in his Jewish identity, his wife and children are still confused. Aisha never converted to Judaism ("It would have to come from the heart, I would not push her, should have to believe in it herself"), and under rabbinic law, the children are not Jewish, either. The girls attended Hebrew school but never had bat mitzvahs (the Jewish coming-of-age ritual usually celebrated at twelve), and Munr hopes, somewhat wistfully, that all four of his children will eventually choose a Jewish identity. In 2008, when Abraham was seven, the family had their first Passover seder together, and one passage in that ritual tells the story of the biblical patriarch Abraham. When the boy heard his name, "he turned to his mother and said, 'Mother, are we a Jewish people?'" As Munr tells the story, Aisha responded, "Whatever your father says, we are that people." But the answer is not that simple, and all of Kazmir's children are still trying to answer young Abraham's question for themselves.

As Munr's family life improved his economic life faltered. Several hospitals that owed him money went into bankruptcy, canceling out their debts. He sold off his remaining contracts for several million dollars and closed down the business. But it was just a temporary setback.

Kazmir opened a second company, Quality Home Care Providers, which supplies equipment, such as oxygen tanks, for homebound patients. The business prospered, but also encountered controversy. In 1994, the *Record*, a daily paper in Hackensack, reported that Kazmir's company was under investigation by state regulators for a variety of violations, including the use of unlicensed therapists. The man who had enjoyed the patronage of "the Chaudhry" back home and understood the value of powerful friends was already courting local politicians. The *Record* said that Kazmir and his associates had contributed to state assemblyman Patrick Roma just before Roma complained to regulators that they were harassing Kazmir. Without admitting any wrongdoing, Kazmir eventually paid a $26,000 fine to settle the charges. When I asked about the incident, he gave a benign explanation: An employee whose license had lapsed applied for a new one. The state agency "cashed his check but did not issue the license. In my mind the person was licensed, his check was cashed, the mistake was done in paperwork." But because the *Record* was following the story, Kazmir decided to cut his losses and pay the fine: "If I go back to court, we would win, but every day will be a media story." Kazmir resented the *Record*'s coverage for another reason: "The reporter focused on the Pakistani father–Jewish mother angle. I lose a lot of business because of that." He grew agitated as he explained: "I'm in America but we're still anti-Semitic here and I'll tell you why. I have a home-care company, and a lot of my business comes from the Muslim doctors. When they find out I have a Jewish mother I lost a lot of my business." In northern New Jersey, he explains, "big Muslim doctors have a very strong following [and] they told the discharge person in the hospital, 'Why you giving business to a Jewish doctor?' My response was, give the business to the company that provides the best of care, not based on [who owns] the company."

Always on the lookout for a new business opportunity, Munr was recovering from surgery in 1998 and walked on crutches into a CVS pharmacy to fill a prescription for the painkiller Percocet. The pharmacist, he says, "hands it to me and says, 'Here's your Percocet.' There are a few people listening and that's not good. There's no confidentiality." He went home and thought about the incident: "I came up with the idea of home delivery of prescriptions. You can talk to a pharmacist in the privacy of your bedroom. So that's how I started that business." He called it Direct Meds, and it operates this way: a doctor faxes a prescription to the company's modest office on a busy street in Leonia, New Jersey. Direct Meds promises delivery in under four hours within a twenty-mile radius, but it's also licensed to fill prescriptions around the country through UPS. Prior to every refill, a pharmacist calls the customers and discusses their medication. "This is personalized service. I love it," says the entrepreneur. "To me this is also education. That's how you can cut health-care costs."

Munr sees a lesson here: "If you focus and you believe, and you're straightforward, you succeed. This is the best place; this is what this country is all about. That's what I tell people in Pakistan what America is about. I'm an immigrant and I'm proud." But he's not always proud of other immigrants. He tells the story of waiting in the airport in Karachi for a flight to America. He overheard a fellow passenger, surrounded by his wife and children, saying: "'When I go to America, I'm going to have a taxi. I'm going to get Medicaid, we're going to get housing, we're going to get free health care. If I make cash money I will send the money back.' And I'm just thinking, he wanted to take from the system, not contribute to it. What kind of message are you giving the children? That's the wrong message. And that all goes through education."

From his first days as an immigrant, Munr was interested in American politics. "The most important issue in my life is the state of Israel," he says, and it was a Middle East issue that turned him from a Democrat into a Republican. In 1986, after a series of clashes with the Libyan leader Muammar Qaddafi, President Reagan launched an air strike against the Libyan navy, sinking two warships. "I hate Qaddafi," says Kazmir, and Reagan's military action convinced him that the Republicans would more vigorously defend American—and Israeli—interests against Muslim fundamentalists. "That made me a Republican," he says. On the national scene he became a large contributor to George W. Bush's campaign in 2000 and his office is decorated with photos of himself with the president. "I support him and I have a good feeling about him. I go with my gut feeling," says Munr. "I think he's an honest guy and that's really important." His feelings for Bush were enhanced by the president's response after 9/11: "On the war issue I totally believe. I do support him." As late as mid-2008, when much of America had turned against the Iraq War, Kazmir's support remained unshaken. Interviewed at the Republican convention, where he was a first-time delegate, he told a reporter for a Jewish community newspaper in New Jersey, "We are fighting a difficult enemy. This world doesn't understand. I grew up with anti-Semitism. I think what Bush is doing in Iraq—it is the greatest thing he is doing. If you just walk away from the war, you are giving weakness." For similar reasons Kazmir strongly supported John McCain for president. "We are naïve; people are very naïve here," he told me. "We're dealing with a very difficult world. I'm really worried."

If he is a devoted hawk on foreign policy, Kazmir follows a more moderate line on domestic issues. "I am not a religious right-wing Republican," he says. "I consider myself a Christie Whitman Republican," a reference to the governor of the New Jersey in the 1990s, who has clashed with party conservatives. He cochaired the finance committee for Whitman's successful run for governor in 1993 and he and his family have donated generously to many Republican candidates over the years, from former senators Elizabeth Dole, Rick Santorum, and Alfonse D'Amato to New Jersey congressmen Steven Rothman and Rodney Frelinghuysen. These political connections have paid dividends. Governor Whitman appointed him to the state lottery commission and Representative Rothman praised him lavishly in the *Congressional Record* when Kazmir received an honorary doctorate from the Rabbinical College of America. His White House ties certainly didn't hurt when Direct Meds received a low-interest federal disaster loan for $747,000 after 9/11, making Kazmir the largest beneficiary in New Jersey. "We lost a lot of business," he explained. "We couldn't deliver medication" in places like Brooklyn and Jersey City because "the police blocked off areas." And once customers start using their local drugstores again it is hard to get them back.

Kazmir's list of charities and awards covers several pages. *Tzedakah* is a concept he lives by every day. But no endeavor moves him more deeply than the school in Lahore. He's financed it personally (with the help of a guaranteed loan from the Overseas Private Investment Corporation) and he's planning others in Jordan and Cairo. As a Jewish immigrant from a Muslim country, who is deeply devoted to the survival of Israel, he always comes back to the importance of education as a counterweight to Islamic fundamentalism. "The point of the school," he says, "is to show that their thought does not work, their thought is wrong." But the school is not just political, it's personal. He's never forgotten his Muslim grandmother denouncing his Jewish mother as a *kafir*, or infidel. Giving Pakistani children a Western education is his way of changing the mind-set his grandmother reflected. The economic turmoil of late 2008 hit Munr hard: "It cost me a lot of money, but I'm going to continue. I refinanced my properties; they're not going to stop me." He takes comfort in the counsel of his rabbi: "No matter what we do, people are going to hate us. So why don't we do good?"

10.

Pablo Romero

MEXICO

After finishing medical school I had one of those recurring dreams. Somebody came up and said, since I hadn't gone to high school, nothing else since then was valid. Everything was null and void. I had to have a high school diploma and I didn't have one. I think those dreams eventually went away.

Pablo Romero was only eleven when he finished the sixth grade and dropped out of school. Continuing his education would have required a long bus trip and money his family did not have, so he went to work at a brick factory in his home village of Santa Rosa Jauregui, Mexico. He made ten pesos, or about eighty cents, for a twelve-hour day, and one of his jobs was hauling the bricks from the ovens and stacking them up in waiting trucks. "Carrying bricks is not easy, because your hands become real raw," he remembers now, almost fifty years later. "I used to get home and tell my mom, the tortillas had to be cool, not hot, because if you ate them hot they would hurt your fingers."

Two years later he joined his father in America as a bracero, a migrant farmworker. The Romero family eventually settled in the California town of Salinas, made famous by the novels of John Steinbeck, and Pablo spent his teenage years toiling there in the fields and packing sheds. Eventually he was drafted into the army and sent to Germany, and the experience changed his life. He read every book in the post library, traveled all over Europe in a secondhand Opel, passed his high school equivalency test, and impressed his commanding officer. "The captain told me, 'You're pretty smart; you're going back to California and I'm going to go back looking for you,' " recalls Pablo. "'If you're still working in the fields, I'm going to kick your ass. You'd better do something with yourself.'"

He did. A program at the local community college aimed at underprivileged Chicanos got him started. That led to a scholarship at the University of California at Irvine and a medical degree from UC San Francisco. Today he runs a family practice in Salinas, where most of his patients are farmworkers: "I tell you, at times I feel like a bit of a thief because everything's been so amazing, it's worked out so well." But there's a hole in his history: eleven years that he spent stacking bricks and cutting lettuce, instead of reading books and attending classes. And those years left a scar on his psyche: "After finishing medical school I had one of those recurring dreams. Somebody came up and said, since I hadn't gone to high school, nothing else since then was valid. Everything was null and void. I had to have a high school diploma and I didn't have one. I think those dreams eventually went away."

Pablo Romero calls himself a mestizo, from the Spanish word meaning a descendant of both European and Native American bloodlines. His great-grandfather on his mother's side, Antonio Beltran, was a Spanish settler in Mexico who raised fighting bulls. "A tall guy with a white beard," Beltran married an Otomi Indian woman, a member of the tribe that provided foot soldiers for the Aztec armies. "The more hair the more European, the less hair the more Indian," says Pablo.

"You look at my family there's always the struggle of less hair and more hair." The 1920s brought upheaval and revolution to Mexico and Pablo's grandfather, Joaquin Beltran, was a mule driver for the army and often traveled ahead of the troops to set up camp: "He remembers going to battlefields where there would be many people dead, from gunshot wounds and machetes, and slaughtered animals. The stench was incredible." The Beltran family once owned a lot of land, but Joaquin drank heavily and squandered it away: "They essentially became pariahs; they had little in the way of anything." Pablo's grandfather was eventually given "a little bit of land" by the government and he scraped out a living growing corn and beans and raising goats. His grandmother contributed what she could, making baskets of tortillas for a rich family. She received no money, just a few of the leftover tortillas, but they helped feed the family: "They were living on the edge at all times; there was never any fat in there at all."

Joaquin was an "absolute tyrant" to his daughter Maria Felicitas, Pablo's mother, especially when he was drinking. A "bit of a rebel," Maria left home at seven or eight and hired out as a maid in the provincial capital of Queretaro, about fifteen miles away: "She remembers the cruelty of some of the places she would work at; she would not be allowed to eat anything until four or five in the afternoon." Many of her employers were doctors and she was not thrilled at her son's decision, many years later, to attend medical school: "I think she was afraid I'd turn into the same ogre she had as a boss." Maria eventually returned home to be closer to her mother and went to school at night, entering kindergarten at age seventeen. A year or so later she was working as a maid for the local church when she met Vicente Romero Naranjo.

Pablo knows little about his father's family, which ran a small inn for travelers, mainly mule drivers. His grandmother on that side, Manuela Naranjo, could read and write—one of the few villagers in Santa Rosa Jauregui with that skill—but her views on child rearing were heavily influenced by the church: "The priests at that time were telling the peasants, 'You don't need to learn to read and write. The teachers were communists, Jews, who were going to take your children and corrupt them. So hide your children.'" The priests told the peasants "not to trust anybody who had any learning," and that included doctors. The brainwashing was so effective that Pablo's father "spent a good part of his childhood hiding from the teachers so he wouldn't be corrupted. He was also hidden from vaccinations. His mother would take him to different towns and hide him." So Pablo had to overcome antimedical animosity on both sides of his family: "I think if my grandmother knew that I'd become a doctor she would be very disappointed. She had no use for doctors."

Given that background, it was no real hardship for Pablo's father, Vicente, to drop out of school at an early age, after his own father died. A distant relative hired him as a sales clerk but his skills were so limited that he could not multiply numbers, only add them. (Years later Pablo was teaching a niece multiplication when his father overheard them and asked to learn: "My father thought that was the greatest invention ever. He said, 'This is incredible!' He felt so lucky that he learned that.") Pablo's parents met each other when she occasionally shopped at his store. Since public contact between single people was discouraged, they would leave messages for each other, tucked into the stone walls of the church. They wanted to get married, but as their son tells the story, "My grandfather in his infinite wisdom decided my father was not a good man to marry because he didn't work with his hands, he didn't work with the plows, he didn't herd goats." Vicente asked the priest to plead his case with his prospective father-in-law, but old man Beltran kept avoiding the conversation. Finally the priest threatened him: if you're not home when I come again, "I'm going to marry them regardless." Pablo's grandfather finally gave in, but there was no money for a lavish wedding, so the priest performed a simple ceremony after Mass one Sunday: "Nobody showed up;

maybe my grandmother and a couple of other people." There was no reception, and the groom could barely afford a one-night honeymoon a few miles away. The next day the newlyweds moved in with Vicente's mother and went back to work: "It was a tiny little house, and with two women there was a lot of turmoil. My grandmother felt my mother was an intruder and they didn't get along very well. At one point my mother was ready to say, 'I'm done, I'm going to leave, I don't care what happens.'"

In 1950, the year Pablo was born, his father decided to leave his family and head to the United States for work: "He had no profession in the town, no assets, his salary at the store was meager, just enough to eat, and he did not want to stay the rest of his life with his mother in the same house with his wife." Under the bracero program, workers could legally enter the country and sign contracts that ranged from three to eighteen months. The elder Romero roamed the West— Montana, Colorado, Arizona—working the crops as they came into season. California was a frequent stop, and he loved the weather in Salinas, but not the strawberry growers he worked for: "He remembers them being quite cruel. The workers were not allowed to eat any of the strawberries. They used to give them whistles, and they had to whistle all the time, so the bosses knew they were not eating strawberries." He also worked the sugar beet fields in Spreckels, a town south of Salinas dominated by huge brick ovens used to process the beets. Years later, when the ovens were being dismantled, Pablo bought a load of the bricks—which originally came from England as ship ballast—and used them to pave his patio.

Vicente Romero was a small presence in his son's life: "I knew him very little growing up; he was always gone. He'd come in, stay a few months, and sign up again. It was tough. We would see him as an intruder half the time. We were getting along fine. Why does he have to come in? Why doesn't he just send the money?" That money enabled the Romeros to leave Vicente's mother and buy a small house of their own, but it leaked all the time: "We used to sleep under the bed when it was raining; that was the driest part of the house. It was so crazy, oh my God." Pablo's father wanted to raise pigs to earn extra cash, but "he wasn't there to take care of them. When it rained it was a mess. Pigs are filthy, filthy animals." The "intruder" would occasionally bring home presents for his kids—Pablo treasured a train set "that I kept forever"—but Pablo's daughter, Kaija-Leena, remembers a family photo, taken when her father was about two. He's holding a ball and looking "stricken, very sad" for the camera. The ball was just a prop and he had to give it back. "I grew up thinking, if you're a good person God takes care of you," says Pablo, but village life taught a different lesson. At holiday time "the rich kids, who were always obnoxious to their mothers and everybody else," got bicycles as presents, while Pablo and his brothers and sisters received an orange and some sugarcane: "I said, 'C'mon, there has to be more to it than that. How much better can I be?'"

Early on, Pablo's mother saw a spark in her son, and asked a neighbor to teach him reading and writing even before he was old enough for school: "The ruler kept hitting me in the hands so I had to learn quickly," he recalls. She scrimped enough to afford Catholic school, and when he entered first grade at age five, many of his classmates were ten years older: "That made me a very, very fast runner, because some of those fifteen-year-olds wanted my pencil and my book. I would race home or else my things would be stolen." Pablo was under constant pressure from his grandfather, Joaquin Beltran, to drop out of school: "He wanted another hand, to carry goats and that sort of thing. That's what he knew." His parents pushed back, insisting their son continue his education, but once he finished sixth grade, his options dried up. The money Vicente sent home had to support eight kids: four boys and four girls. The closest seventh grade was miles away—"you had to go to the city, take a bus and pay money"—and even though Pablo desperately wanted to stay in school, he could not figure out how: "I looked into every detail, what it would take for me to go the city and do that. But I realized the structure wasn't there, the money wasn't there. I was the oldest boy; you were expected to contribute to the economy of the family, so when I finished the sixth grade I went to work."

Santa Rosa Jauregui was known for brick making, and the process was an ancient one. Clay was mixed with water and horse manure (which contained straw for strength) and poured into molds to dry in the sun. After that the bricks were fired in an oven powered by diesel fuel mixed with more horse manure. One of Pablo's godfathers owned a brick company and gave the boy a job. One of his tasks was driving out to local farms, shoveling the dung into burlap sacks, and carrying it up a ramp into a truck. Old, dry droppings were easy to handle, but if the manure was fresh, or moist from the rain, the task was much messier: "When it was a little bit wet, you'd put it on your back [in the burlap sacks] and it would run down your legs. I remember getting back to town at the end of the day and skirting around the streets to get home and take a big bath. My friends who were with me in school would run away from me. I was not a good sight." Loading the trucks when an order came in was just as hard. The boys worked without gloves, tossing and catching the rough bricks with their bare hands. The process essentially "sanded" the skin off your fingers. For the privilege of ending the day with stinking clothes or aching hands—or both—Pablo earned less than a dollar. And if he overslept by even five minutes and missed his ride at 6 A.M. he got no work and earned nothing: "Then I had to go home and look at all the long faces. There were a lot of kids still depending on the money I was making."

In the fall of 1963, as Pablo was turning thirteen, his father was home between contracts and decided to go to Mexico City to renew his passport: "My mother said, 'Why don't you take Pablo to the city with you and show him around?'" They traveled by bus, and after Vicente finished his business, he took his son for a stroll along the

Paseo de la Reforma, the main street of the capital. As they passed the American embassy, Pablo's father turned to him: "And he goes, 'Would you be interested in going to California?' And I said, 'Well, yeah, I would.' I was actually dying to do something, I was getting bored with the work I was doing. I was super restless. I was burying myself. I just didn't think carrying bricks was a very challenging activity, and physically it was a pain. I knew that I could do better." By then Vicente had spent so much time in America that he'd qualified for a green card, or residency permit, so processing his son's papers went smoothly. Within a month they were on a train together, headed for the U.S. border: "It was three days in third class, sleeping on wooden benches, just disgusting. But I was totally excited."

They crossed into California at the town of Calexico and boarded a bus for Salinas, where they'd look for work. Pablo noticed that the bus station was more "clean and orderly" than Mexican versions. By now it was winter, and Salinas was "all green, very rainy and cold." Vicente checked in at a farmworkers' bar and found out who was hiring. Soon they were in a pickup truck, with Pablo in the back, headed for a labor camp outside of Castroville, in the middle of an artichoke field: "I thought we were in the middle of Mars. I'd never seen an artichoke in my life. I thought people got tortured with those things. The next day we went to work, cutting broccoli and other weird things I'd never seen." The trip to the fields took ninety minutes, riding on wooden benches in an old bus. The broccoli was so cold, sometimes covered with ice, that the newcomer's hands quickly turned red and raw. A fellow worker named Paul, the first black man Pablo had ever met, "was very gentle and spoke some Spanish." He "had pity on me" and gave the teenager some "old raggedy gloves" to ease his discomfort. Quickly they settled into a routine: ten-to-twelve-hour days in the fields, six days a week, then back to the camp. On Sundays father and son would walk into Castroville, about four miles away, attend Mass, and cash their checks. Vicente would send most of the money home to

Mexico, holding back enough to buy himself "a couple of beers" and Pablo a "thing of chocolate milk." Then "we'd walk back to the bar-racks on Sunday evening and get ready for work on Monday."

The next year Pablo's mother moved to Salinas with two of his siblings and the family rented a small apartment. The teenager was shrewd and ambitious, and soon figured out that "the best possible way to make money was to work with the lettuce." The lettuce fields were highly stratified. On the bottom were the cutters and packers, who spent all day stooped over for lowly wages. At the top were the box makers and closers, who got paid by the piece and could make a lot more than the field hands. Pablo couldn't crack the box-making guild but he did win a tryout as a box closer: "You have to be very fast with your hands and you have to be gentle with the boxes; you couldn't hurt them too much." Closers also had to be good with tools, oiling and sharpening their stapling guns every evening. After Pablo's first week as a closer, "I got up in the morning, my hands were so swollen I couldn't bend my fingers." Closers work in three-man teams, and if one of them lags behind, the whole system staggers: "They were patient enough with me, I was fourteen. I was able to stay with them. Once the second generation of calluses came in, then I was able to do it." A year before Pablo was making eighty cents a day. Now he could bring in $150 or even $200 on a good week, but he was still a teenager, who sometimes had trouble getting up for work. A friend named Felix, a fellow box closer, would come by every morn-ing and serve as chauffeur and cheerleader: "When my fingers were supertired and hurt, when I couldn't even bend them, he would say, 'C'mon, you can do it.' Even if I was out of it entirely, he used to come in and wake me up to take me to work." The money was good but the work was so stressful it induced nightmares: "Being behind, you can't catch up with the crew: that was always the nightmare, not being able to say current. Even if you worked harder and harder and harder, you never caught up."

In the early days, Pablo always turned his check over to his father, but after his mother moved back to Mexico, the two workers had a showdown: "I remember him coming into town, taking my check, and saying, 'Well, take a dollar for yourself.' After a whole week's work, a dollar to go the movies, which cost seventy-five cents; the rest went for M and Ms and a Coke. He would then go out and have food and beer with his friends, so at one point I got into an argument. 'You know what, this is not fair. We're both working the same hours. I make as much money as you do.'" When Vicente said he needed Pablo's check to "take care of the kids," his son lashed back: "They're your kids, not mine." Vicente responded with a slap across Pablo's face: "I was just being a totally obnoxious kid, and he might have had a couple of beers. I'm sure he regretted it and so did I. But he was a very powerful man, and so was I. We didn't talk to each other for the next two months and I kept the checks. I said, 'If you don't talk to me I'm not going to give you the money.'"

As the tension mounted, Pablo decided to travel back to Mexico and visit his mother and younger siblings in Santa Rosa Jauregui. After six weeks or so, his mother was returning to Salinas but Pablo could not face his father: "I dreaded coming back to see him, because I knew we'd get in argument." As they headed north toward America, Pablo told his mother he was going to Arizona, not California: "Where is that?" she asked. "She had no idea." When he arrived in Phoenix he went "looking around for Mexican faces" but saw only Indians. He found a cheap hotel and in the morning "I was out of money; that's all I had." Finally he ran into a labor contractor he knew from Salinas: "He asked me if my father knew I was there. I said he should know by now because my mother told him. So he said, 'I have a job for you.' He put me in the back of a pickup and off we went, to a labor camp near Phoenix." Even though he was penniless, "the labor camp had food so it didn't matter." After two weeks he got his first check and called his mother to say he was safe: "She was very stressed, but I stayed there, and made enough money to buy my first car." It was a 1964 Corvair. Pablo had just turned fifteen, old enough to get a driving permit in Arizona, and after the lettuce season ended he drove to California's Imperial Valley and worked there another three or four months. He then returned to Salinas, and in the meantime "my mother had worked on my father to be a little more understanding." A truce was reached and he moved back into the family apartment.

Over the next few years, the family saved enough to buy a small house and bring the rest of the children to California. There were two bedrooms for eleven people. The parents took one bedroom, the four girls another, and the four boys shared the living room. A wayward uncle floated around as well, but he often "got mad and slept in the toolshed." Green card holders are subject to the draft, and with the Vietnam War consuming more and more recruits, Pablo eventually got a letter from the Selective Service. Since he spoke no English a friend translated: report to the induction center in Oakland: "They did a lot of testing, all in Spanish. I came back home and that was it." A few months later another letter arrived. By now it was midwinter, few farmworkers were around, and Pablo had nobody to translate for him. The second letter looked like the first so he assumed he was being summoned for more testing. He parked his car near the Greyhound station and took the bus to Oakland, but something different happened when he got there: "Next thing I know, we get herded into a long skinny room, with an American flag at the front. There are some officials there, there must have been fifty or sixty people in the room, and the guys in the front had their right hand raised. I'm in the back with American Indians who have their arms crossed, with blacks who had a fist in the air, with hippies who had this peace sign, and with a whole bunch of people who had their middle finger up in the air." Pablo emerged from the room totally confused. He found a Marine named Gonzalez and asked him in Spanish what was going on: "He said, 'You're in the army, you've been inducted.' I said, 'Oh my God.' I had no idea, no idea." That night the new soldiers were shipped by bus to Fort Ord, not far from Salinas, for basic training. When they stopped at a coffee shop along the way Pablo called his father and said, "I'm not coming back. I'm in the army. Can you pick up the car I left at the bus station?" Pablo's father had been strongly influenced by Cesar Chavez, who was then organizing farmworkers into their first union, and he responded angrily at the news: "My dad at the time was very left-leaning. He said, 'I can't believe this; it's ridiculous. This is not good; Vietnam is not good. Tell me where you are and I'll pick you up and take you back to Mexico.' But I said 'No, let it ride. Let's see what happens.'

"No one likes basic training," notes Pablo, but he got lucky. Many of his comrades were college boys from the Midwest who had joined the National Guard: "These guys were all well spoken, their diction was perfect, and some of them took it on themselves to teach me English. So that was good." His father visited six weeks later and again offered to spirit him out of the country, but again Pablo resisted: "The army did a very good job of teaching you the domino theory. I was sure that if we didn't stop the communists in Vietnam they would take us over. So I told my dad, 'No, the world's falling apart and I'm going to save it. I'm going to Vietnam and take care of it.' He thought I was crazy." Then came artillery training at Fort Sill, Oklahoma, and there he "ended up in a company of hillbillies, and I had no idea what they were saying." All the English he'd learned at Fort Ord was useless. He was "back to square one" and it took him weeks to get up to speed. He started going to movies to improve his language skills, but he found one so confusing "I could make no heads or tails of it." The film was Catch-22: "I've gone back since then and it still makes no sense!"

Pablo thought he was headed for Vietnam, but several foreign nationals in U.S. ranks had defected to the enemy and the commanders decreed that no noncitizen could enter the war zone without top security clearance. So when his company shipped out for Southeast Asia, Pablo headed to West Germany. It was midwinter when he arrived with a buddy, a soldier who had never been out of Iowa before. They wore only jungle fatigues, no one showed up at the station to greet them, and "that fellow from Iowa was practically in tears. We had no idea what to do. We thought we'd freeze to death." Then Pablo heard someone whistling an old Spanish bullfighting song. When he tracked down the whistler and explained his plight in Spanish, the man took the boys to a police station. The American base was called and the stragglers were retrieved. For four or five months Pablo "felt cheated" that he'd missed out on Vietnam, but his feelings faded when he started talking to returning GIs and realized that the war was "not as rosy" as the lecturers back in the States had made it out to be.

Germany opened Pablo's eyes and tested his talents. The base employed many Spanish exiles who had fled the Franco regime, but there was no one to translate for them or understand their culture. One small example: the base menu contained a lot of corn, but the Spaniards considered the dish an insult. Back home corn was fed only to animals. Pablo stepped in, acting as a bridge between the workers and base officials, and the commanding officer took notice. As one of the few soldiers with a truck driver's license, he started receiving sensitive assignments, transporting equipment and documents around Germany. And his love for learning, snapped off when he was eleven, started blossoming again: "I just read and read and read. I was always reading in the library. I read every book in there." Pablo's years in the fields had taught him a lot about machines, so he bought an old car and went foraging in the base junkyard for parts. After rebuilding the engine and transmission, he and three buddies started making field trips all over Europe—Munich, Amsterdam, Paris. And everywhere he went, he read about the country's history and culture. "The four of us were a mini U.N.," recalls Pablo. "A black guy from Maryland, a super-blond kid from Oregon, a Puerto Rican, and me." They would pinch gasoline from the post, and stay in cheap hostels or sleep in pastures: "All my money, which wasn't much, was used for travel." On one trip they went to Spain with some workers from the base, "who opened doors for us; everyone was very, very welcoming." Pablo also took classes to improve his English and decided to get a high school certificate: "I took the test and I passed it, just to see if I could do something."

People have always seen promise in Pablo and watched out for him. The first was his mother, who made sure he could read and write even before he entered school. Then came Paul, the black farmhand who gave him his first gloves; Felix, who rousted him out of bed and saved his job as a box closer; and the base commander in Germany, who urged Pablo to "do something with yourself." After Pablo left the army he returned to Salinas and went looking for work. He took a test for the postal service and failed—his English was still not good enough. When he filed for unemployment benefits, a guardian angel stepped forward, in the unlikely guise of a government bureaucrat. Hartnell, the local community college, was starting a new program called "Chicano Readiness," and the clerk urged Pablo to apply: "Go see this fellow, Joe Martinez, at the college; see what he tells you."

Pablo was eager to resume his education, but he still felt an obligation to his family, particularly his younger brothers and sisters: "I came out of the army and said, 'Okay, I can work and you can go to school,' but they said no." His siblings liked their paychecks too much to give them up. So Pablo went to Hartnell and looked up Martinez. Chicano Readiness was for students who had left school and "fallen out of the cracks." It was designed to ease their way back, through special classes and personal tutoring, and Martinez agreed that Pablo was a good candidate. He took some tests and was still "very rusty," especially in English, but his math skills were solid and he enrolled in classes. For his first exam in American history, Pablo pleaded with the professor to take it in Spanish, "and he said okay, but one only."

A self-paced math course, however, that was supposed to last four or five months took him only two weeks. He was on his way.

Still, there was a problem. After entering the army, Pablo had failed to pay taxes for the last year he had worked in the lettuce fields, and he owed the government about a thousand dollars: "So I had no choice but to work to pay back the taxes." He took classes at Hartnell in the morning, then worked a full shift in the lettuce fields, then studied deep into the night: "I never went to bed before midnight and I never got up after five." But the torturous schedule was worth it. He paid off the government and excelled in the classroom: "I felt at the time that I had been given some sort of incredible gift. I could just sit there and learn and learn and learn. It was opening all kinds of doors. I always felt like a kid in a candy store. I felt bad about not being able to contribute more at home but I really loved this stuff, so I got a little selfish. By then I knew the fields were just a means to an end." But one thing was missing: he never got a chance to enjoy campus life: "I was in the library. I was hiding, hiding to study, to stay away from every other stuff. I had no time for any social life whatsoever."

As he was finishing Hartnell another mentor entered his life, a counselor from the University of California at Irvine, located hundreds of miles south of Salinas in the center of Orange County: "They had one of those career fair things. They had all these different recruiters, and I have no idea why someone from Irvine came up here. But he did." The man urged Pablo: apply here, you'll get a good scholarship. So he sent in the forms and received back an invitation to visit the campus. A reception at the dean's residence was part of the tour: "He had a beautiful house, and we show up there and they have all these maids with little aprons and black dresses—very, very formal—and I'm thinking, Oh, what did I get into?" Pablo also had to make a presentation about why he deserved a scholarship. It worked. He won a full ride, and in the fall of 1974, as he was turning twenty-four, he became a full-time college student for the first time. By then he had become a "great farmworker," an expert box maker, and his last paycheck was for $1,600: "So my father looks at the check and says, 'So what are you going to make next week?' So I said, 'Well, next week I'm going to be paying money to go to school. I'm not going to be making anything. I'm going negative.' And he goes, 'That's kind of dumb.' He still thought I was making a mistake."

Pablo had no trouble with the course work at Irvine, but campus life required a huge adjustment. Back in Salinas he had lived at home, eleven people in two bedrooms, and worked all afternoon in the fields and hid away in the library at night. Now he was living in a dorm with younger and wealthier kids and he found them "extremely immature and difficult to deal with. I was impatient with the fact that they were so silly and stupid. There was a war going on in Vietnam, there was poverty in the world, and they're just having a good time." For many of his classmates, "their biggest challenge was getting money from their parents." Pablo was getting nothing from home. His scholarship paid his college bills but if he wanted spending money he had to earn it. So once or twice a quarter he would use his trucker's license and pick up a job driving a rig back east. He'd clear about six hundred dollars per trip, and many of them were made over holiday breaks: "I remember spending Thanksgiving in Albuquerque, at a Denny's at a truck stop, having turkey dinner." Occasionally, Pablo would escape to Mexicali, a town just across the Mexican border, and spend a weekend drinking beer, eating crayfish, and fixing cars with his old farmworker pals: "I had to get away from the brats. I was not fitting into the social scene. UC Irvine was a wonderful place but it was full of brats, rich brats, and I didn't mix with them at all."

One female classmate was always "making faces at me and being friendly," so Pablo asked her out on a date, to hear the classical guitarist Andrès Segovia. When he picked her up a man answered the door: "So we left and I said, 'Who's that guy?' and she said, 'Well, I live with him.' I said, 'You mean like brother and sister?' and she says,

'No, not like brother and sister.' So we went and saw Segovia and I said, 'You know what: let me put a stop to this thing. I don't need this excitement in my life.' So I went back to my books." Another student invited him to meet her parents, and he recoiled at their large house with only four people in it: "It was a beautiful home, but you felt like you were a statue, and if you moved something it would break. It was not my idea of fun; it was absolutely unbearable." Looking back on his two years at Irvine, Pablo says, "I never got used to the fact that people could look down on me. It's a very discomforting feeling—you're weird, you're different. But I said to myself, I've made it this far, no way in hell is anybody going to put me down. I'm as good as anybody else and I've never asked for any favors."

Pablo gravitated to science and math courses, and joined a club for Chicanos interested in those subjects. At one meeting a professor of organic chemistry gave a "pep talk" urging the students to consider medical school. Since his family had always hated doctors, this was not an easy sell. But when the professor asked him how many Mexican doctors practiced in Salinas, he had to answer zero, and the question left him shaken: "So I asked, 'How do you do this? How do you apply to med school?'" He was told to take the medical school admission tests, and he sent out a bunch of applications. The first school he heard back from was Cornell, a flat rejection, and while it hurt at the time, he now feels "it would have been a terrible mistake" to leave California and go to school in New York. He was interested in Case Western, but he could not afford to fly to Cleveland for an interview, so he picked up a trucking job and drove east. He got as far as Chicago when the truck broke down. Pablo had to crawl underneath the cab to fix the problem and his jeans and sweatshirt got covered with oil. He'd brought no extra clothes with him and finally pulled into Cleveland on Sunday night. Since his appointment was for early Monday morning he had no time to shop, so he showed up for the interview in his disreputable clothes, while the other candidates glistened in their well-groomed three-piece suits: "I spent the first ten minutes explaining how I got there. I wasn't staging a protest. I just didn't have any other clothes." He might have been the only med school applicant in the history of Case Western to drive to his interview in a long-haul freight truck, and to the school's credit, they were "very enamored" of his tale and let him in. But Pablo's parents were getting older. His father had spent years in the fields, wrecking his back by chopping weeds with a short-handled hoe, and diabetes made his health even worse. So Pablo decided to stay closer to home.

His interview at UC San Francisco's medical school did not go well, however: "I almost got into a fistfight with the interviewer. He was a black hematologist, and somehow I knew a lot about hematology and so got into all sorts of arguments about hematology and sickle cell and I was sure he was going to throw my application in the garbage." He didn't. The doc loved Pablo's spirit, gave him a "glowing review," and practically "drafted me into UCSF." It was, he says now, "the best thing that ever happened to me." Another good thing happened that year as well: Pablo met his future wife.

After graduating from Irvine he decided to give himself a treat and take a brief vacation at the Club Med in Cancun. He financed the trip by driving a truck to Miami, where he was supposed to catch a ferry to the Mexican resort, but when the boat got canceled he took a plane instead and sat next to a woman named Patricia Blumberg, who had just finished college in Connecticut and was also on holiday: "She was extremely nervous about flying and she was not touching her lunch, so I said, 'You're not going to eat that?' We started talking, and I tried to divert her attention but my ulterior motive was to steal her lunch." She stole his heart instead. Patty was a "nice working-class girl," the daughter of a fish truck driver with a rich ethnic heritage: Irish, Swedish, Slovak. She had worked her way through state schools and was thinking of moving to San Francisco, where her sister lived. They spent a few days together, touring the sites around Cancun, and then parted: Patty back to Connecticut, Pablo to the Mexican city of Chiapas to visit an uncle: "Something was happening. We hit it off. I started thinking about her and dreaming about her in Chiapas." Med school started in August. Patty moved west in October, and the couple started dating: "I was extremely leery of getting serious, because my mother told me, if you get married you'll never graduate. I don't know who made the rule but that was her rule—Mexican folklore, I guess." But he got serious anyway.

Introducing his Anglo girlfriend to his Mexican parents gave them "a bit of a shock" but his mother's main concern "was whether she was Catholic or not." Patty "passed muster" on the religious test and then started talking to Mrs. Romero in Spanish, another big plus: "She tells me now, in retrospect, that she was very stressed at the time, very afraid of rejection, but my dad always loved her." They were married during Pablo's last year in med school.

Pablo found UCSF far more compatible than Irvine. Instead of feeling socially inferior to a dorm full of "rich brats," he now reveled in the "inherent equality" of med school: "There was always an odd person who stood out as a jerk, but the rest of us had proven ourselves; we'd gotten through college and gotten great reviews from everybody and it was time to relax and just learn." But racial prejudice still lurked in some corners, and Pablo was stunned to learn that he had failed a test in vascular surgery, a subject he enjoyed and knew well. The professor summoned him to his office "and he starts yelling at me—the reason med school is going to crap is people like me who were probably admitted under some special program for minorities." Pablo protested: I know the subject, something's wrong, can I see my test. When the professor handed it over Pablo pointed out the problem: two pages were stuck together; several questions were left ungraded. The professor took the test back and read Pablo's answers: "He looks

at me, throws me the test, and says, 'Get out of here. You have an A.'
There were a few leftovers in med school who felt I shouldn't be there,
but too bad. I was there."

As graduation approached Pablo toyed with the idea of specializing
in surgery. He had always been good with his hands—even if cutting
broccoli was not quite the same as cutting bodies—and he liked the
fact that surgeons could fix something tangible with their work. But
the pull of home was strong: he decided to take a year learning family
medicine at Natividad Medical Center in Salinas, with an assurance
from his old professors that he could return to San Francisco and take
up surgery at any time. That never happened: "As soon as I came back,
and started seeing patients, I realized, this is the reason I studied medicine. I realized, this is ridiculous, I've been running around in circles,
and here I am, running into all sorts of people that I know, that I've
known for a long time, that I know from the fields; I know their parents. How much more natural could it be than to take care of all of
them? These people would say, 'We're so happy you're here; we're so
happy you can take of my baby.' And people were going up to Dad and
saying, 'It's so nice your son is taking care of my grandma.' You hear
more and more of that and you think, maybe this is a good thing."

After completing three years of residency at Natividad, Pablo
set up a private practice within sight of the hospital with two other
Latino doctors. In the beginning, he'd work twenty-four-hour shifts
a few times a week at the hospital emergency room to pay the office
rent, but soon the practice was up and running and he could ditch
the outside work: "It didn't take long, thank God. Those twenty-
four-hour shifts were murder." The best description of daily life at
Pablo's office, the Santa Lucia Medical Group, comes from his daughter, Kaija-Leena, in her own application to medical school: "I thought
all offices bustled, day and night, well past 7 or 8 P.M. with the chaos
and noise of colicky babies; toddlers with silver-capped teeth hanging from the door handles; young, smooth-faced teens with bulging

bellies and prematurely wary looks on their faces; old men stooped and grizzled, bent over at the waist from years in the fields; female farmworkers wearing unwitting burkas from the neck up, fashioned out of pieces of colored cloth and bobby pins to protect their faces from the sun, and topped off with mesh caps. I thought all patients dropped off gifts of tamales, boxes of artichokes, or free Christmas trees in exchange for services rendered and that all doctors arrived at work early and left late to accommodate the relentless need; that everywhere, no matter how efficiently the physicians and medical assistants worked, the tide never subsided; that wave after wave of new, sick and often scared patients poured through the door hundreds in a day, thousands in a week."

Pablo's presence in the community could make life difficult for his three daughters. (Kaija-Leena, the middle child, named for a Finnish friend of Patty's, is now in medical school. Liliana, the oldest, and Marisol, the youngest, both work in the film industry in Los Angeles and want to make a film of their father's life.) As Pablo tells it, "The kids used to think something weird was going on. My girls, when they were learning to drive, would be by themselves, so they'd think they can get away with anything. Maybe they'd go too fast around a corner and so-and-so would tell me, 'Oh, I saw your daughter, and she was going rather quickly around the corner, tires screeching.' I'd get home and say, 'At the corner of so-and-so this morning, why were you going so fast?' Their eyes would open up. What do you mean? How do you know? Who told you? And I'd say, 'People tell me, so you always have to be good.'" Pablo's daughters don't think he always understood their lives. He knew who he was, a full-blooded Mexican who immigrated to America and made a great success of his life. They were born here, half Mexican and half white, and had to find a different identity.

Their mother "worked very hard to give us a sense of pride about being Mexican," says Kaija-Leena. "She went to great extremes to find dolls that were brown-eyed and brown-haired and brown-skinned."

But it was not easy in the 1980s "to find non-blond Barbies," so Patty would put nylons over the blue-eyed versions "to make sure their skin looked brown. She really, really made it a point of making sure we never felt we had to look blond or blue-eyed in order to feel beautiful." Going back to Connecticut to see their mother's family could present pitfalls: "They would all ask us where we had gotten such beautiful tans and my mom would say, they're not tan. She worked really hard not to get insulted." Visiting their father's family in Mexico could be treacherous in other ways, says Kaija-Leena: "I remember my seventh or eighth birthday in Mexico, somebody brought me a cake, and all the kids were blown away; they had only seen cakes sold by the slice and here I got a whole cake for my birthday." Some of the guests could only afford small presents, such as plastic hair barrettes, "and I remember thinking, You have to be excited about these barrettes. But I didn't know how."

For Pablo's daughters, race and culture were a continuous and confusing part of their lives. Kaija-Leena remembers the annual Thanksgiving pageant in elementary school, "and always angling, every year, to get to be an Indian and not a pilgrim. I really don't know why, but I remember that it was highly important. We'd also chase this one blond neighbor around the yard, playing General Custer. The blond kid always had to be General Custer and he always had to run away from us." The Romero girls were, after all, directly descended from Aztec warriors. But since their father was a doctor, many of their neighbors came from the wealthy landowning families of Salinas, and the youngest child, Marisol, was once invited to fly on the Antle family plane for a weekend at Disneyland. The Antles were the biggest lettuce growers in town, and not many years before, Marisol's father and grandfather had worked in their fields.

In the fourth grade, Kaija-Leena was sent to a private Catholic school in Monterey, where many of the students came from wealthy communities such as Carmel and Pebble Beach, and the girl from the farming town encountered prejudice for the first time: "Because I was from Salinas, they thought I was poor, or dodging gunshots on my way to school. All of a sudden, I was going into this environment where being Mexican seemed like a liability. That was really shocking to me. I just didn't understand it. I came from this place where my dad was a doctor, being Mexican was something to be proud of, and there were these people telling me that wasn't the case." When Kaija-Leena invited a classmate home to Salinas the girl's parents apprehensively called Patty: "Her parents were saying, 'We don't want her to get hurt,' and Mom was saying, 'What do you mean by that? I'm insulted that you would even think I would bring my child to a violent area, much less your children.'" A few years later Kaija-Leena had a summer job in Monterey, doing office work for a doctor friend of Pablo's: "I remember showing up. Most people treated me with kid gloves, and I had a slightly inflated sense of myself. I remember meeting the manager's cousin or boyfriend, and he asked me where I was from and who my father was. He said, 'Dr. Romero,' and I said, 'Yeah,' and he said, 'That means you're a beaner.' And I remember thinking, Whoa, this is not the message here. The message is that I'm really important, my dad's important. It was his way of putting me in my place and being obnoxious but I just went to the bathroom and cried and cried and cried. It was silly anger, but he could reduce everything my dad had done to one word. I suppose it's still there, lurking in my mind still, about who I am and what I do. It's still there in what other people see."

As a teenager, Kaija-Leena felt that her sisters "were the best refuge for questions about identity. I didn't really feel my dad got what we were talking about. Dad's experience was really an immigrant experience; he was surrounded by people who understood what he was going through. But I didn't know anybody who was half Mexican, the daughter of a doctor, going to an elite private school. In fact I've yet to meet somebody with that experience. There was a certain feeing of being alone." But the sisters had each other and asked themselves the same questions: "How do you build relationships with other people? Do you try to isolate yourself? Do you become kind of militant and fixated on your ethnic heritage or do you totally ignore it? Or do you build an identity somewhere in between? At different points in our lives, my sisters and I have had different ways of answering the question, 'Who are you?' "

Pablo always had a clear answer to that question, and he agrees with his daughter that the "immigrant experience" was central to his life. "It's a weird thing," he says, "but I feel bad for the Mexican-Americans, the people who are second generation here, who get eaten up so early in life, who get to feeling like they can't do as well as others." Perhaps, he seems to be saying, it was better to grow up in Santa Rosa Jauregui than in Salinas. He was never called a "beaner" there or made to feel bad about his origins (despite the kids who got bikes for Christmas): "I grew up in a town where I was as good as anybody else. I was poor like everybody else. There were no class distinctions, I wasn't second place to anybody else. I was always extremely confident and that's what propelled me." But if his origins gave him confidence, a part of Pablo is still uncomfortable in the larger American society. He's still the college student who found that visit to a rich Anglo's house "absolutely unbearable." Kaija-Leena recalls her father attending a birthday party for a friend of Marisol's. Instead of mixing with the other parents he spent the whole time chatting with the family's Mexican gardener: "I remember just cringing at the story and thinking, Oh my God, my dad is so unrefined, so unable to participate socially with other people." But the story doesn't "bother Dad that much." His own sense of identity remains solid; he's happy talking to the gardener. And that self-direction, says his daughter, "has made him capable of gliding above" a lot of insults "in a way that my sisters aren't capable of."

The Romeros wanted their daughters to attend college back east.

"Mom was from there," says Kaija-Leena, "and she thought it was important to get a different perspective. Every place is not like California." After Liliana chose New York University, Kaija-Leena went to Harvard (Marisol stayed on the West Coast and went to the University of Southern California), but she had to fight the impression that she was a token, that she was only accepted as a result of affirmative action. When a friend got turned down by Harvard his mother told her, "What do you expect? He's a white male," and she reacted vehemently: "I got really defensive, because I was a really good college applicant. I wasn't a really good Mexican college applicant, but nobody could see that." Cambridge, Massachusetts, was definitely different from California, starting with the weather: "I would call home to talk about how cold I was. I was wearing flip-flops in the snow because I thought I could walk on top of the snow, sort of like snowshoes."

And the daughter of a doctor had a different social life than the son of a farmworker who had spent every possible minute in the library. Kaija-Leena called home one Friday night and told her father she was going out: "And he says, 'Why aren't you in your dorm? Don't you have homework for Monday?' And I was like, 'Dad, of course I have homework, but it's Friday!' And he was so shocked." Her family provided money for essentials—doing laundry, visiting her aunts in Connecticut—but then she asked for an allowance, saying "What if I want to get a cup of coffee, or go out to dinner? And Dad said, 'There's a dining hall.' And I thought, What? I remember feeling, all of a sudden, that I had jumped to the middle class from my parents' working-class, working-poor roots." Kaija-Leena finds it "inconceivable to imagine" what college was like for her father. Pablo had been "really lonely" at Irvine; "he was in on Friday night and not going out to dinner; he went out to dinner once a quarter because that's all he could afford." Now she was at Harvard, "this magnificent magical place," and Salinas was very far away: "I was this child he didn't recognize anymore because I was capable of navigating this world that he felt so displaced in. That, in and of itself, was a weird experience."

Harvard might have been a "magical" place but it was also a stratified and snobby place, and she still felt defensive about her background: "My ethnicity and my father's story, therefore, felt like a bit of a liability: a secret that I wanted to avoid discussing lest I fall in my peers' estimation." She started dating an Anglo, a fellow student who had grown up in France with "jet-setting expat" parents. But he was not considered an "immigrant." That term, she felt, "only applied to those of us too brown, too poor, or maybe just too grateful to have left our native land." Her biracial background complicated things even more, and she "was trying very hard not to be lonely" on a campus where few people shared her experiences. Then she found a group of women, "pretty feminist but not militantly so," who all had "a little bit of a twist to their stories": one was half West Indian and half Irish, another a Sikh from Canada, a third came from a Moroccan Jewish family that had emigrated to Israel. They became roommates, and one of the women started a campus group called Remix, open to other students of mixed race and ethnic backgrounds. "We all felt like outsiders and really found solace in one another," Kaija-Leena recalls. "They made me feel capable of being there. Our group looked like they were out of a Benetton ad. Every one understood the idea of negotiating an identity from the disparate parts of your experience."

Pablo Romero's daughter had one more step to take in "negotiating an identity" for herself. She had always "rebelled against the idea of going to medical school because my parents wanted me to so badly," and perhaps for that reason, she had performed badly in her freshman science courses. But the pull was always there, even when she tried to deny it. During college she spent time in Mexico, volunteering at a home for patients with severe neurological disorders; in Chile, she assisted in group therapy sessions at an orphanage. But the final link snapped into place after graduation, when she worked in her father's clinic, developing a project on obesity among Latino youths. When Pablo started training at Natividad Medical Center in Salinas, he quickly realized that he had found his life's work. And his daughter, who was born in Natividad, came to the same conclusion, working with her father across the street from that same hospital. As she wrote in her medical school application, she "overcame the bad taste in my mouth from freshman general chemistry," because she felt "compelled by the health problems of [my] community to become a doctor." Not only that, she decided to study at UCSF, her father's old school, entering in the fall of 2007. Back at Harvard, she had felt ashamed of her father's story, but now she asked Pablo to come speak to her fellow students about his life in medicine. As the event approached she panicked: "I didn't know if anybody would come." She bought sandwiches for thirty, and was stunned when twice that many crowded into the room, eager to hear from the farmworker who had become a physician. A circle had been closed, a tradition upheld. "I got tears in my eyes," said Kaija-Leena, and her father felt the same way: "I felt like a king talking to Kai's classmates."

Part V

T H E
WOMEN

In the last twenty years "the feminization of migration" has occurred in America, according to demographer Susan C. Pearce. Women now account for a clear majority of the legal immigrants entering the United States, and they "are more likely than in the past to be single, to have few children, and to join the labor force." That trend is reflected among illegal migrants as well. Sociologist Katherine Donato told the *New York Times* that as many as 45 percent of the undocumented workers crossing the border from Mexico are females, more than double the rate twenty years ago. "They come to find work in the booming underground economy," the *Times* reported, "through a vast network of friends and relatives already employed here as maids, cooks, kitchen helpers, factory workers and baby sitters. In these jobs they can earn double or triple their Mexican salaries."

Many of these immigrant women are such strong figures that they have also spawned a "feminization" of the arts. Korean-American filmmaker Grace Lee, for example, traveled the country interviewing women who shared her name. But even the strongest women can face a special set of problems in a new land, and they often start with children. Normaeli Gallardo, a single mother who left two young daughters back in Acapulco, tearfully told the *Times*, "My heart broke; my heart broke. But I had to give them a better life." Children born on American soil automatically become citizens and that can cause a different form of separation. Elvira Arellano became a folk hero to immigrants after she was arrested for using a false Social Security card and threatened with deportation. Instead of abandoning her seven-year-old son, Saul, who was born in the United States, she sought sanctuary in a Chicago church. *Time* magazine named her one of the "People Who Mattered" for 2006.

Saul Arellano is one of four million citizen children born to illegal immigrants, according to the Pew Hispanic Center, and my young friend Renata is another. Her mother immigrated illegally from South America more than twenty years ago, and after 9/11 led to a crackdown on undocumented workers, Renata says that "being an immigrant required constantly obscuring the truth and lying outright in order to keep our lives on course." After she was admitted to an expensive private school, Renata discovered that her mother's status barred the family from getting financial aid. "I filled out the form for my mother, who cannot read English," she told me. "When I reached the question on the form, 'Are you a U.S. citizen or legal permanent resident?' I checked 'yes.'" As a teenager she became adept at bribery—loan officers, motor vehicle inspectors—to keep the family functioning. At one point she drove her mother hundreds of miles out of state to get her a new driver's license in a jurisdiction that did not ask too many questions. But a life of deception leaves a mark on children like Renata. By honoring and obeying their parents, they have turned into lawbreakers. "Can we be good daughters and sons to our parents," she asks, "and to our nation at the same time?"

Female immigrants, particularly those fleeing war-torn countries, often carry deep emotional and physical scars. Dr. Mary Bradmiller, who treats many Somali refugees at Hennepin County Medical Center in Minneapolis, sees many cases of depression and posttraumatic stress disorder caused by "domestic violence, child protection issues, war trauma, nightmares, flashbacks and separation from their families." A study of Somali and Eritrean refugees found that almost half the women had been tortured or raped. Even those without a troubled past can be vulnerable to abuse. A Miami man was indicted on multiple counts of sex trafficking for forcing immigrant women into prostitution. Violent spouses, or bosses, often go unreported to police, says researcher Melissa Nalani Ross at the Center for New Community, because immigrant women "have no way of fighting back, they are alone, they are stuck in conditions that are horrific."

Marie Aziz reflects the feminization of immigration and knows what it's like to be alone. She fled an abusive marriage when she was a pregnant young bride. Then she fled the Soviet occupation of Afghanistan with a three-year-old daughter and very little money. She found work with a company selling equipment to security and intelligence agencies and when her daughter was sick, Marie brought her to work and had her nap on a pile of bulletproof vests. A direct descendant of the last king of Afghanistan, who was deposed in 1929, Marie was so destitute at one point that she literally pawned the crown jewels to pay the rent. Eventually she became an executive of a major economic consulting firm, sent her daughter through law school, and brought her mother to America. "I come from a very strong family, the women especially," she says, "and I take great pride in that."

Ulla Kirschbaum Morris Carter also comes from a line of strong women. She was a girl in Germany during World War II when her father was killed fighting in France. After the war her mother supported the family by resurrecting a failing printing business and occasionally cadging coal from barges that passed through their hometown of Dusseldorf. At twenty-one Ulla struck out on her own, moving to Cairo to work for an Egyptian businessman of dubious reputation. After fighting him off—and fleeing his house—she made a life for herself in Egypt, where she met and married an American newspaper correspondent, Joe Alex Morris. When Joe was killed covering the Iranian revolution for the *Los Angeles Times* in 1979, Ulla had little choice. With three daughters to support and no college degree, she moved to Los Angeles and took a job with the *Times*. She was a reluctant refugee, a new widow savagely sundered from the life she loved, and her daughter Karin spoke for the family: "I hated it here; I couldn't stand it. From the moment my father was killed, there was a complete sense of helplessness." Karin eventually married an Israeli immigrant with Kurdish origins; Ulla married a photographer and jazz musician. And this German woman, who met her American husband in Cairo, moved with him to Beirut and Athens, owned a house in Italy, and now lives in California, finally has a granddaughter. Her name is Silan, which means "wild rose" in Kurdish.

The three Kemal sisters were all small when their parents left Burma and settled in California, but they reflect a fact described by Susan Pearce: "Immigrant women often find the United States to be especially liberating . . . when compared to their home countries." Their mother still sees herself as a "guest" in America; she never learned to drive or develop marketable skills and cleans office buildings for a living. The sisters are all professionals—teacher, social worker, test manager for a drug company—and are working toward graduate degrees. But they have used the "liberating" climate of America to assert their Muslim heritage and adopt the hijab, a distinctively American version of "feminization."

11.

Marie Aziz, Mariam Aziz
Mahmoudi, and Mahera Loynab Aziz

AFGHANISTAN

*One month I didn't have the rent, and I was too proud to
ask for help. I had very nice jewelry, a huge emerald, a huge
diamond, and some other things. There was a pawnshop at
Eighteenth and M. I went there and gave all that and got one
thousand dollars and paid the rent. The next month they sent
me a letter: you have a month to give them the money to get
your jewelry back. But I didn't have the money, so it all went.*

Marie Aziz remembers the day in 1980 when she decided to leave
Afghanistan for good. The Russians had invaded the country, and
their MiG fighter planes frequently flew low and fast over the capital
of Kabul, frightening the local populace. Marie was standing under
an acacia tree in the garden of her house, with her daughter Mariam,
then three years old. A sortie of fighters screamed across the sky and
Marie remembers: "Mariam was very scared, and I said, 'I have to

save this child.' I couldn't let her live in those conditions. That was the last straw." Marie belonged to what had once been a powerful and privileged elite. Her grandmother on her mother's side was the daughter and sister of kings. Her grandfather on her father's side had been Afghanistan's first ambassador to the United States. But she felt she had no choice: "I'm not the kind of person who will say, 'I'm going to sacrifice my life for my country.' My ancestors gave their lives but I was not thinking about that. I was saving me and my daughter, so I had no regrets. All I wanted to do was get out as soon as possible."

Marie's escape took her to Rome, where she was declared a political refugee, and then on to America. She settled in the Virginia suburbs of Washington, a single mother too poor to support herself and too stubborn to ask male relatives for help. Her daughter Mariam, now in her early thirties and a trademark lawyer for the U.S. government, recalls: "I always felt it was just me and my mom, just the two of us." Through a series of low-paying jobs she usually managed to make ends meet, but not always. Finally she was forced to sell off gifts she had received from her mother and grandmother—family heirlooms that were literally the "crown jewels": "One month I didn't have the rent, and I was too proud to ask for help. I had very nice jewelry, a huge emerald, a huge diamond, and some other things. There was a pawnshop at Eighteenth and M. I went there and gave all that and got one thousand dollars and paid the rent. The next month they sent me a letter: you have a month to give them the money to get your jewelry back. But I didn't have the money, so it all went."

A few years later Marie read an ad in the newspaper: an international consulting company was looking for someone who spoke French or Arabic. Since she knew both, she got the job, and from that day on, the family's fortunes improved. She brought her mother, Mahera, to America and sent her daughter to law school, and one Sunday afternoon I talked to these three women, from three different generations, about their old country and their new lives. All are

American citizens, all are glad to be gone from their dangerous and devastated homeland, and yet all of them have left a shard of their spirit back in Kabul, buried in the soil like a piece of broken pottery. They talked about the roses that bloomed in their garden, the melons and grapes and pomegranates that tasted sweeter than any Virginia version, the songs and poems of Farsi writers they had memorized as girls. To make her point, Marie quoted some famous lines from Rumi, a thirteenth-century mystic who was born in Afghanistan and later moved to Turkey:

> *Listen to the song of the reed,*
> *How it wails with the pain of separation:*
> *"Ever since I was taken from my reed bed*
> *My woeful song has caused men and women to weep.*
> *I seek out those whose hearts are torn by separation*
> *For only they understand the pain of this longing."*

These women inherited a long family legacy that is heroic and progressive, brutal and bloody. But every generation seemed to produce strong females. Marie's great-grandmother was the wife of King Habibullah, who ruled Afghanistan from 1901 to 1919. The queen was a noted horsewoman, says Marie, and "on several occasions, when she was mad at her husband for putting so many people in jail, she would just go, with her entourage, on her horse, to the prison, and say, 'Open the doors.'" Habibullah was assassinated on a hunting trip and some histories say his son, Amanullah, who succeeded him to the throne, was part of the plot. However he got the job, Amanullah, Marie's great-uncle, was a forward-thinking ruler heavily influenced by Kemal Ataturk, the founder of modern Turkey. He abolished the Muslim veil for women and opened schools for girls while his wife, Queen Soraya, often appeared in public with her face uncovered and encouraged Afghans to educate their daughters and read about "the valuable services rendered by women . . . throughout history." Meanwhile Amanullah's sister, Marie's grandmother, had married the governor of Kabul, Ali Ahmed, over her brother's objections. That's a risky thing to do, Marie notes sardonically, when your brother is the king: "But we have a tradition of disobeying in our family." (Also a tradition of innovation: Marie's grandmother founded the first hospital for women in Kabul, which is still operating today.) Amanullah appreciated his brother-in-law's talent and used him to negotiate Afghanistan's independence from the British, but the king also saw Ali Ahmed as a rival, with his impressive landholdings and impudent manner: "He was not as reverent to the king as he should have been."

The monarchs modernized too quickly for their country's potent tribal and religious leaders. They were denounced as *kafirs*, or infidels, and overthrown by rebel forces (with British help) in 1929, ending the family dynasty. Amanullah and Soraya managed to flee the country and escape to Rome, but Ali Ahmed was seized by the rebels and put in front of a firing squad. Marie's mother, Mahera, was five or six at the time and still remembers the sound of the cannon that blew her father apart. Ahmed's widow "somehow collected the pieces" and buried her husband, but she and her children were immediately placed under house arrest by the general who had seized power: "He was always worried about my grandmother; he thought she was inciting some people against him, which was not true. My grandmother never did that; she was too afraid." The house arrest lasted for four years. No visitors of any kind were allowed, not even tutors for the children: "They had absolutely no communication with the outside world." Then the general-turned-king was assassinated, his nineteen-year-old son assumed the throne, and the restrictions were rescinded. But even after their release, life was hard. Despite her wealth and family connections, Marie's grandmother was a grief-stricken widow raising three children by herself in a male-dominated culture. When her daughter Mahera, Marie's mother, turned eighteen she was married off to Abdul Hai Aziz, a twenty-three-year-old professor of law and economics.

The two were actually distant relatives, but the Aziz branch of the royal family had lost favor with Afghanistan's rulers in the nineteenth century and been exiled to Iran, where Abdul Hai's father, Marie's paternal grandfather, was born. After the family returned to Afghanistan, that grandfather, named Abdul Hussein Aziz, joined the diplomatic service and sent his son abroad for his education: a French lycée, the University of Strasbourg, a graduate degree from the London School of Economics. When Abdul Hai returned home and took up his teaching position, his marriage to Mahera Ahmed Loynab was carefully arranged by their parents; the couple exchanged photos but no words before the wedding. From a political viewpoint, joining the two families made sense, but personally, says their daughter, her parents "had nothing in common." Her father was worldly and well educated, with a youthful fling as a "playboy in France" in his past. Her mother "was an extremely beautiful but very protected" young woman, who never resumed her formal schooling after her family's isolation under house arrest. Still, the attractive young couple became a fixture of Kabul's social scene, spending most nights out, at dinners and parties and concerts, while a squad of nannies cared for their growing brood, three girls and a boy. One of the girls was named Marie, a Western, Christian name, but her grandfather always called her "Zermina," a name from his tribal language, Pashto.

After World War II that grandfather, Abdul Hussein Aziz, was appointed Kabul's first ambassador to Washington. (Eventually he became the senior Muslim envoy in the capital and laid the foundation stone for Washington's first mosque, which still occupies a prominent place on Massachusetts Avenue, the city's "embassy row.") In 1948 the ambassador asked his son to join him as a representative of Afghanistan's Ministry of Commerce. Marie was three at the time: "I remember it very well. I have a picture of me standing on a chair, looking very teary-eyed and unhappy. That was the day we were traveling from Kabul, to come to the U.S., and the reason I was so unhappy is that I loved my nanny so much, and I had to say good-bye to my nanny." The family stopped over in Pakistan, where Marie remembers sleeping under a mosquito netting in a bed too high for a small child. She fell out and rolled under the bed, "and when my mother came to look for me, she couldn't find me." After landing in New York they took a train to Washington, and Marie spent the trip playing with coloring books: "I was so stupid. I colored the arms of a girl, one yellow and one pink. And that is how we came to Washington."

The family moved into an apartment building, the Wardman Park, right off Connecticut Avenue and within walking distance of the embassy. Marie developed a passion for American ice cream that almost did her in. She was walking along the avenue one day with her nanny, an African-American named Miss Queen, and demanding ice cream from a nearby drugstore. When Miss Queen said no, the willful child dropped her nanny's hand and ran into the busy street: "Cars were coming on both sides. Miss Queen started to scream." A policeman pulled her out of danger: "When Miss Queen told my father and mother what I had done, they were very upset with me." During the family's year in Washington, the elder Aziz was transferred to the United Nations and a new ambassador replaced him. That envoy had a daughter in boarding school in Baltimore, and Marie and her mother would often drive north to see the girl: "I used to bug them, because there were so many Howard Johnson's on the road and I would ask for ice cream. Finally my mother decided not to go anymore because I was such a nuisance." That boarding school girl was eventually killed in the coup that brought a communist government to power in Afghanistan in 1978.

Washington was a segregated city in that era but Marie's father was a liberal-minded man. He insisted that the children call their nanny

Miss Queen, and not use her first name, as a gesture of respect. He bought Marie a dark-skinned doll and when she asked him to suggest a name, he said, call it "Abdul Hai" after him: "This was my father's way of teaching us by example." When the family returned to Afghanistan, Abdul Hai deepened his involvement in progressive politics, joining a group of young activists demanding that the country's hard-fisted monarchy accept democratic reforms, such as political parties and elections. This was 1952, Marie was seven, and her father returned home one night from a protest rally badly beaten and bruised. Marie's mother, whose father and grandfather had both been murdered, was deeply fearful for her husband and angrily told him, "You're stupid, why are you doing this? You're not going to succeed, and you're going to jeopardize your life and our life."

The next night, several of the young progressives were nursing their wounds at the Aziz house when they heard a banging at the door. It was the police commissioner, backed by a truckload of troops. He arrested the men and hauled them away. "My mother started crying; she was very upset they were taken away," Marie remembers. Then her mother got a call from the governor of Kabul, telling her to bring clothes for her husband to the prison: "My mother started shouting at the governor, 'Go to hell!' She called him all sorts of things, venting her frustration. I never heard my mother speaking so much obscenities to the governor of Kabul! But he said there was nothing he could do; the order had come directly from the prime minister."

Marie's father spent a year in jail with about thirty other political prisoners. She visited him every weekend: "We used to go with much excitement. I loved seeing my father, and the prison yard became a playground for the children of all the prisoners." These were privileged inmates, they could receive food and clothing from home, "but still it was very hard." The prison was "very primitive," with simple wooden beds and not much to do. Deadly scorpions infested the place, and the prisoners amused themselves by playing jokes on each other.

Abdul Hai woke up one day to find a scorpion twitching on his chest. "He got extremely scared," until he saw a string attached to the insect and leading out the door. He realized the scorpion was dead, and the string was making it move. "Farouk you bastard!" he screamed at his friend, a noted historian and the prison's most creative trickster.

During that year, the prime minister who had ordered Abdul Hai to jail asked his father, Abdul Hussein, to become ambassador to Iran. "Of course my grandfather refused," says Marie. "Can you imagine?" When Abdul Hai was finally released he went directly to the house of his father, not his wife, a reflection of the relationship that commanded his deepest loyalty. The older man had grown up in Iran and he followed an Iranian custom, walking around his son, crying and muttering a prayer: "May all the evils come to me." The son then knelt and kissed his father's knees, a gesture of respect and affection. "When I think about it, it's so emotional," says Marie. "These hard men, these proud men, you would never see them cry or do things like that." In fact, "My father did not cry when he saw my mother; he only cried when he embraced his father." Abdul Hai spent another year under house arrest. He had no job and no income and survived economically only because his wife sold off pieces of her family's land. In the evening, Marie's father would dress in Afghan garb, sneak out, and walk to his father's house. The strolls violated his parole but the "government closed their eyes" and let him do it.

After the house arrest ended, Abdul Hai returned to government service, eventually rising to become the country's minister of planning. But something was missing in his life. This man who had studied in Europe and served in Washington really wanted to become an international civil servant: "He was sick of the politics of Afghanistan, of the people involved, of the corruption. He was very upset by that. He wanted to make a leap, but he never could do that." He was offered several posts, by international aid agencies and even the United Nations, but his own government refused permission and he didn't have the strength or will to fight back. "In some ways," says his daughter, "he should have said, 'To hell with all of you, I'm going,' but that never happened."

When Marie was ten, her grandfather moved to India as Afghanistan's ambassador and her family joined him there for several months. In New Delhi the girl was introduced to American movies and "fell in love" with the actor Gregory Peck. Heart problems then forced the elder Aziz to retire from the diplomatic service and he was in Europe getting treatment when he died of a massive heart attack. Marie's father plunged into a "very deep depression" that shadowed her teenage years. Her mother's mother lived with them and made Marie's life miserable: "She was very restrictive. She kept saying, 'If you become pregnant I'd rather see you dead than alive.' To this day I think those things had a very bad psychological effect on me." So it was no surprise that when Marie approached college age, she decided to return to the United States. She loved American ice cream and Gregory Peck and wanted to get away from home: "It was a way out, to be on my own." Her older brother was already studying in Italy "and I wanted to be like him; he was my model." Her domineering grandmother tried to dissuade her, offering a diamond ring if she stayed: "I said, 'Keep your ring. I'm going.'" Asked if she was tempted by the offer Marie responds with heat: "Absolutely not. What would I do with a piece of stone?"

She had an English tutor named Daisy Paul, the wife of an American economist who consulted for the Afghan government, and Mrs. Paul had strong family connections to Bryn Mawr, a well-regarded women's college outside of Philadelphia. Marie won a scholarship from the college, plus a Fulbright grant from the American government, and arrived on campus in the fall of 1963. Her father came to Washington for World Bank meetings and dropped by for a visit before heading to Europe. He died suddenly in Paris on October 28, probably a victim of the same heart condition that had killed his father. But more than forty years later Marie is not convinced. Many other relatives have met violent deaths; her father had sworn political enemies, and she says: "I think my father was somehow assassinated, but I cannot prove it." French doctors wanted to perform an autopsy but were blocked by Afghan authorities. When her father's body was returned to Kabul, thousands of mourners proclaimed that "the friend of the poor has died." Abdul Hai was "not a communist," his daughter insists today, "but he was very much a Social Democrat."

Marie had been a college student in America for just a few weeks and she made a poor decision: she did not return home for the funeral: "I was mad at God. Why did you do this? Whenever I prayed, I prayed for my father as if he were alive. I had this thing with God: I wouldn't accept that he [her father] was dead. He was alive. I never went to a funeral, I never grieved, I never saw his body." This is one of the most difficult dimensions of immigration, missing funerals and other family rituals, and the wound of separation can take a long time to heal. Marie believes that her pent-up grief finally burst open years later, contributing to a mental breakdown.

Adjusting to college was hard enough for a freshman in a new country, even without the loss of her father. She had one advantage over the other students: she had read major European writers (in Farsi translations) and "the other girls didn't know who Dostoyevsky was." But her grasp of American history was woefully weak and she had to find a high school textbook to bring her up to speed. Social life was even more troubling. "Everything was new to me," and her first night on campus, she went timidly down to dinner and sat at a round table for eight in the dorm dining room. "I felt very foreign," Marie recalls, but another woman "also behaved as if she didn't belong." Her name was Olga Dubynin. Her family had fled Russia and opened a shoe factory in Brazil: "She behaved like I did, a little apprehensive, not knowing the people, feeling as if we were left out. That's how I felt and I saw that Olga looked more scared than I did." They formed an immediate friendship that continues to this day.

Boys were an even bigger problem: "Of course on Saturday night everybody went to their boyfriends. This is why a girls' school is not good. If you had a date on Saturday night, that was a sign of prestige, but if you didn't, oh you poor thing. So I stayed home and read Oscar Wilde." She went to a few mixers but felt, "I was in a market; someone was appraising you." She had a few dates but "none of them really appealed to me that much." Because of her family background, and intense involvement in politics, "I was so much more mature than the boys I met." Besides, "I never cared for football or basketball or baseball; that was not my interest at all. My interest was to go to the Philadelphia Academy of Music and listen to Eugene Ormandy, but these young men would rather go to football games." After a lot of lonely Saturday nights, she found some older students who also preferred ballets to ball games and started joining them for weekend jaunts to Philadelphia. Then one of them invited her to lunch, and after the meal "a woman came and started to preach about Jesus Christ." Marie was raised in a Westernized, secular household but considered herself a Muslim (and still does): "I listened to all that and raised my hand and said, 'That's very interesting, but I don't believe Jesus Christ to be God.' The woman responded, 'Do you mean that Jesus is lying?' And I said, 'No, I'm just telling you what I think.'" Afterward, Marie told her friend, "I will never forgive you. You knew why they were having this lunch and you didn't tell me." She continued to receive "numerous invitations" from the missionaries, but threw them all away. Eventually the woman apologized for bringing Marie to the lunch and the two students resumed their friendship.

Still refusing to confront her father's death, Marie never returned home during her college years. She spent summers taking courses at Harvard and George Washington, and after getting her Bryn Mawr degree, headed to Northern Illinois University in De Kalb, sixty-five miles from Chicago, for graduate study in trade and economic development. "I wanted to have the flavor of the Middle West, but I did not like that flavor," she admits. The land was too flat, the cornfields too close. Occasionally she traveled to Chicago, to do research or visit the Impressionist collection at the Art Institute. And she finally met a few men she liked, one from Sweden, another from Morocco, "but I never had the feeling I wanted to marry them." She thought about working for the World Bank, but her student visa did not allow that, and her emotional problems, slowly building since her father's death, started to crest: "I was confused, especially when I got depressed. I didn't know what I wanted at that point." So she left Northern Illinois without finishing her degree and in 1968 returned to Kabul. She would not see America again for twelve years, until she returned as a refugee.

"When I went to Kabul I was absolutely astounded," Marie recalls. "I left a house that was very civilized, a cultured, happy place, and I went back to a place where my mother had abandoned everything. My mother had gone into such a deep depression after my father's death, she had given up her zest for life, the joie de vivre was no longer there. So that was very shocking to me." The men in the family, Marie's father and grandfather, had gathered vast collections of crystal and china during their many trips to Europe. But those men were dead now, and their trophies were packed away in boxes, never to be used. When Marie tried to unearth them, her grandmother—now old and paranoid—would snap: "Don't use them; people will steal them." But Marie insisted that the family "go back to the life we had." She ordered renovations on the family house that included a new room for herself, with a private entrance onto the terrace. She started using the china and crystal at family gatherings and dinner parties. And she went to work, taking a job with a German company that had a consulting contract with the country's agricultural development bank.

Marie admits that her royal blood boils easily, and she clashed with the German team leader: "He was ordering Afghans around and I didn't appreciate that. I had a big argument with him. He said, 'So-

and-so is not obeying orders,' and I said, 'That's the problem with you Germans; you obeyed orders and look what happened.' And of course he didn't like that." She left the Germans and concentrated on volunteer causes such as literacy and family planning. Then she heard that the Iranian ambassador to Kabul was looking for an aide, an Afghan woman who knew the local language and culture. She took the job and thrived in it. The ambassador was a poet, and they would recite verses in Farsi to each other: "That was the best year of my professional life, because he appreciated me. He knew who I was and what I was and what I was trying to do." Her family connections opened a lot of social doors: "I was beautiful and I was wearing beautiful clothes, because the embassy was paying me a lot. Everybody was looking at me and I enjoyed that." The ambassador also trusted her to represent him at meetings around the capital, and on a visit to the deputy foreign minister, an old friend from student days, he greeted her by saying, "So now you're coming on a diplomatic mission!" The whole experience was "very enjoyable" but it did not last. It was 1973, the king was ousted in a coup led by his prime minister, and the new foreign office decided that an Afghan woman of Marie's royal lineage should not be working for a foreign power. The government had closed the borders and stopped issuing passports, so Marie proposed a deal: I'll quit working for the Iranians if you give me a passport and permission to leave. But there was a hidden motive behind her offer.

For the first time, Marie had fallen in love. He was an American, a veterinarian from Minnesota named Rick who was serving in Afghanistan as a Peace Corps volunteer. He was also a musician, a guitar player, and they met when a mutual friend asked Rick to teach Marie's sister the instrument: "He played Simon and Garfunkel and he knew a lot of country music, and with the American background I already had, I had such a good time with him." But their romance was hampered by her family's snobbery. When Marie told her mother

she wanted to marry Rick, she replied: "Couldn't he be a medical
doctor, rather than a vet?" Even today Marie is aghast at that reaction: "Can you imagine that kind of thinking? The doctor of animals
doesn't count." Conditions "were getting terrible in Afghanistan"
during this period, and it was too dangerous for the young couple
to go out alone together: "We went on picnics and to the movies, but
we always blended in with other people. He was tall and very broad,
with very blue eyes, and he could not pass for an Afghan at all." Marie
realized that she could not be with Rick and stay home: "I didn't want
to go through the scandal, the daughter of so-and-so is marrying an
American, a non-Muslim, and all those things." His Peace Corps tour
was up in a month anyway, so they reached an understanding. After
Marie made the deal with the foreign office to quit the Iranians, she
took her new travel documents and bought an airline ticket routing
her through Berlin and Geneva and on to Washington. She would go
to Germany, where her aunt was living; he would write to her there
and they would make plans to meet in America. But the lovers were
betrayed, and never saw each other again.

Marie arrived in Berlin and moved in with her aunt: "One week
passed and two weeks passed and three weeks passed and I did not
hear from Rick at all. So I said to myself, Well, it's because I was a
Western-educated woman and for him that was interesting, but now,
he's back in his own country . . ." Her voice trails off, the memory
still pungent with loss: "He was also younger than I was, and that
was another chip on my shoulder." As the weeks went by, her aunt
came up with a different plan: marry an Afghan, a medical doctor
named Mahmoudi. He was living in the German city of Hannover.
His wife had died in a car crash, leaving him with a seven-year-old
son, and he desperately needed help. The doctor was actually a distant
relative. Marie had known him years before in Kabul, where he had
introduced her to cigarettes when she was twelve. She was like a fly,
trapped in a web. There was nothing for her in America, and nothing

for her back in Afghanistan: "I don't know what happened. I said yes; we had a very simple ceremony in Hannover."

Within a week she knew she had made a serious mistake. Dr. Mahmoudi lived with his mother, a "terrible woman" even more overbearing than Marie's own grandmother, who had made her life so miserable back in Kabul. The doctor himself had "a very foul temper" that he often directed at his son: "He would get upset at the boy and throw his slipper at him. There were times when I stood in front of the boy and I got the slipper. I just saw this dysfunctional family, and I didn't want to have anything to do with them." So she confronted her new husband: "I said, 'Couldn't you divorce me now?' This was a week after the wedding. He said, 'Are you crazy?' And I said, 'I don't think we can live together.' "

A short time later, Marie went to Berlin to visit her aunt, the one who had made the match with Dr. Mahmoudi. She went out to a wine bar with her sister Leila, who was a student at the Freie University in Berlin, and poured out her story: "I was crying in my wineglass, how miserable I was, and she said, 'What would have happened if Rick had written you a letter?' And I said, 'Things would have been very different, but this is a moot question. Why are you saying this?' And she said, 'Well, he did write. We opened the letter.' This is like a story from the nineteenth century but it happened." The aunt had intercepted the letter and asked her son, who knew English, to read it. Then she drew Marie's sister, and her brother who lived in Switzerland, into the plot: "They had a phone teleconference and decided for my own good to simply cover it up. Leila, with me crying in my wineglass, told me that. And after that I went into an extremely deep depression. My stupid aunt! I never thought the family would betray me the way they did. I just cursed them, I really did." Why had her family acted that way? "They thought it was better for me to marry an Afghan, rather than an American, and a medical doctor rather than a veterinarian. My aunt said, 'How could I face the relatives of my husband if they knew you had married an American?' See how small they were thinking! This woman had lived all her life in Germany; you'd think she'd be broad-minded. But she's still a small thinker!"

Marie returned to her husband in Hannover and found out she was pregnant. When she was five months along, she spent hours at a café, composing a long letter to Dr. Mahmoudi's brother, who lived in Hungary. The gist of it: "My life is miserable with your mother here; could you please take her for a while. I'm pregnant, I have to live with your brother, please help me." When she returned home her husband "attacked me and hit me in the stomach." To this day she does not know why, but suspects her mother-in-law was spreading stories about her. "He thought I would be like a *mauchen*—*mauchen* in German means a little mouse, and I was *not* a *mauchen*. I ran out, and went to a neighbor's house and called the police." When the cops came she told them her story: "The police said, 'Dr. Mahmoudi, are you a man?' and he said, 'Of course I'm a man,' and the police said, 'No, you're not, because if you're a man, you would not have hit your wife.'" The police advised her to get her belongings, leave the house, and call a lawyer: "I wanted the German police to do more: I wanted them to arrest him, but they didn't. So that night I walked out, went to a hotel, and called my uncle in Berlin. And I said, 'Could you please send me two thousand marks, because I know I will need the money, I need to see a lawyer.'" Marie's tribal instincts for revenge also kicked in. She called an ambulance from the same hospital where her husband worked. She wanted to make sure the baby was all right, but she also wanted to make sure the hospital learned of the attack. They did—and fired the doctor.

When Marie's mother and sister in Kabul learned of the incident, they immediately flew to Berlin and urged her to return home. But her mental stability was beginning to crumble. After a big fight with her aunt, the one who had brokered the marriage, Marie stormed out of the house and went to get her hair done. When she emerged from the shop, she saw a bus labeled "Tiegel Airport" and suddenly jumped aboard. She still had her original airline ticket, the one that was supposed to take her to Rick in America, and at the airport she went to the Air France counter and asked if the ticket could be rerouted to Paris. The airline agreed and she got on the next plane: "I think by then I was totally gone." Arriving in Paris with no money or luggage, she took a taxi to the Georges V, a luxury hotel where she had once stayed with her father: "So I was trying to trace him in some way, in my convoluted mind." She also thinks she was trying to frighten her family: "It was my way of revenging what they did." When she got to the hotel and couldn't pay the taxi, the police were called. They brought her to Sainte-Anne's, a psychiatric hospital, where she was heavily sedated. Back in Berlin her family was frantic. She had disappeared without a trace, but the police said, "She's an adult. If she doesn't want you to find her, we can't help." At Sainte-Anne's, Marie kept asking to make a phone call, to alert her family, but was denied permission. Finally, after a week of confinement, she was allowed to write a letter, and a few days later her brother arrived in Paris to collect her. She kept insisting that she wanted to go to America and have her baby there, but her family disagreed: "They said, 'You are not in a position to be all by yourself and having a baby.' And I think it was the right decision." She returned to Kabul with her mother and sister, and a few months later, in December 1977, her daughter and her divorce papers arrived at about the same time: "That was my adventure with marriage. It was bad from the beginning."

Kabul was bad, too, and getting worse. Marie found work with a Canadian development team but once the communists took over in 1978, she worried that she'd be forced to spy on her employers and quit. Before the Russians invaded a year later, her younger sister Hawa escaped the country by fleeing across the mountains to Pakistan, but with an aged mother and young daughter, Marie could not follow that route. To complicate matters, Marie's mother was dithering over the decision to depart. But after those MiG fighters buzzed her garden, terrifying her child, Marie was determined to escape, even if it meant leaving her mother behind. Passports and exit visas were hard to obtain, but Marie cleverly took advantage of a loophole in the rules. Afghans with spouses abroad were allowed to leave, and since Marie's divorce had taken place in Germany, there was no record of it in Kabul. So she was able to convince the foreign ministry that she was still married to an Afghan living in Germany. One problem: the Germans had taken in so many Afghan refugees that they were getting sticky about visas, so at the last moment Marie changed her destination to Rome. She remembers an airport bristling with Russian soldiers, their guns drawn. Mother and daughter boarded the plane and Mariam, then age three, started sobbing, because she was leaving her nanny and grandmother behind: "I asked for a glass of Coke, and the Coke saved her from being too upset. She loved Coke, which I did not allow her to have most of the time." As she left her homeland for good, Marie thought of her father, now dead seventeen years: "He loved Afghanistan but in many ways he wanted to escape and do something else, and I don't think he ever escaped. In my life, circumstances were very different. I could run away from Afghanistan. I made the leap that he couldn't."

Marie had relatives in Rome—her great-aunt, the sister of the exiled King Amanullah, was still alive and living there—but she was now on her own. The paperwork was endless, but she finally obtained a hearing before the U.N. High Commissioner for Refugees and made her case: my child and I are in danger back home, "I come from a prominent family, my family is being ridiculed" by the communists. After the U.N. officially declared her a political refugee, she went for an interview at the American embassy. She remembers with a laugh that the official read from a standard list of questions including, "Do you believe in polygamy?" She replied: "As a woman, of course not." There was no real problem: she was healthy, she had an American college degree, the Carter administration was sympathetic to Afghans fleeing the communists, and it was twenty-one years before 9/11. Now, says Marie, "Everyone is conscious—you're a Muslim so you're a terrorist. But that didn't exist then." She still faced one more hurdle: she needed a sponsor to gain entry to the United States. She had an uncle living in the Washington area but he refused: too many other relatives were coming, he said. 'We cannot help you, too.' So she turned to Robert Nathan, a prominent economist and an old friend of her father's. When he learned of her uncle's attitude he immediately stepped in and said he'd sponsor her himself. Her passage was arranged by the International Rescue Committee, a private agency devoted to helping refugees, and she and Mariam boarded a charter flight filled almost entirely with Soviet Jews. She still has her boarding pass on Alitalia Airlines stamped "AZ 701, Gate 1, 29 Sept 1980." But the flight was actually delayed a day by a strike in Rome and she finally arrived in America on October 1, two months after leaving Kabul.

Marie chose the Washington area for several reasons: Nathan was there, and a growing community of Afghan exiles was already settling in the Virginia suburbs. But money was a huge problem. Her family wealth was almost entirely in land—not an easy asset to convert into cash with a communist government in power. Marie actually had two uncles in the area, but one had already turned his back on her, and the other was equally stony: "I was almost penniless but he didn't offer to help, either." So as soon as she landed, she started looking for a job. She found one at a company that sold countersurveillance equipment near the Watergate building made famous by the scandal that had driven President Nixon from office six years earlier. She started as a receptionist, making $12,000 a year. But given her background, she related well to the company's clientele, and was soon promoted to sales representative with a $20,000 salary: "We had customers from the mafia to kings." She spoke some German, which helped when a wealthy German publisher purchased a high-powered flashlight for his wife, designed to blind attackers, and a scrambling system to disguise his phone conversations. Her French was fluent, a big advantage in selling scrambling systems to the Moroccans. As a Muslim, she could relate to emissaries from the Turkish embassy, who bought $300,000 worth of bulletproof vests to protect their diplomats from Armenian terrorists.

Still, her budget was tight: "My life was very, very simple. I didn't have much clothing. I never bought anything secondhand for Mariam but that was my pride. Mariam always wore very nice clothes. I bought groceries and that was it. No luxuries, nothing." She made some friends among the Afghan émigrés but "I was not part of their social life. For me, being a woman alone, having a child and a very small income, I could not compete with their social life. I didn't see much of them." Mariam was in day care at a local church, but when the child got sick, Marie had no choice: she had to bring her to work. Mariam would take naps under her desk or on a pile of bulletproof vests in the storeroom. When I started to ask how this great-granddaughter of a king adjusted to her new status, Marie cut in: "You mean being a worker? Being a proletariat? I still am a proletariat. When you get to the point where you just have to survive, you don't think about the past. Thinking about the past would have depressed me, but I didn't have time to be depressed."

After several years Marie realized she had no future selling bulletproof vests. Wanting to utilize her expertise in economic development, she contacted an agency that sent her on temporary assignments to a law firm and the World Bank. The tasks were interesting but the pay poor, and it was in this period that she had to pawn her jewelry to pay the rent: "I was extremely unhappy, especially because these were things my grandmother had given me and also my mother had given me. But I was so desperate. Otherwise I would have been homeless; they would have thrown me out. You know how it is in this country: you don't pay the rent, you're out the next day." But Marie realized that many of her countrymen were even worse off: "So many rich Afghans had lost their homes, their jewelry, their sons and daughters. I thought, At least I'm alive, Mariam's alive. Those were beautiful jewels, but so what? As life went by my sentimentality disappeared. I became more hardened."

She worked briefly for a small economic consulting firm, writing reports on the price of wheat for a large French bakery. But when her boss asked her to perform some personal tasks, she angrily replied, "I am not your servant." The boss's wife sniffed that Marie "had not adjusted to her station in life," but a woman who grew up in a house full of servants was not about to pick up anybody's dry cleaning. She soon got fired, but the experience gave her a taste of economic consulting, and that's when she got hired by Chemonics, a company that mainly does development projects under contract with the U.S. government. It was a good fit. The company was filled with foreign nationals like herself, and she was assigned to work with an Egyptian Copt, stirring up business in the Middle East. Her breakthrough came when the company won a contract from the Persian Gulf country of Oman, which wanted help in protecting its traditional fishing industry. As a Muslim, she understood local sensitivities and always dressed respectfully, in long sleeves and long skirts. She impressed a government minister when she told him frankly, 'I understand Arabic, so don't speak it if you don't want me to understand.' The man switched to Swahili for private conversations but later told her bosses: "You were smart to send a Muslim woman here; all those men loved her." Her big breakthrough came back in Washington, where the head of Chemonics was hosting a party to celebrate the contract with Oman. By this time Marie's mother had moved to America, and had bought her daughter a new jacket for the occasion. She also gave her a pendant to wear, fashioned from a gem that once adorned a royal tiara owned by Marie's grandmother. Her boss noticed the jewelry, but also her diplomatic skills. After all, she had first come to Washington as the three-year-old granddaughter of the city's senior Muslim ambassador. The guest list included Omanis and Americans, politicians and economists, and "very smoothly, I got all these men together to talk. The boss saw that and noticed what I was doing. They were all looking at me in a different light."

Marie eventually rose to a senior position at Chemonics. She's lived all over the Middle East, guiding development projects from Egypt to Morocco, and while her company spends American taxpayer money, she feels that her background gives her an advantage over native-born colleagues: "I have an understanding for other people and respect for their culture that Americans don't have." She lectures young people when they come to Chemonics: "Our client is not only USAID [the U.S. Agency for International Development], our client is the people for whom we are working. This is something they don't realize." And she is quick to jump on anyone who uses the term *locals* in front of her: "I never use the word *locals*. That kind of language is condescending, I just don't like it."

One incident shadowed her long career at Chemonics. In 2003 she was sent to Afghanistan, to head a project on agricultural development. It was her first trip back in almost twenty-four years and when she saw the mountains of her homeland and its shattered capital she started crying, and didn't stop for a week. Finally a Turkish colleague told her, "You can't help anybody by crying all the time," and she mastered her emotions. But she soon realized that the project was a disaster. She won't go into details, but the Bush administration was pushing hard for visible results and Marie felt that "most of what we did was for show," not for any long-term benefit. She was supposed to stay a year but came home after four months.

Today, the three Aziz women are all on their own. Mahera, well into her eighties and long widowed, speaks little English but doesn't have to. She lives in a senior citizens' complex in Virginia with many other Farsi speakers, and Marie says she gets all the gossip about life back in Afghanistan from her mother. Marie never remarried, and when I ask about Rick, the one love of her life, she says, "for many years I did not try to find him." When she finally did, "he was already married, and I have very strong ethics about married men, so that was the end of it." Mariam is still single but has dated Afghani men and says that marrying one would make life a lot easier: "You don't have to explain everything."

These are strong women, who draw inspiration from their female forebears: the queen who rode her horse to the prison gates to protest her husband's penal policies; the queen who dared to show her face in public and say that girls should be educated; the daughter and sister of a king who gathered up the pieces of her murdered husband's body and prepared them for burial. "It's an amazing story and an amazing history," says Mariam, the government lawyer. "I come from a very strong family, the women especially, and I take great pride in that. There are very few men in our family. I was raised by a single mom and I've seen how women carry the family, emotionally and financially." Marie, too, is proud of her royal ancestors and their heroic deeds. But she also knows that her greatest accomplishment was private, not public, carrying the family on her back when no men would help her. She recalls the day, in her garden in Kabul, when the Russian fighter planes frightened Mariam: "I was standing under that tree and saying, Now I have to save that child. Well, I did."

12.

Ursula (Ulla) Kirschbaum Morris Carter

GERMANY, EGYPT, LEBANON, GREECE

Karin Morris—LEBANON, GREECE

Moshe (Kushi) Gavrieli—ISRAEL

*I think there was a lot of inner conflict about coming here.
It took me years and years and years to be able to say, with
a lot of peace internally, I'm American. I couldn't even say it,
I never felt it, and for years I was convinced that I was just
temporarily here and I was going to move on and go back to
other countries I had been living in, where I really wanted to be.*

The first time Ulla Kirschbaum saw an American, she feared he
was about to kill her. It was January 1945, she was eleven years old,
and her family had already been bombed out of two houses in their
hometown of Dusseldorf. She had been sent to live with relatives in
a remote corner of Germany that her mother thought was safe from
attack. But it was not. The Nazis had built a secret airstrip in the area,

to guard an underground bunker containing critical documents, and now the advancing American forces were searching for it. Ulla was on her way to school, crossing a snow-covered field with a friend named Bernd. "Suddenly," she wrote many years later, "we heard the well-known droning sound of approaching planes. Out of a clear blue sky, whizzing noisily and dangerously low overheard, a group of American dive bombers appeared. We knew they were American because we could see their insignia. Even the pilots' faces were visible. Bernd and I threw ourselves facedown into the snow—no bush, no tree, no place to hide. We were terrified and cold." How close did they come? "These dive bombers came incredibly low," she told me. "You couldn't see whether the pilot had brown or blue eyes but you could see the face." Only for a moment: "Then as fast as they had appeared they climbed back into sky. Gone within seconds."

The Americans would be back. A few weeks later they seized the famous bridge over the Rhine at the town of Remagen, just a few miles away, and Ulla and her family knew the war was lost. "We lived in fear and terror of what might happen to us," she wrote. "Would the Americans take revenge on the civilian population? We knew the American troops were more disciplined than the Russian troops, but that was little comfort considering that they were our enemies all the same. Nazi propaganda had succeeded in making the prospect of military defeat a terrifying vision." That vision was not realized, but the fear remained. When the American forces finally arrived, "there were all these healthy, good-looking boys in crisp uniforms," Ulla recalls. "One was envious of them. They weren't starving." The Americans set up camp nearby and placed the family under house arrest. When the soldiers offered Ulla oranges and chocolate, her aunt snapped, "You don't want to take this from these enemies." And she replied, "No, of course not."

Fourteen years later Ulla married one of those "enemies," an American newspaper correspondent named Joe Alex Morris Jr. For their entire married life, they wandered the world, renting temporary houses, taking temporary assignments—Cairo and Beirut, Bonn and Athens. Like every immigrant who marries a foreigner they had to face an immutable fact: no matter where the couple settled, at least one of them would always be a stranger. And their children would always balance between their two worlds, never fully at home in either one. Ulla tells the story of living in Germany when her middle daughter, Karin, was six years old and attending a British school. The Duchess of Kent paid a visit and asked every first-grader their name and nationality. Karin answered: "My name is Karin, I am American, and I come from Washington." When Ulla heard that she admonished her daughter: "Washington? You have never even visited Washington, let alone come from there!" The little girl replied: "Every child said only three words: their name, nationality, and the city they came from. I am American, and every American in my class said Washington. How could I tell the duchess that I have an American passport, but I am half German, half American, and I was born in Beirut and I really don't know where I come from?"

In 1979, the Morrises were living in Greece, refugees from the civil war that was lacerating Lebanon. Joe was on assignment in Iran, working for the *Los Angeles Times* and covering the uprising that drove the Shah from power, when a single stray bullet killed him instantly. Ulla was on a ski trip when she heard the news and after a torturous drive back to Athens she finally reached her two younger daughters, Karin, then fourteen, and Julia, thirteen (the oldest, Maria, was at boarding school in Switzerland). As she recalls, "Trying to be brave and wanting to comfort me, the first thing I remember Karin saying was 'Don't worry, Mommy, we can help; we don't need to take lunch money to school every day—we can make sandwiches at home.' Then the question I had feared: 'But where are we going to live?' Without their father and breadwinner they thought they would immediately be impoverished. They already understood correctly that we could not stay on in Greece: we had to find a new home somewhere. Home? Where was home?"

For most immigrants, America is a distant, driving dream. Often they scrape and struggle for years before finally making the journey. For the Morris family it was the opposite. They were unwilling and unhappy immigrants, moving to southern California within weeks of Joe's death because that's where the *Los Angeles Times* offered Ulla a decent salary and a dollop of security. America represented a "lost dream," a lost future. As Karin put it, "I think there was a lot of inner conflict about coming here. It took me years and years and years to be able to say, with a lot of peace internally, I'm American. I couldn't even say it, I never felt it, and for years I was convinced that I was just temporarily here and I was going to move on and go back to other countries I had been living in, where I really wanted to be. So that identity shift took a really long time. It almost didn't deeply sink in till I had kids." Ulla, too, eventually came to terms with the disruption and despair of her husband's death. In 1985 she married Bill Carter, a photographer and jazz musician, and moved to a sunny, sprawling house in the hills south of San Francisco. Now in her mid-seventies, she has an American husband, four American grandchildren, and the same shimmering blue eyes that thawed the heart of that orange-offering American soldier so long ago. She became an American citizen just before the last election and voted for the first time. Still, there's a hole in her history. "I have no roots," she said, gazing out a picture window just a few miles from the Pacific. "Here, I don't have anybody with whom I share a past. There's nobody who knows anything about me, beyond the time that they met me, unless they ask me and I tell them the story."

That story begins in Dusseldorf, a city near the Ruhr district that served as headquarters for many of Germany's heavy industries. Ulla's father, Hanns Kirschbaum, was a photographer and artist who took over his family's printing business; her mother, Maria Liesenfeld, was a talented pianist whose hopes for a concert career ended at nineteen when she fell down the basement steps and shattered her arm. As a girl Ulla lived in the same small apartment building that housed her father's parents and the family enterprise. Her first memories involve running across the street to purchase hot rolls for the family's breakfast: "They were oval-shaped and golden brown with a crusty top created by a cut through the middle of the dough before they were baked." The warm scenes and smells of a placid childhood started dissolving in November 1938, just after her fifth birthday, when Nazi gangs trashed countless Jewish homes and businesses during a rampage that came to be called Kristallnacht (or "crystal night," named for the broken glass that littered the streets of German cities). The Catholic Kirschbaums had many Jewish neighbors and Ulla says, "The one thing I remember is seeing this piano flying over a balcony and crashing into the street." She also remembers the fires flaring in the streets that night: "It was the books burning; they kept throwing all the books people owned into the fire." Many years later, when Ulla asked her mother about those days, and how her family felt toward the Nazis, she received few answers: "My mother was very angry with me, she didn't think she deserved to be questioned on this subject. The war was not happily discussed in any family. There were too many losses; too much trauma had happened to every family."

The Kirschbaums' trauma began when Hanns was drafted into the army in 1940. Already thirty-seven, "my father was basically an artist, that was his life," says Ulla. And with two small children at home, "he really wasn't a soldier at heart; he never would have gone into the war voluntarily. That wasn't his thing at all." After the fall of France, Hanns was assigned to a military police unit in occupied Brittany, but his duties were never quite clear: "We think they sent him off on intelligence missions. They couldn't tell us, ever." Soon British bombers were raiding Dusseldorf, and one night in 1941 the warning sirens went off at three in the morning. Ulla's mother grabbed her children and hustled them into a basement shelter that had once stored coal and potatoes. "Closing my ears with my index fingers, I tried to shut out the swelling drone of the planes," Ulla recalls. "The noise grew more intense. A powerful explosion nearby made me hold my breath, then a second one. The house shook dangerously, but it stood." Then a third bomb, a direct hit: "The lights went out and we all clung to each other in total darkness—darkness that was darker than black. There was only dust, noise, shock, terror, lack of air, and fear of death." The family stumbled to the street. Fires raged everywhere. The Kirschbaums were alive only because the bomb that hit their house had failed to explode. But it was still dangerous. "Get away! Quick, quick, move on!" the police shouted. "It might explode at any moment." Ulla recalls: "'Move on' was easier said than done. Where to go? We had nothing but the clothes on our bodies. We started walking away from the burning street and our house with the unexploded bomb."

Her "gypsy life," as Ulla describes it, started that night and has never really ended. The family moved in with the Liesenfelds, her mother's parents, ten blocks away, but the apartment was small and soon they left for the countryside, where a series of relatives took them in. In May 1943 they were back in Dusseldorf, living again with the Liesenfelds, when Ulla made her First Communion. Her father couldn't get home from France but sent a pair of small gold earrings as a present. Family friends sent traditional gifts, potted plants of azaleas and cyclamen. That night the house was bombed "and of course, all this disappeared." Ulla's school was destroyed as well, so the entire student body was evacuated to the hill country about fifty miles south of Dusseldorf. Now nine, she was housed with a farm family and given many chores: cleaning the pigsty, peeling potatoes, washing the kitchen floor every morning before breakfast. That meal was no treat, either, featuring warm milk fresh from the cows, and the city girl was "ready to gag just smelling it." For Christmas 1943,

Hanns returned home from France for a brief visit and Ulla was allowed to leave school early to be with him. A few weeks later she was
back in the hill country when she received a call from her mother. "It's
Daddy," her mother whispered down a faulty line. "Daddy is dead,
killed in France."

The family never learned exactly how or why he died. Hanns was
found in a ditch by a German military chaplain. Perhaps he had been
on an intelligence mission; perhaps he was killed by partisans. When
the family received his personal effects, they included a heavy wool
sweater he had been wearing under his uniform. There was a sharp
cut on the left side, near his heart. "That's why we assume he might
have been stabbed," says his daughter, "but this has never been con-
firmed." The belongings included Hanns's wedding ring, still smeared
with blood. Maria, then age thirty-four, would never marry again
and would never see her husband's grave, but her daughter would.
Hanns's body was moved twice, but in 1964 it came to rest in a cemetery in Brittany built by the Americans. A few years ago, Ulla and
her husband, Bill, made "a little pilgrimage" to the grave site and she
was pleased at the setting: "A few French ladies would come with
their children and play there. It was very quiet, very nice. There were
quite a number of graves for unknown soldiers but in my father's case
they had everything. His birthday was right, they even spelled his
name right." Bill said of the trip: "It was something Ulla needed clo-
sure on for many years, and I think it gave some of that. It's like she
had been holding her breath all that time." Today a picture of Hanns
Kirschbaum in his military uniform hangs in the Carter house in
California and Bill admits, "Even I do a double take once in a while."
But the photo, he adds, dispels the image of "evil Nazis" usually de-
picted in pop culture: "Here's a guy, with the swastikas and collar and
everything, and he's just playing with his child."

After finishing the school year in the hill country, Ulla was ready
for upper school, or gymnasium, and her mother sent her to yet an-

other new place: the home of great-aunt Hedwig and her husband, Paul, in the town of Andernach, in the district that was supposed to be safe from air raids. The tranquility didn't last. For the third time, bombs smashed a house Ulla was living in and her aunt and uncle decided to evacuate to a mining camp about two hours away that Paul had run for years. It was now abandoned, with all the miners off to war, and the family moved into three tiny rooms that had once served as a barracks. There was no electricity or indoor plumbing. Water had to be hauled by wagon from the nearest village, fifteen minutes away.

The only heat in the sleeping quarters came from a woodstove, and water kept in a basin overnight would sometimes freeze. They had to break the ice in the morning before washing their faces.

Ulla was living in those barracks the day the American dive bombers sent her sprawling into the snow. A few weeks later her uncle Paul, then almost sixty-five, was called up to help defend the Siegfried Line, Germany's last defense against advancing Allied troops. Hedwig and Ulla were left to survive the winter alone, and when spring arrived, and a friend came to borrow Paul's truck, Ulla was allowed to go along for the ride. From her perch in the rear she heard the familiar scream of approaching aircraft. She pounded furiously on the cab, hoping the driver would stop, but the old rattletrap made so much noise he couldn't hear her. So she leaped off the back and into a thick green bush. I'm saved, she thought to herself, only to realize that she had landed smack into "a large cluster of wild blackberries, thorny, prickly and outright painful." Then a spring storm ripped the tarpaper off the roof of the barracks, and eleven-year-old Ulla was assigned to climb a precarious ladder and fix the hole. From her vantage point she saw, for the first time, the remnants of Germany's retreating army: "The soldiers came running up the hill, begging for civilian clothing—anything to replace their uniforms." Hoping to avoid capture by the Allied forces, the soldiers wanted to ditch anything they had with military markings—clothes, boots, bikes, even a bar of margarine. One wanted to hide in a haystack behind the barracks "but my aunt insisted that he would get us all killed if he were found out."

As the Siegfried Line collapsed, Uncle Paul suddenly returned. He decided all the family valuables—jewelry, cameras, watches—should be buried in the mine. Everything was packed into a large casserole and placed in a deep hole. The bike, the margarine, and anything else associated with the fleeing German troops went in as well. About the only thing the family held on to was a pair of field glasses, which Aunt Hedwig often used to watch Ulla as she trekked to the nearby town for water. Big mistake. A few days later, as Hedwig was peering through the binoculars, the first American troops arrived. When they spotted her, surveying the landscape from her hilltop, they jumped in a jeep, raced to the barracks, took away the field glasses, and placed the family under house arrest. A few hours later, when Ulla needed to use the outhouse, she timidly knocked on the door. When it opened a crack, "I stared into the dark eyes and the face of a black soldier. I had never before seen a black man and was startled." So was he. But he finally understood her sign language—and her urgency—and let her out. The mine's main product was volcanic lava, used in road building, and one day a detachment of Americans showed up. They needed lava for a construction project. Uncle Paul directed them to a section of the mine, away from where the family valuables had been hidden, but the leader said he knew mining, his father had a similar business, and he would pick his own spot to dig. So he did, right on top of the buried treasures. Soon the casserole and the bike emerged and as Ulla recalls, "that did not go over well." The Americans confiscated everything and tightened the guard.

At about this time, Ulla's two cousins, "beautiful and blond," returned from nursing duty in a military hospital. Several of the American soldiers guarding the family "made big advances" toward the girls: "They were the victors. They were certainly not like the Russians,

but you can have what you want when you are the victorious army."
Aunt Hedwig, "Brunhilde-like, marched herself down to the camp"
and told the commander to keep his men away from her daughters.
Whatever Hedwig said in her poor English apparently worked, and
the guards were removed. Still, Ulla wanted to go home. She'd been
away for most of four years and all civilian communications had been
cut off. But there were no trains, no buses, no public transportation
of any kind. Another problem: while Americans controlled the Andernach region, Dusseldorf was in the British sector. Aunt Hedwig
did her Brunhilde act again and "extracted a promise" from the local
commander to take Ulla by military truck to the edge of the American zone. There she could catch another ride with the British. After
reaching Dusseldorf she headed for her grandparents' house, but she
was not sure if it was still standing, or even if her relatives were still
alive. At the end of the street she caught sight of three large chestnut
trees that had long loomed over the house; they were still there, she
thought, so the house must be, too. It was. She ran up the steps to the
second floor and into the arms of her mother, who didn't even know
she was coming.

Peace was almost as brutal as war. The Kirschbaums were eventually able to repair their old home and move back in but they could
keep only two rooms for themselves; strangers who had lost everything occupied the others. (Ulla recently found herself chopping vegetables in her daughter's crowded kitchen and complaining that she
might have to go back to her postwar tactic—using the toilet seat as a
cutting board.) "Those years were sheer survival," she recalls. "There
were harsh winters and not much food. Every day was a day to survive and organize something that would keep you alive." Rations
were strict, and hungry men would "sneak around" at night, stealing food. At school, the children competed for kitchen duty and the
chance to scrub out the soup pots: "If it was a sweet soup, a milk soup,
there would be a big crust around the rim of the kettle. You could

trim off this stuff and eat it. This was the best part, because it was like crisp bread." The Kirschbaums were fortunate: they had relatives who owned a small grocery store in a rural area near Dusseldorf. As a black market blossomed they could sometimes trade for food with the local farmers—a set of bedsheets, say, for ten eggs: "The farmers took everything. We didn't have very much but certain things survived. We traded only for food, because everyone was hungry." Hungry and cold, because fuel was also in short supply. Ulla's mother befriended a barge captain who ferried coal to the industrial plants in the Ruhr region. When he came through town, she would ride her bicycle down to the port, sneak under the barbed-wire fence, and come home with a small sack of sooty black treasures.

Emotional hardships were as draining as physical ones. Every family was coping with grief. Ulla had lost a father and two cousins, two uncles were still in POW camps, and the dying hadn't ended. A young cousin who survived the war was playing hide-and-seek on an abandoned anti-aircraft battery when a shell lodged in the gun exploded: "They didn't want to tell me but later on I did hear that he was really ripped into pieces, a shoe with a foot in it, that kind of thing." One day a relative was running a small store and a former soldier came in, just released from a Russian POW camp. He was over six feet, but weighed less than a hundred pounds; his head was shaved and his glasses gone. There's another of those poor bastards, thought the woman at the counter. But then he spoke to her: "You don't recognize me?" It was her brother. Surviving soldiers often faced great difficulties adjusting to civilian life: "Women had become very self-sufficient and independent, even though they had been brought up in earlier years to be very obliging and obey their husbands. They ran families and worked in factories, and then these men came back and they thought they could step right back into where they left, and that did not work in many cases. Divorce was not common, but there was a lot of hardship, a lot of rough feelings, because these women, many of them, didn't want to just give up what they had learned and accomplished." Ulla recalls that "plenty of women were willing to have an affair with an American soldier" as a way of supporting themselves. Many became pregnant, and if their lovers were black, they were often too embarrassed to keep their mixed-race offspring. Ulla's great-aunt was a nun who ran an orphanage near Dusseldorf, and these German women would drop their babies off at the door: "I would call them the 'chocolate babies' because they were so beautiful."

Ulla's mother, Maria, had no husband but she did have the remnants of the family printing business. She borrowed five hundred dollars from an uncle and soon it was up and running again, crafting letterheads and advertisements for small companies that were just starting to regenerate. Maria noticed that one of her employees, a talented graphic artist, was always staying late. One day the police showed up and said to Maria, "You're under arrest." It turned out the artist was designing counterfeit ration cards. Maria got off, but the artist went to jail. Ulla resented another employee, a young man she felt was "always pursuing my mother" with the aim of taking over the business for himself. Then, when her mother went into the hospital for an eye operation, the man came into Ulla's room one night and tried to assault her. "I couldn't stand him," recalls Ulla, who was fourteen at the time. "After my mother came back I went and stayed with a girlfriend. I didn't want to see him again. I basically at one point said to my mother, 'Either I go or he goes.'" Those years left deep scars on Ulla: she can't stand loud noises and compulsively stocks her house with extra food. She keeps a flashlight in every room and when her children visit, she packs them off with bags of rice and other supplies. "It was a society of survivors," says her husband, Bill. "Surviving women held things together and I think that affected Ulla's character. She's a survivor. Whatever happens she starts looking at the practical side and that was very good preparation for the rest of her life."

Those postwar years contained occasional moments of joy. Ulla remembers her grandmother tearing apart a bright red Nazi flag and making her a dress from the cloth: "She took off the swastika and burned it in the kitchen stove and she made me the most beautiful dress, red with a blue belt, and blue trim on the bottom, and puffed sleeves. It was the best dress I ever had." Maria scrounged a piano from somewhere and the family would gather together and sing as she played—folk songs, operettas, pop tunes. "Ulla lights up when she hears a Franz Lehar waltz," says Bill, referring to the popular composer of *The Merry Widow*. "She dances around the room." She joined the Girl Scouts through her church and left Germany for the first time to attend international jamborees in Sweden and Rome. She found a boyfriend and joined a kayaking club. The cultural influence of the American "enemy" was growing steadily. A "bargain basement" opened in a big department store ("It was unheard-of in Germany, a store that had a lower basement with cheaper things"). And one of her friends in the kayaking club played a new song on a piano, the "St. Louis Blues": "I'm not sure I called it jazz, but I remember thinking, this was a marvelous tune." The American jazz musician Lionel Hampton played a concert in Dusseldorf and "people were standing on the seats, it was so incredibly exciting."

But most of life was pretty drab. When Ulla finished high school at age seventeen she wanted to train as a physical therapist, "but you had to go to school and pay money and none of that was available to me at the time." Maria's eyesight was failing, she was afraid she'd lose the printing business, and Ulla was left with no choice: "I really needed to have a job so that my mother could live in peace and know that I wouldn't starve if she were to remain blind, which was a strong possibility at the time." So "very reluctantly" she left school and took a clerical job with Eikomag, a big iron and steel company. She lived at home, gave most of her paycheck to her mother, and took classes at night to learn technical English. "The war robbed you of your youth," she says now. "I wanted nothing more than to learn ice-skating but

I never had a pair of skates in my life. There were all these things we couldn't do, or didn't have the means to do." In 1955, when she was twenty-one, she went to a trade fair and met the Egyptian representative of Eikomag, who offered her a job in Cairo. "My mother was very distressed," Ulla recalls. "She said to me, 'No decent German girl goes to the Orient.' She was just in hysterics." The Egyptian, a Mr. Abbas, had a terrible reputation and a German businessman who lived in Beirut told Ulla's mother, "I would break her neck, if she were my daughter, rather than letting her go to Cairo." But Ulla was determined: "I wanted to get out of Germany; to me this was very simple. In 1955 we still had POWs in Russia, we were still in the postwar era, a lot of places were still in ruins. We were in this rut, everything had to be rebuilt and redone and everything was work, work, work, work. It was not that much fun for me. I just wanted out, and this was my way out." In February 1956 her uncle took her to the train station, where she started a journey that would take her to the Italian port of Genoa, and then by boat across the Mediterranean to Egypt. Her mother was too upset to see her off.

For good reason. Her fears proved correct. Abbas was as sleazy as advertised. For months he kept Ulla isolated, in his office or apartment, and made increasingly urgent demands for sex: "I felt like a bird in the golden cage: I was imprisoned. I had no privacy. Mr. Abbas entered my room whenever he desired to do so. He never left me alone." An aide to Abbas, a Christian named Odsi, privately warned her that his boss had done this before, with other young women from Europe, and said, "This is not a good place for you." When Abbas wanted to take Ulla with him to Saudi Arabia, Odsi objected: "Under no circumstances can you go with him. You will never return. He wants to present you to one of his business partners in exchange for more contracts." She managed to avoid the trip after a "bitter fight" but then Abbas asked her to sign a "visa application." Don't do it, said Odsi, they are actually marriage papers. Finally, she found a way out. Through a sympathetic German businessman who worked with Abbas, she met an official of the Egyptian tourist ministry named Talal. One day, after her boss left her alone for a few minutes, she called Talal and asked him to meet her on a street corner near her apartment. She raced home in a taxi, jammed her belongings into two suitcases, and found the Egyptian waiting at the appointed spot: "He jumped out when he saw me, helped me with the luggage, and drove off. We had not spoken a word so far. I had climbed into the backseat and lay flat on the floor. I was so terror-stricken and afraid that someone might recognize me that I never even lifted my head off the floor. I was close to a nervous breakdown." Talal took her to a small guest-house, calmed her down, and promised she would be safe. She never saw Abbas again. But instead of leaving Cairo, she decided to stay, and found a job with a German company. Why didn't she go home? "That would have been admitting defeat. I was much too embarrassed to go back."

Once free of Abbas, Ulla came to love Cairo. She traveled often—from the temples of Luxor up the Nile River to St. Catherine's monastery deep in the Sinai Desert. She acquired a fiancé, a German businessman who had fought on the Russian front as a teenager, and one day the couple was visiting a journalist they knew based in Cairo. The journalist briefly introduced Ulla and her boyfriend to an American correspondent, Joe Morris, who worked for the *New York Herald Tribune*: "We rode down in an elevator together, and the story goes that Joe remembered me from this dark elevator ride, which is totally ridiculous." Her relationship with her German fiancé was already disintegrating. He was deeply tormented by his war experiences and as Ulla recalls, "I had this feeling that I could help him out of this nightmare, but it was not possible for me." After she broke her engagement, Joe came courting and five months later, in March 1959, they were married. But it was not easy. For one thing, Joe was not baptized, and before they could have a Catholic wedding, he was required to receive religious instruction. Ulla dispatched him to a German priest she knew in Cairo and got very worried when Joe didn't return for hours. The priest turned out to be a big baseball fan and the two men spent the time discussing their common devotion to the Boston Red Sox. To many Germans, Americans were shallow shysters who could not possibly appreciate the heritage and history of Old World Europe. "It was difficult to explain to some of my friends and family that there were Americans who were well educated," says Ulla. "They had this vision of Americans, that they're just go-getters, all they want to do is move fast and make money and drive fast cars. People had this idea that they knew nothing of our culture." One friend wrote to her: "You're marrying an American, just think of all the things he will be missing, and you will be losing." In fact, Joe had graduated from Harvard, spoke several languages, and loved classical music. But he had trouble with his own family as well: "Joe had to explain that he was getting married to a German and a Catholic. Everything was wrong. There was still this sentiment against Germans and on top of that, his family was not religious."

Ulla eventually grew close to Joe's father, a noted journalist and author, but she had a harder time feeling affection for his homeland. In August 1959 the newlyweds came for a visit and she saw America for the first time. One day, as her husband was visiting the *Tribune*'s Washington bureau, she ventured out to see the capital on her own: "Bus number thirty-nine was to take me back to the Shoreham Hotel where we stayed. I consulted a pleasant-looking African-American bus driver, who was sitting comfortably behind the wheel that reached right up to his rather ample girth. 'Can I come with you to the Shoreham Hotel?' I asked in my best English. He smiled broadly and without hesitation, his deep baritone voice audible to every passenger on the bus, boomed: 'Anytime, baby.' I blushed, feeling my face turning a dark red while all the passengers roared with laughter. I knew then and there that I had a long way to go before I would feel comfortable with the language and the way of life of my husband's country." Two years later the *Tribune* summoned Joe back to New York and that move launched "a terrible year for me," Ulla recalls: "This is after Cairo, where I had a wonderful life. People pay you compliments and I was used to all this nice treatment. I come to New York where everything is rough and different and nobody cares whether I'm there or not."

She arrived with an eight-month-old baby, and Joe had to leave immediately to cover the Bay of Pigs debacle: "Here I am in New York, I don't know east from west or one road from another, and I'm supposed to find an apartment and I don't know where to begin." They were staying in Greenwich Village, with Joe's cousin, and given the soot that blanketed the city in those days, Ulla was appalled to find her daughter Maria "covered in black" whenever she crawled on the floor. Eventually she found a place in the Village but New York prices badly stretched their budget: "Joe was making good money but it was never enough to live in New York; we could hardly afford to go to the theater and have a babysitter, so we couldn't enjoy what New York had to offer. I felt terrible, I was a mother with a child, I wasn't working, I didn't know a soul, and I didn't know what to do with myself, other than clean house and watch the baby. It was a dreary time." She always felt like she was doing or saying the wrong thing. In one particularly painful incident, a drugstore clerk asked if she could help her. "No, thank you, I have already been served," Ulla replied. At that point the clerk blew up at her for using the word *serve* instead of *help*: "These kinds of cultural differences shocked me. I thought I had said the right thing but she said it was an insult." Joe's career situation made life even drearier. Afraid the *Tribune* would fold (which it did two years later), he jumped to *Newsweek*, where he helped put out the foreign section. But he hated the work: harsh deadline pressures every week, while editing stories instead of writing them. And everybody got sick. Maria, the baby, was hospitalized twice before doctors figured out she could not tolerate wheat products. Joe came down with mononucleosis, his temperature shot up to 104, and Ulla had to sit by his bedside with a bucket of water, bathing him constantly to bring down his fever. Then he collapsed over the steering wheel of his car, a victim of "complete exhaustion." When *Newsweek* offered to make Joe their Middle East correspondent, based in Beirut, the family grabbed the chance to escape: "Coming back to the Middle East was a wonderful thing for me; it was a relief to get out of that terrible city."

If the Morrises had a spiritual home, it was Beirut. It was dazzling, and a bit decadent, and it didn't belong to either one of them. There was no family nearby, but no expectations, either. They were on their own; they could be themselves, a German-American couple that did not have to choose between those two identities. Eventually Joe left *Newsweek*, joining the *Los Angeles Times* and returning to his real love, daily reporting. Two more daughters, Karin and Julia, were born in Beirut, but foreign correspondents cannot stay in one place forever. In the early 1970s the Morrises moved to Germany, a very different and more livable country than the one Ulla had fled in 1955. Joe was so fluent in the language he appeared regularly on German television. However, they were headed for a new assignment in Moscow when Joe was diagnosed with lymphatic cancer. German doctors "operated on him without telling me," says Ulla. "I couldn't find him. I had no idea what had happened to him." When she finally tracked him down, "he looked like death" and his editors decided to fly him back to Los Angeles for further treatment. He was given a fifty-fifty chance of survival and spent four months in California recovering. Meanwhile, Ulla and Joe had decided they could not just float forever from house to house and country to country. They needed a base, an anchor. They bought a ruined farmhouse in northern Italy and started to fix it up. "Italy took on more urgency when Joe was diagnosed with cancer," recalls Ulla, "because he said, 'If I can't travel anymore, maybe I can sit in Italy, on the hill, and write.'"

When Joe returned to duty the *Times* canceled his Moscow assignment; the health care there was too precarious. Instead they sent him back to Beirut. But it was 1975, and Lebanon soon erupted in civil war. When the local schools closed down, Maria was packed off to Switzerland and the two younger girls were sent to a British boarding school in the mountains—an eerie echo of Ulla's search for sanctuary in Germany more than twenty years before. But just as war had found their mother, wherever she fled, war found Karin and Julia as well. Roads started closing, their school started emptying, and long after most other foreigners had left the country, the Morrises realized they could not stay. Their first goal was the island of Cyprus, just off the Lebanese coast, but planes had stopped flying there. Planes were still going to Greece, however, and the family caught the last flight to Athens before the Beirut airport was engulfed in fighting. They landed with almost nothing and moved into "a miserable apartment that was much too small for us," Ulla recalls. I was the *New York Times* correspondent based in Athens at the time, and my wife and I had met Joe at various gatherings of foreign journalists. Not long after the Morrises arrived, they came over for dinner and I met Ulla for the first time. They were so destitute that as they left that night, we handed them a stack of towels to help furnish their new place. A friendship flourished between the two couples, and when we had our next Passover seder, in the spring of 1977, Ulla asked to be invited. This daughter of a Nazi soldier, who had spent most of her adult life in the Arab world, wanted to know more about our Jewish ritual.

A few months later we moved back to America, and the Morrises rented a large, comfortable house in Athens, but Joe was hardly ever there. An absent husband facing constant risks had started to wear on Ulla and she remembers the day that "a strange feeling of foreboding, totally incomprehensible and difficult to understand," had taken hold of her. That night she managed to speak to Joe by telephone from Tehran, and when she voiced her anxiety, he urged her to take a break, go skiing. So the next morning she left the house early and drove to Delphi, the ancient site of a Greek oracle, now a popular winter resort. Ulla occasionally saw a ski patrolman cruising the slopes and saying he had a message for a "Mr. Morris from the American embassy." But since she was not a mister, and had no connection to the embassy, she ignored the messenger. Late in the afternoon, as she was preparing to leave, something nagged at her brain and she asked about the message at the ski office. A woman produced a pink slip containing two phone numbers: her home and Joe's office. It took her half an hour to get through. The call was answered by Clair George, an intelligence officer in the American embassy and a close friend from Beirut days. Twenty-five years before, her mother had told Ulla over a crackling telephone line that her father had died a violent death in France. Now George had to tell her that her husband had died a violent death in Iran. When she finally got back to Athens, the details overwhelmed her. Getting Joe's body out of Tehran, in the middle of a revolution, was an intimidating task. Hawthorne (Hawk) Mills, the deputy chief of the U.S. mission in Athens, asked gently where Joe would be buried. "Well," she replied, "Joe told me some time ago that he would want to be buried in Ameno—in the cemetery near our old farmhouse in Piemonte. It's a beautiful cemetery." Mills was incredulous: "Ameno? You mean in Italy?" Ulla: "Yes, Italy—why not?" Mills: "Joe was shot in Tehran. He is a U.S. citizen who worked for an American newspaper. You are German and you live in Greece. How can we possibly get Italy into this mix? Please, call Joe's father—he is waiting for your call." When she finally reached Joe Sr. he told her: "Bring Joe's body to Connecticut—we'll deal with the details later." That's what they did. Joe's funeral was held in Guilford, in a lovely old church bordering the town green on a brisk, brilliant winter day. Like dozens of other friends, my wife and I flew up from Washington for the service. There was Ulla, mourning her husband in a strange building in a strange country. "I felt completely detached," she recalls.

"I had never been in this church before. There was nothing comforting or familiar." A few days later she went to the funeral home to pick up Joe's ashes. Along with an urn, the director handed her a small envelope. Like her mother before her, she found herself holding her dead husband's wedding ring.

Now Ulla had to answer her own question: Where was home? Friends in the German foreign ministry offered her a job. Others suggested moving to Washington and working for the World Bank. But while she had strong language skills and vast practical experience she had never been to college and her "qualifications were not very clear." The *Los Angeles Times* was willing to put a "protective umbrella" over the family, hiring Ulla in their public relations department and providing health insurance for her children. So while Los Angeles "was like a foreign country to me," she says, "I felt my hands were tied. This was the only place I could go." But everything went wrong. Ulla's boss felt she had been "shoved down his throat" and didn't speak to her for three months: "I used to go out to lunch and walk around the block and take deep breaths and think, I'm just going to die here because of him. This is what the children experienced—a mother who came home and was really down." At a friend's suggestion Ulla moved to San Marino, an upscale, conservative suburb east of Los Angeles that only aggravated the family's alienation: "The children felt like fish out of water. I brought them to the wrong place. San Marino was this nicey-nice Republican place, where all the girls wore little pink shirts with puffed sleeves. This was an extremely painful time for all of us." Ulla came home one day and found a letter Karin had written to a friend and left on the kitchen table: "The worst part is my mother, she is so gloomy." This stoic German woman who had survived three bombings as a child could cope with the practical problems of life in a "foreign country," but not the emotional problems. "Joe had a great sense of humor, he was funny, he could play with the children," Ulla recalls. "I wasn't any of this. I tried to be a good mother but you can't replace this person. At one point Karin said to me, 'Well, if Daddy were alive we wouldn't be living here, right?' And I said, 'You're probably right; this would not be our place.'" Karin shares that memory of misery: "I hated it here, I couldn't stand it. It just seemed like life as we knew it had been ruined. From the moment my father was killed, there was a complete sense of helplessness."

All Karin knew of America were brief summer holidays with grandparents in Connecticut "watching a lot of TV and eating Lucky Charms." As a teenager in Greece she had developed "a lot of distaste" for the Americans she met there: "I thought they were sort of stupid; they were really partiers; I had some really bad sexual experiences with some of the guys." And she had absorbed the strong anti-American feelings that were rippling through the Middle East in those years. Arabs hated Americans for favoring Israel, Greeks hated them for siding with Turkey, and twice during her stay in Athens Karin was "kicked out of taxicabs when the drivers found out I was American. I came to identify being American with something that was not desirable in a lot of ways. From then on I would tell someone I was Australian or British, but I would never say American." San Marino High did nothing to improve her view: "The schools here were so academically inferior to what I was used to, students at my age level were far behind me." They also asked a lot of dumb questions: "People didn't even know where I'd lived most of my life. People didn't know what languages were spoken there. I had kids saying things like, 'Do they drive cars in Greece? Do you have electricity? Do you live in a hut?' I was really shocked at the ignorance." Those experiences hardened her hostility and made her feel, "That's *not* my culture, I'm *not* part of that. So my identity for a long time was international. I didn't identify with any one country. I just knew that I didn't identify with being an American."

Karin's reaction to California was "complete defiance." She felt she had to choose between two dominant cultures at San Marino

High, the "preppy cheerleaders" or the "east-enders, the kids who were anti-mainstream, the drug users and the smokers and the motorcycle riders." She "really quickly" joined the second group and started "doing a lot of things my mom never even knew about, a lot of dangerous things." She dated a drug dealer, smoked and sniffed what damaging substances she could get her hands on, drove cars when she was high: "I'm kind of amazed Mom didn't take me to a hospital. It was a time of darkness for me." The worst moment came at graduation: "I was totally drunk, and I had to pee." So Karin and a friend, who was equally smashed, "ran down behind the bleachers" and squatted there to relieve themselves: "A lot of people saw that; my mom was mortified." The principal upbraided Ulla after the ceremony: "What kind of mother was I? Did I have no education? How did I bring up my children? I was really in tears; he was awful." Karin went off to the University of California at San Diego and strongly identified with the left-wing, blame-Washington culture she found on campus. She read books like *Food First* by Frances Moore Lappé, a highly critical account of America's worldwide agricultural policy, and fell under the influence of a "solidly socialist" professor who urged her to drop marine biology and study "third-world" development: "I very quickly moved into this frame of mind that America is the evil empire." After her sophomore year she decided to study at the American University in Beirut: "I was pretty deeply unhappy with my life at that point. I wanted to get out, and it was almost like, I want to go home again, to go back to what was familiar for me." But once again, war intruded. It was the summer of 1982, Israeli troops were invading Lebanon, and Karin got only as far as Turkey. Clair George, the intelligence officer who had told Ulla about Joe's death three years before, urged her to summon Karin back to California: "If you let this kid go, you must have lost your mind. You've already lost a husband. Do you want to get your daughter killed?" Very reluctantly Karin turned around. Eventually she earned her degree from UC's Berkeley campus, and got a job helping poor immigrant women from Latin America. For fun she would hang out in a club called El Rio in the Mission district of San Francisco, a popular spot with young immigrants—legal and illegal—from all over the world. There she met Moshe Gavrieli, known to everyone as "Kushi." At first she didn't know he had been part of the Israeli army that had occupied Lebanon in 1982 and prevented her from going "home again." In fact Karin didn't know he was Israeli at all. "When she met me, she thought I was Persian," laughs Kushi. "If she knew I was Israeli she never would have started with me." Karin agrees: "I wouldn't have given him a second look." When did she find out? "After it was too late," says Kushi.

Kushi traces his origins to the Kurdish region of Iran. His parents were born in nearby villages but did not meet until after their families had immigrated to Israel in 1952. Virtually the entire Jewish population of the area moved at the same time and "just left everything," says Kushi. "My mom says they didn't even sell their house." The Kurdish settlers were "promised" places in Jerusalem, but instead were sent to a farming community in the Negev Desert. "They all know each other" and still speak Aramaic among themselves, a dying language that survives from biblical times. Kushi's parents had each been married before. They eventually produced a total of ten children with various partners, and as he recalls his childhood, "Growing up in a village, at the time I thought it was very boring. But I'm looking at it now and I think it was really wonderful." He often got up at 5 A.M. to help with farm chores—the area grew flowers for export to Europe—and played soccer with his pals until dark: "We had the ultimate freedom there." But even in the desert, Kushi could not escape the tendrils of war. During the 1967 conflict he recalls watching an Egyptian plane fall from the sky as his mother herded her kids into an air raid shelter. At eighteen, like most Israelis, he entered the military and spent several months manning an antimissile battery in Lebanon's Bekaa Valley, a few miles from the Syrian border. When he got out he wanted to travel, but his family was "pretty poor" so he found work as a security guard along the Egyptian border: "We were licensed to kill; we had permission, seriously." After he'd saved some money he headed for Europe with a friend, sleeping in cars, showering on beaches, cadging food where they could: "I never had a desire to come to America." But his wanderings took him to South America, and when some friends he made there moved on to California, he decided to pay them a visit: "I fell in love with San Francisco. I had such a great time; it was such an international city. Immediately we had lots of friends, all these Indians and Spaniards and French and Africans. We were all meeting in the same nightclub and dancing. I grew up in a village where there was not much going on, so for me it was like, wow, a big eye opening." His friends started a painting business and he just tagged along: "In Israel I never held a brush in my hand, but I worked with them a little bit and learned the trade." He overstayed his tourist visa, living in California illegally for a year, then returned to Israel, got a new passport, and headed back to San Francisco. It was then that he met Karin Morris: "I had seen her in the club a few times; I was actually dating a good friend of hers." They started a "very hot" relationship punctuated by "these enormous drawn-out arguments about politics," she recalls. After three or four months he was arrested and deported. He was probably a victim of mistaken identity; the immigration officials were looking for someone else with a similar name. But it didn't matter: "We were crazy about each other, so I feel like I'd been kicked out of here. It was not my choice. It was like, something was wrong about the picture." Over the next nine months Karin visited him twice in Israel, and this granddaughter of a Nazi soldier who had spent most of her childhood in the Middle East was deeply offended by her boyfriend's homeland: "I really couldn't stand how they thought about and talked about the Arabs."

But the heat in their relationship had not abated, and they hatched a scheme to get Kushi back to California: he would fly to Vancouver in western Canada, where Karin would meet him, and they would sneak across a remote section of the border on foot. But then they realized that there was "not a heck of a lot of enforcement at the border." Kushi had obtained yet another new passport and when he presented it at the crossing point, the guards lacked computers and did not know that he had previously been deported. So he slipped back into the country in a "half-legal" manner. Then the young couple proceeded to do "everything backwards." Karin got pregnant, creating a new urgency to legalize Kushi's status, but she considered marriage a "death trap" and even tried to bribe her younger sister, Julia, into marrying Kushi instead: "I think we even offered her like a trip to Israel so he could deal with his papers." When Julia backed out, Karin grudgingly agreed to a wedding six months after their son, Jobi, was born. "The main reason we got married was to fix my papers," says Kushi, but the wedding caused him considerable grief with his family back in Israel: "My dad gave me a really hard time. He kept telling me, 'How am I going to walk in the streets of the village when my son marries a non-Jewish person?'" So imagine how Kushi felt when he first saw the photo of Ulla's father in his German uniform: "I was taken aback. You know, it's a very sensitive issue to discuss." But that "very very odd" heritage gives Jobi a big advantage in a popular parlor game. Each contestant tells two lies and one truth, and the others have to guess which is which. No one ever guesses that Jobi is correct when he says, "My great-grandfather was a Nazi." Kushi has insisted that Jobi and his sister, Silan (her name means "wild rose" in Kurdish), be raised as Jews. When the boy turned thirteen in 2008 the family celebrated his bar mitzvah at an old Turkish fort near Kushi's home village, complete with "Kurdish musicians in full regalia," reports Ulla, "plus fireworks and enough food to feed an army."

While he now has a green card, entitling him to permanent resident status, Kushi has resisted becoming an American citizen: "It would be very weird for me to have an American passport. I'm an Israeli;

it doesn't matter how many years I'm going to be here. There's one home for me and that's Israel. I'm working here, I'm making a living, but where's my heart? It's there." But where this couple will live—or even if they will stay together—remains unsettled. As they talked about the future, it sounded like they were repeating lines they had recited many times before. Karin: "Living in your village would be like death for me; it's too far away, it's too isolated." Kushi: "It would be heaven for our kids." Karin: "I don't know, possibly, but I don't think I would be happy there." Kushi: "We are in a comfortable place of work, and economics, but I can easily move somewhere else and not feel that I'm missing this place." Karin: "Yeah, me too. There's really a part of me that wants to raise my kids in another place in the world."

In recent years Ulla Kirschbaum Morris Carter has achieved a measure of peace, marrying again, visiting her father's grave, planting flowers in her garden, becoming an American citizen, working for researchers at the Hoover Institute on a three-volume history of postwar Germany. But in a sense she's still living a "gypsy life," still looking for the home that was smashed by British planes in 1941. The police told her that night to "move on," to get away from an unexploded bomb. She's still moving.

13.

Haaroon, Malak, Khalida, Ameera, and Deeba Kemal

BURMA

My mother has this immigrant mentality—always be nice, don't say anything bad, because they can always send us back. And I always say, "You know, Mom, there's freedom of speech in America." But she would say, "No, no, we're immigrants."

From the day Haaroon Kemal and Malak Marwan got married in Burma in 1975, the young couple planned on moving to America. Malak's family had once been rich, owning land and buildings and car dealerships, but their fortune—and their future—had been confiscated by Burma's dictatorial rulers. At the time of the wedding, Malak's older brother had already settled in Southern California and was slowly sponsoring the migration of his nine siblings. Haaroon had grown up poor and was eager to join his wife's relatives in a new land. "One of the forces that united my mother and father was immigration," says the Kemals' oldest daughter, Khalida. "America was well known as the land of prosperity and opportunity. Who doesn't want to come here? That was the attitude."

But when they arrived in 1983, what Haaroon saw horrified him. The freedoms he sought in the New World threatened the values and traditions he carried from the Old World. In one incident now cemented in family lore, Haaroon visited an old friend shortly after arriving here. The friend was sitting on the floor when his son entered the room, plopped down on the couch, and put his feet on the coffee table, right near his father's face. In the Muslim culture showing someone the bottom of your shoes is an enormous insult. "My father saw that and said, 'This is what I see in America. This is what I'm not going to let happen to my children,'" says Khalida.

It didn't help that Haaroon was raising three daughters in Orange County, whose lithe and lubricious teenagers have been featured in the popular TV drama *The O.C.* As Khalida notes, "In our culture, girls represent [a father's] honor to some degree. We had to make sure we were very pure, so nobody could raise a finger to him." To protect that purity, Haaroon set down strict rules: no shorts, no skirts, no alcohol, no pork, no shopping malls, no English at home, no bawdy movies or TV sitcoms, and above all, no boys. "If we had even a group project with a guy no, no, no," says Ameera, the middle daughter. "That was really tough. Nothing. No communication. Anything that looked like a man, no communication. He protected us to the point where we were in this bubble wrap." When it was time for Khalida to enter college, she wanted to live in the dorms at the University of California at Irvine (UCI). Haaroon was "very apprehensive, very scared," says his daughter. "Of course anyone would be. You're going to leave your home, your life, anything could happen." But his wife pushed him to agree: "Let her have her wings, let her try that."

Haaroon was right. In college, his daughter did start asking questions and redefining her values: "When I went to UCI I started thinking a lot more. You're now away from your parents, you have your own identity, you no longer have a watching eagle above you, you're making your own decisions." But here's the surprise: she became more religious, not less, more Eastern, not Western. Instead of adopting the shorts and skirts that were banned at home, she put on the hijab, the headscarf that marks a devout Muslim woman, a garment her own mother seldom wore. And Haaroon, once again, was horrified. "When I put this on, my father was very upset," recalls Khalida, who now teaches at a Muslim school. "He was like, 'This is America, you can't do this here.' And my answer was, 'Precisely because this is America I *can* do this here.' The First Amendment gives me the right."

The Kemal family's story in America is marked by ambivalence and anxiety, by constant tension between enduring traditions and enticing opportunities. Like so many immigrants before them, the older Kemals never felt completely comfortable in their new country. Deeba, their youngest daughter, says: "My mother has this immigrant mentality—always be nice, don't say anything bad, because they can always send us back. And I always say, 'You know, Mom, there's freedom of speech in America.' But she would say, 'No, no, we're immigrants.'" Her mother, adds Deeba, feels "like she's still a guest in America." But the three sisters don't feel like guests: they're members of the club, and they have created their own identity, a very American identity, weaving threads from their past into the fabric of their future. When they were all still living at home and speaking among themselves they'd skip rapidly through five different languages: Urdu, Gujarati, Burmese, English, and Spanish. "We took the pieces that were necessary and that was our communication," says Khalida. "It was amazing."

The elder Kemals are both Surti, people from the Surat region of the Indian state of Gujarat. The Surti in Burma migrated there more than a hundred years ago but they've maintained a very cohesive community. They continue to speak Gujarati, even though most of them have never seen that ancestral homeland; they've maintained their Muslim faith in a largely Buddhist country; and they've often married each other. Haaroon's parents, for example, were distant relatives with the same last name. And the Surti take pride in their ethnic heritage. "We don't have that Asian look," says Khalida. "You look at us, we look Indian, our race is Indian, but nationally, for generations now we've been in Burma." In fact, if the Surti have absorbed any outside bloodlines they are probably Turkish, not Burmese. Ameera notes that two of her uncles are "ridiculously fair," with blue and green eyes: "There's some mix somewhere. You don't see Indian people with blue eyes!"

Many Surti families prospered in Burma, few more than Malak's people, the Marwans. "During the industrial revolution my grandfather built a great empire, a great amount of wealth," says Khalida. One of the largest buildings in Rangoon bore the family name and when motor cars became "the hip thing," the Marwans captured the market: "It was such a well-known, wealthy family that my mother and her siblings were transported in special cars with special drivers. The protection was provided so no one would kidnap them and blackmail the family to get money." Haaroon's family was just the opposite. Both his parents died young and his grandmother took in sewing to feed her grandchildren. He dropped out of school after the fourth grade, traveling at a young age to neighboring countries such as Bangladesh, looking for work. For a time, Haaroon and his brother ran a successful food store but their partnership "fell apart over family issues" and they lost the business. By the time his match with Malak Marwan was arranged he was running an eyeglass shop in a bazaar. He was not exactly a great catch but the Marwans had fallen on hard times themselves. "Their wealth had disappeared by that time; the government had taken everything," says Ameera, and inflation was devouring whatever was left. Malak's mother was in declining health, she wanted to see her children married before she died, and Haaroon met the three basic requirements: he was a man, he was a Surti, and he was willing to move to America. "Surti people tend to stick with Surti people," explains their daughter Khalida.

The young couple's finances continued to deteriorate. Haaroon lost his shop and moved his wife and young daughter "to this shack type of place" with a leaky roof. Her mother, says Khalida, "would put containers wherever she could and with that water she'd wash clothes and take showers." When Ameera, the second daughter, was born, Malak didn't know where to hide her baby from the constant leaks. To feed her children, she'd pilfer mangoes from a nearby tree and mix them with rice. Meanwhile, other members of the Marwan family were getting sponsored and moving to America and Haaroon's resentments multiplied. As his daughters tell the story, "Dad was always saying, 'When are we going to go? How come this family is going before us? Why can't we be first? Why isn't my support here?'" A third daughter, Deeba, came along, and she was less than a year old in late 1983 when the Kemals finally made it to America, eight years after their marriage.

From the beginning, Haaroon did not adjust well to his new homeland. He suffered from a "pavement-of-gold imagination," as his daughter Ameera puts it. "There was a gap between his expectations and what life became," adds Deeba. "He thought as soon as he arrived in America he would be offered a job. It would be easy." But it was never easy, starting with his first moments on American soil. The family members who were meeting the Kemals brought only one car to the airport and only Malak and the three girls could fit inside. Haaroon was put on a bus and told when to get off. "I wonder how this processed for him," muses Khalida. "He would have expected a car, not a limousine, but a car, and a good introduction to the city. And instead here he's on a bus and doesn't know where he's going." Then it got worse. At a family dinner a few nights later, Haaroon sat at the table expecting his plate to be cleared by someone else. As Khalida tells it, "One of my aunts said, 'In America you have to get up and put your plate in the sink and wash it yourself.' And that was an insult. I think he still feels that's an insult to this day."

With little education or English skills, Haaroon had trouble finding a job. "People kept asking, 'How many years of experience do you have?'" recalls Khalida. "And he'd say, 'I just came to America,' and they'd say, 'Well, we can't hire you.' He kept saying, 'How can I get any experience if no one will give me a chance?' It was tough on him. I can appreciate his struggle, I really can." Finally he found work, assembling television sets in a factory, and often he'd take a second job just to meet expenses. But there was little left over, and when he wasn't able to sponsor his relatives to join him in America, tensions flared. "There was this 'You must be rich, why aren't you helping us?' type of attitude," says Ameera. Khalida adds: "I think from the beginning this disappointment increased and increased. Suddenly you're doing two jobs and you don't have a car and you can't sponsor your own family, either. And it hits him that it takes so much energy, so much effort." The disappointment was aggravated by embarrassment. "He's trying to get this reputation in Burma, on the other side of the world, that 'I'm in America, I'm earning the honor of being here,'" says Khalida. But the failure to finance his family's migration stained his stature: "This disconnect between my father's impression of what is going to be, and what happened, caused him a lot of grief. He still holds on to a lot of feelings of anger." (While the entire Marwan clan, Malak's family, settled here, only one of Haaroon's relatives, a cousin, ever made it to America.)

Not only did Haaroon disappoint his own family, he battled with his wife's people. They helped out enormously—bringing groceries, guaranteeing his apartment lease, translating documents—but he still felt slighted. Your brothers, he told his wife bitterly, should have "put me back in school," to learn proper English and more marketable skills. Haaroon's daughter Khalida has little patience with her father's feelings: "It's not my uncles' job to make sure he gets his degrees, it's his job. They did their part by sponsoring him here." It was a complex relationship common to many immigrants: Haaroon needed assistance, but he hated asking for it, and whatever his relatives supplied was never enough. Khalida describes what he went through: "I think for my father there was this internal struggle, of independence and yet needing help. Who wants to have help? And yet you are put into a position of feeling the weight of people who are helping you, and sometimes you can't cope with that. Add to that the struggle of being an immigrant, the struggle of a new language, that separation from the umbilical cord of Burma. It's like being a plant, pulled out by your roots and put in a different soil and asked to grow."

Money was always tight. "We were lucky, we had everything we needed," says Khalida. "Sure, we couldn't get Nike shoes, but who cares for Nike shoes?" Her sisters were not quite so upbeat. Ameera remembers wanting a fancy JanSport backpack, but it cost twenty dollars, far too much for the family budget. The one she had, "everyone thought was very tomboyish," with an emblem resembling a military insignia. So she devised a way to carry the pack on one shoulder "and I would put my hand to hide the emblem. Things like that did happen." Deeba remembers: "We didn't grow up with a lot of money. Sometimes I wouldn't have the best clothes on and sometimes the boys in junior high would make fun of me." One day Haaroon was picking her up at the bus stop and saw the boys "pointing and laughing and he got so mad. He got out of the car and said 'Hey, you leave my girl alone,' and from that day on they didn't bother me."

Then Haaroon hurt his back carrying televisions and could no longer work. Malak tried to help out but the only job she could find was cleaning office buildings. Since she did not know how to drive, she often woke up at 2 A.M. to take three buses to work. Deeba recalls: "She made sure that at least breakfast was made for everybody, then she'd catch the bus and walk and walk and walk in the cold. She didn't want to be a bother to anyone. I remember sometimes she would come home saying, well, she had her food, but she would share it with some of the other people because they didn't bring their food. My mother was a very sacrificing person. After long days at work she'd have to catch two or three buses back. It's just very heartbreaking. I don't ever recall my mother getting a good night's sleep." During the hardest times the family relied on public assistance, and using food stamps crushed Haaroon's pride. One day he went to buy cooking oil, but he knew somebody at the store that offered the best price, so he faced a choice, says Khalida: "Either pay more, or go to the cheaper store and have your honor and respect at stake. I'm not sure the decision he made but it was a struggle for him. There were some very, very tough moments."

For the Kemals, the cultural struggle was, in some ways, even harder than the economic struggle. And one symbol of that struggle was Malak's failure to learn how to drive. Back in Burma, she had even mastered a stick shift, and driven in Rangoon's dreadful traffic, but somehow, in America, she never qualified for her license. When I asked her daughters why, they offered a variety of reasons. Khalida: "It was a new land, a new place, homesickness, everything put together. She never took that step. There were so many factors I can't isolate one. Suddenly she comes to America, she has three kids, she has all these hurdles to overcome; this was one that fell through the cracks." Ameera says her father was a "very authoritarian figure" who forced her mother into a life defined by her children, her home, and her husband: "It was very difficult for her to break out of the mold that she was in. Independence kind of never existed for her." Deeba says that "coming to America almost took away the confidence" that her mother had displayed back in Burma. For a woman who always felt like a "guest" in her new land, perhaps a driver's license was a sign of belonging she could never imagine, or accept: "Maybe it's because of a sense of humility. That's how my mother felt about America."

If Malak felt a sense of humility about America, Haaroon felt a sense of fear—that his culture would be lost, his authority questioned, his honor blemished, his daughters violated. One sign of that fear: he banned English from the household, demanding that the girls speak only Gujarati in front of him. "He wanted to make sure we learned the language, so we didn't lose it," says Khalida. "At times, if we spoke English in front of our father, he would get upset, so we had to consciously remember." In fact the girls spoke different languages to different parents: Gujarati to their father and Urdu, a form of Hindi, to their mother. "It's so weird," mutters Ameera. "It's so weird." But Haaroon had more in mind than preserving the Gujarati language. English symbolized what he detested in America—lax rules, rebellious children, immoral attitudes—and he was determined to bar the door against those influences. Deeba puts it this way: "He would visit the houses of other immigrants and their sons and daughters would say, 'Hey, Dad, what's going on?' He didn't like that at all. He thought it was so disrespectful. So he would come home and say, 'You guys are not speaking in English.' Just the concept of 'hey,' that word is so informal in American culture. In Burma, or in our culture, 'hey' is like you're being disrespectful."

Today the Kemal girls are grateful they were forced to learn Gujarati, but the absence of English at home came with a heavy price. Haaroon is still uncomfortable with the language. He still can't grasp the idioms and sayings he would have easily picked up from his daughters, and this deficiency has always deterred his integration into American life. "He would always say he sacrificed learning English for us," says Deeba. In many ways, banning English was a decision that Haaroon now regrets. As Deeba puts it: "He really questions whether he should have done that. He saw people around him who were going ahead of him because he had language problems. He had to make a hard decision in his eyes, whether to allow his children to become Americanized. But he says today, maybe he should have allowed English."

This lack of English meant the Kemals depended on their children to connect the family to the larger world, even when they were very young. And that did not always work out well. During their first year in America, one of her uncles told Khalida to give her father a message: daylight saving time was ending, the clocks had to be turned back an hour. But she went to sleep before her father returned home, and as she tells the story, "My father is extremely punctual about getting to work on time, because he wants to keep his job and keep his reputation strong. But because I failed to pass the message on, the next day, when he went to work, everybody was there, when he was used to being the first person. He was shocked that he was late. He was so upset, he was so angry, the change of time caused so much tension in our family, in our parents' relationship. I was known to be extremely responsible—that's why they gave me the information—but I had no idea what was going on. Even today, I feel the pain in my heart when I think about it. Because of me my father was late. But what does a six- or seven-year-old know about daylight savings time?" A few years later, the Los Angeles Angels baseball team—which played in Anaheim, just a few miles from the Kemals' apartment—was handing out free tickets to good students in the local schools. Khalida received two, but knew nothing about baseball and gave hers away to a classmate. "When I came home and mentioned it to my father he was so upset," she recalls. "He said, 'I'm in America, I want to go to a baseball game. I had that opportunity and you lost it for me.' I was devastated, and every time I go past Angels Stadium you can imagine how I feel. Oh, if I had only saved those tickets!"

"We became his crutches, and that was very hard for us," says Ameera, "because we were still so young ourselves." One good example was the mail, adds Khalida: "Mail came in the door and he didn't understand it and wanted us to translate it. But just because we go to school doesn't mean we understand an insurance policy. Even junk mail was so important to him. 'Why is this mail coming?

What is the point of this mail?' We knew junk mail was just junk mail, we threw it away, but my father took it so seriously. 'What is 1.9 percent APR? What is all this? Turn the back side and read every single word to me!'" Then there was the address book. Haaroon bought a new one, with a baby blue cover, and assigned Ameera to transfer all the names and phone numbers from his old book. When she put them in, last name first, her father was furious: "That did not work for my father, he was not happy. At all, at all. Every time he would go through that phone book he would need to say something. 'I'm going through this phone book and I don't know what the names are. I don't go by last names.' I was a child, I was trying to do the best I could, but I didn't know that he didn't know the last names of everybody." As she told the story, Ameera's anger stirred: "That stupid blue phone book! Oh my God! I'm never, ever going to buy a blue phone book!"

While their father's depressions and demands clouded their childhood, the Kemal sisters also sympathized with his position. "He was under so much stress," says Khalida. "He felt isolated; he felt compelled to find help but he didn't know where to go. So a lot of times he would say to us, 'You're going to school here, you know what's going on, I need your time so I can understand what I'm doing in this country.'" And that led to contradictory messages. At times he would tell his girls: "I made a mistake by dropping out of school; you have to work hard and get an education so you can 'sit behind a desk,' and not do 'a laborer's job' like me." At other times he seemed to resent their devotion to academics. "Pay attention to my needs," he would say. "You're going to go crazy" if you read all the time. "It was very hard to balance what we were hearing from my father," says Khalida. "He had this ideal way he wanted us to be, and what he wanted us to become, but for him, watching the steps it took for us to get there was too painful, or something. He couldn't tolerate it sometimes. Studying all the time was not okay. He didn't understand what it meant to get an education; he didn't understand how much energy and hard work it took." But their father was saying something else as well: "You are succeeding in ways that I am not." And while he took great pride in their achievements, there was a part of him that felt left behind, overshadowed. His daughters were becoming Americans while he was still an immigrant. "He had this feeling that we were detaching ourselves from him," recalls Khalida. "We had to be the birds that fly away. It was always 'Why aren't you asking me?' He had that feeling that 'my children don't need me.'"

The Kemals' integration into America was impeded by another factor: the brutal dictatorship that ruled their homeland had left a deep imprint. "That dictatorship mentality translated here," says Khalida. "They were always very suspicious of the government." That's partly why Haaroon was so fixated on the mail. He grew up believing that any official communication was to be feared, not welcomed. And like his wife he lived with the dread that "they could always send us back." Deeba puts it this way: "I don't think my family has anything to hide. We came as legal immigrants. But my parents' mentality—back there the government was corrupt—kind of shaded and colored their views coming here. They didn't know if they could trust people." That mistrust didn't just focus on the government, but on neighbors and co-workers as well. Deeba describes herself as a "pretty talkative person" who enjoys the fact that "American culture is pretty inquisitive." But to her father, anyone could be a spy, an informant, a threat: "I think the culture just didn't jibe with him. Everyone is always talking and communicating here, but my dad, if people asked him a lot of questions, I don't think he liked that. He didn't really like people asking him where he worked. I'm sure, in Burma, they had experiences where people who asked a lot of questions would go and backstab them. So they had problems and issues because of the politics back there." Those "problems and issues" came to a head when Haaroon got hurt and had to deal with California's complex workmen's compensation program. "It was terrible. He was accused of lying; he didn't know how to fight the system," recalls Khalida. That system, she insists, always tries "to avoid paying," and it's hard enough for a native-born worker to win a claim: "But for an immigrant it's just mind-boggling. You're lost in a jungle and you don't know how to navigate through it. You don't have a machete to cut through the growth."

There was a profound paradox at the core of Haaroon's attitude toward America. Since he felt "lost in a jungle," he needed his daughters to guide him through that wilderness. But if they became too independent, too immersed in American culture, they could lose their virtue and their dependence, and he could lose his reputation and his authority. "There are so many levels to this," says Khalida. "He wanted to come here because his reputation back home skyrocketed. 'Oh, our brother in America, we have someone in America.' But being here his goal was to make sure his three kids didn't diverge into a path he didn't approve of, like marrying an Anglo, a non-Muslim." Ameera jumps in: "It wasn't just the marriage part. 'I don't want my children to end up pregnant,' that was a very valid fear of his. 'I don't want my children to take any steps that would tarnish us as a family.' Fear of us being girls in America was really very powerful for him."

Today, all three daughters are married to Muslim men. (Only Deeba married a Surti; the other two married Pakistanis.) And as Ameera notes, all of them can now see the value of their strict up-bringing: "When I was younger, it was very hard for me to accept how they kept us so sheltered. But now that I've grown up, I can't say I would have wanted it any other way. If they let the reins loose on me, I don't know if I'd be where I am today." But at the time, living in a "bubble wrap" was a source of endless tension and embarrass-ment. As children, their mother walked them to and from elementary school. When they got home, they were required to change into tra-ditional outfits and were not allowed to go out and play. Most of their after-school time was spent inside, studying. If they left the house, they had to stay within sight of the apartment. TV watching was carefully controlled: *I Love Lucy* was okay, but not *The Simpsons*. American movies were out but occasionally the family would watch Bollywood features together, partly to improve the girls' grasp of Urdu. Dress was a particularly thorny issue. Once the girls reached puberty, shorts and sleeveless blouses were banned. Khalida recalls that in the fourth or fifth grade she wore a yellow skirt to school, and when her father picked her up, he decided the garment was too transparent. "He was so angry," she recalls. "And from that day on, there were no more skirts in the house." Pants became their uniform, but never tight ones, and they were always worn with a long shirt or sweater that came to the knee and covered the derriere.

Once they got to junior high, the girls were allowed to walk by themselves, but they were constantly lectured about the dangers lurking along the way. Khalida: "Every day I was told, if you see a nook or cranny, and you think someone's hiding there, don't pass there. We weren't supposed to walk too close to any cars, because the cars could pull us in and take us away. We weren't supposed to be against a wall because a door could open and pull us in." As for boys, they could talk to them in school, when it was absolutely necessary, but once they left school, all contact was prohibited. No phone calls, not even about schoolwork. "My father didn't really allow us to speak to boys," recalls Deeba. "There was always that fear, well, if he calls for her algebra homework, maybe they'll sit together and study, and maybe he likes her, and maybe he says it's okay to kiss her. You know what I'm saying? That fear played into our lives." During the period when he was hurt and out of work, Haaroon would sometimes pick up the girls at school, and they lived in terror that he would see them talking to a male classmate. Ameera: "Walking home from high school and knowing my dad might pick us up, it was so important that there weren't guys around us. Oh God, I remember that. That would be a very stressful moment for us if there were guys around." One time it happened: "This guy that I kind of knew made a comment, it could have been something as harmless as 'I'll see you tomorrow,' and my dad was pulling up." Haaroon got out of the car and started yelling at the boy: "What did you say to my daughter?" It was not a high point of her high school career. Neither was the senior prom. She didn't go: "It didn't matter to me. I didn't feel like I was missing something." Ameera did attend a weeklong camp for student leaders during her senior year. There was a dance at the end of the session and she went for a few minutes, but soon returned to her bunk: "I showed my face a little bit, but I realized, this isn't my scene, I don't like it, it goes against what I live."

As the youngest, Deeba chafed a bit more under her parents' regimen: "Sometimes in high school I was like, 'Oh, man, can't we just go to a movie after school like all the other kids?'" And, she adds, "it turns out there were some boys who did like me at the time." One of them, who lived in the same apartment complex, started to walk her home one day: "It was very flattering, of course. It would be flattering to any young girl." Her parents' warnings sounded in her head but she tried to resist them: "I remember thinking, What's the big deal? He'll think I'm a dork. How can I tell him you can't walk with me?" But her determination crumbled, and she told the boy to keep his distance: "It was just so embarrassing." Five minutes later, her father pulled up to drive her home: "I was so happy, because I know he would have made a scene." But if the Kemal sisters had no social life in high school, they found a different identity: the smart girls. "Being the best in the class was our way out," observes Deeba. "It's almost like we became popular because of how much we tried to do really well in class. That shifted away the tension of having to be social." The honors poured in: Most Likely to Succeed, delegate to a statewide political convention, student government offices. Most important of all, college scholarships. As the oldest, Khalida was the first to go. She was still very close to her parents and was required to call home every afternoon exactly at five: "At 5:05 they started getting a little bit antsy and nervous." But by living in the dorms, she found some measure of independence, and like all freshmen, she looked for a place, a group, that could provide a sense of connection and community. She found it in the Muslim Student Union.

The Kemals were always religious people. The girls followed the basic rituals: praying five times a day, avoiding alcohol and pork, fasting during Ramadan. They even learned to recite the Koran in Arabic. But Haaroon only visited the mosque, or *muzjid*, occasionally, "and would pray when he felt like it." Malak seldom wore a hijab or headscarf, and in high school her girls generally left their heads uncovered. But once she got to UCI, Khalida changed: "When you're in a university you're exploring everything, your mind is open, you want to learn as much as you can. And when I saw people wearing the hijab I started asking why." The answer surprised her. These young women didn't feel like "people were oppressing them," they felt that headscarves were "part of the religion," a central part, not a fashion accessory. Khalida started experimenting. She'd wear a scarf to the cafeteria, or to prayers, then would leave it off at other times. "Gradually, I said something is inherently wrong here," she recalls. "If this is part of my religion, why would I pick and choose? That does not make me an authentic person, just picking and choosing things because I want people to like me. Who do I want to like me? God or people? God, of course."

It wasn't that simple, of course. "It was a huge decision for me when I put it on; it was a struggle inside," admits Khalida. "I want to have a great job, and if I put on the scarf, maybe I won't get a job. How am I going to handle myself in interviews? How's it going to be when I run into people? Immediately it sends a message; one piece of cloth can send such a message. People make a decision, 'Oh, you're oppressed.'" She wrestled with her decision for a full year: "Then one day I just put it on and said, 'Today I'm going to go through the entire day with this.' Next day I did the same thing. Eventually it's just like wearing anything else; it's part of me now." Her father was upset for many reasons: he wanted his daughters to succeed in America, he feared they would face discrimination, and he worried that the government could somehow crack down on devout Muslims, especially immigrants who still felt like "guests" in the country. "I tried to explain it to him," says Khalida: "no matter what part of the world you're in, you do what you need to do. Who cares about anybody else? Just being in America doesn't make this something I shouldn't do. Because I'm afraid of what the American government is going to think? Or what the American people are going to think? Or how I'm going to be treated in the supermarket?"

Deeba believes that Khalida's personality reflects her place in the family: "Being the first child, she takes things more seriously." The other two are "more chill" in their attitude, and that's certainly true when it comes to dress. Khalida follows the religious rules closely, making sure her head covering is tight around her face with no hair, ears, or neck showing; her sisters drape their scarves more casually. Khalida's life is defined by her religion: she teaches in a Muslim school, gives lectures around Orange County on how to treat Muslim students, says Arabic prayers under her breath while she drives. Her sisters both work in secular jobs: Ameera is a project manager for a company that tests pharmaceuticals and is studying for a master's in business; Deeba counsels troubled teenagers and is earning her master's in social work. But Khalida's influence weighs heavily on both of them.

Ameera admits she's a "social butterfly" compared to her older sister and says, "My closest friends growing up have always been guys. I feel like guys you can be more chill with." And when she got to college she enjoyed her new freedom: "I strayed away from my education. My first-quarter grades were B, D, and F. I didn't have a boyfriend or go to parties, it was just hanging out. It was really just wasting my time, that's what I got caught up in. But I graduated summa cum laude, so

I turned it around really well." Khalida was her roommate, and her conscience: "I wasn't being her boss, but my goal was to remind her, 'The reason you're here is to get an education; there should be nothing at all distracting you from that goal.' It's very easy to get distracted at a university, very easy, extremely easy." Ameera admits to resenting her sister's attitude: "That was kind of a rough spot for us." And when Khalida started wearing the hijab, Ameera recalls, "I was not very supportive. I said, 'I don't understand, what this is?'" Khalida: "I felt a distance; you were very angry in some way." True, says Ameera: "I was very social." And her sister's censorious attitude, fueled by her growing religiosity, "was a weight on my shoulders. All these friends of ours would ask me, 'How come your sister's not joining us?' I felt very pressured. It was very hard for me to adjust to her personality."

Eventually Ameera, too, was drawn to Islam, and to the hijab, but it was a slow process. One day she was manning a booth on campus for the Muslim Student Union and decided to wear a headscarf: "I felt like people were treating me differently. I felt people who saw me wouldn't approach me. I even made eye contact and several Muslim people were not approaching me. And these were guys. Once you put on the hijab, guys respect that, and say, maybe she doesn't want us to associate with her in that way anymore. But I was like, 'Wait! I don't want my whole life to change!'" So she loosened the pin holding her scarf in place and let it fall to her shoulders: "I was like, I can't do this, and I let it go. Because for me, the social aspect was so large."

Still, she was moving toward Khalida's view that the hijab was an essential expression of her religion. She remembers sitting in a large lecture hall one day and thinking: "I'm trying to be as good a Muslim as possible. I'm not drinking alcohol, I don't have a boyfriend, I'm not eating pork, yet just by sitting here, I'm sinning, because I don't have my hijab on. I was struggling, struggling."

By this time the sisters had a roommate who also wore the hijab, and one day they were all going to a mosque for a religious program.

The roommate offered Ameera a scarf to wear: "I didn't own one at the time so I said, 'No, I'm just going for the program.' But she said, 'You're going to the *muzjid,* you should wear one.' And I'm like, 'Okay, fine, just give me one.' So then we went in a big van with a bunch of people, guys and girls, and I received a pretty warm reception: 'It's good you're doing this.'" Wearing the hijab on campus had brought her cold stares and a sense of exclusion; but here, in this van, with a smaller group of more devout students, the scarf earned her warm praise and a sense of acceptance. After the religious program the van dropped her off at the science library: "At that moment, that is when I made the decision. I said, you know what, now that I'm going into a public forum, outside of the Muslim community, I'm just going to keep this on. I told myself, I'm not going to take it off. And I never took it off after that." Still, the doubts lingered. She came back to the apartment and complained to her roommate, "I don't know why I'm doing this. I wasn't ready. It's so hard." And her roommate responded: "'The fact that this is hard means your intention is really true. You're not doing this to please people, you're doing this to please Allah. Nobody said it would be easy. It's not about the people here, it's between you and your god.' And I said, 'Okay. I'm just going to keep doing this. I'm going to keep doing this.'" Deeba's decision was easier because her sisters were already covering their heads when she got to college: "My sisters have always been a tremendous role model for me." But she worried about another stigma: if she wore the hijab, fellow Muslims might shun her as marriage material. "I know girls who want to get married," she says, "and if they wear the hijab, they wonder if proposals will be coming their way. Sometimes the guy's family wants the girl to take off the hijab because they think she's super-religious and this doesn't fit with the marriage thing. There are all these different stigmas."

Haaroon worried that when his daughters put on the hijab, his fellow Surti would be critical. "He was very upset," recalls Khalida.

"He was like, 'What are the Surti going to think? What's the community going to think?'" But the reverse happened, says Ameera: "The reception he got from the community was like, 'Wow, you did a really good job with your kids.' It increased his honor." Then 9/11 happened, sharply altering the image of Muslims in America. Khalida had graduated, and was working at a large insurance company, and on the morning the twin towers fell, she neglected to turn on her car radio. So when she got to her office, dressed in her hijab, she didn't know what had happened. "People were passing by my cube and looking at me really strange, and I'm smiling as I do normally," she recalls. Then she was summoned by her boss: "One of my coworkers had complained on me about something. I had said something that had made her antennas go up. She went to the manager and the manager pulled me in. I was in shock." Remembering that day, she says: "They were just ignorant, honestly. I don't blame them, because I could see how they would feel I was a threat. My goal was not to add to that threat. My goal was to make a case that I have nothing to do with this. Just because I'm the same religion, I have nothing to do with this. Not everybody will like you, but I felt a little bit like I had been hit under the belt."

The elder Kemals were deeply alarmed at the anti-Muslim sentiment spawned by 9/11. "Our parents said, 'Take off the hijab,'" recalls Ameera. "They really wanted us to." Adds Khalida: "They said, 'Even in Islam you can do things to protect yourself. You don't have to do this. Allah knows this is a tough time.'" The sisters resisted that advice but finally reached a compromise with their parents. They went to Target and bought long-sleeved sweaters with hoods, which could hide their scarves when they went out in public. Ameera was still in college, so she had less of a problem, but she does remember a moment not long after 9/11 when a bunch of Muslim students wearing hijabs were gathered at a campus hangout. A man and a woman passed by and yelled, "Go back to your country!" And one of the women, who had been born in America, shouted back: "I *am* in my country!" In recent years, all three have had similar experiences. Khalida: "Before 9/11 I was ignored a lot, in the grocery, running errands. Now it's not like that. Now you see their glances stay on you longer. And in the background it's the eagle and the flag. What they're expressing is, we will never forget, that kind of thing."

The two older sisters still live near their parents in Orange County, where a woman in a headscarf is a familiar sight. But Deeba moved to Minneapolis, where there are fewer Muslim immigrants, and she encounters more frequent comments. One day she went to a "high-class grocery store" to buy saffron for a popular South Asian dish called *biryani*: "I wanted to see how strong the aroma was. I didn't open the bottle, but I put it up to my nose, and this guy came from out of nowhere and he said, 'Don't do that!' really loud. 'We don't do that in this country! Why are you doing that? You have to buy that! That's not how we do things in this country!' He said it in such a vindictive manner. People started to crowd around and actually, my heartbeat started to race. He said it so loud, and he said it to attract attention, and I felt like I was in the spotlight, and I wasn't doing anything. I'm just trying to smell the aroma of the saffron to make *biryani*. Of course, I went to the manager and said this person is harassing me, but he said he couldn't do anything about it."

These are three intelligent, articulate young women, and it bothers them that so many Americans are still so ignorant of the Muslim culture. Some people see their headscarves and assume they can't speak English. Khalida was in a store, talking on her cell phone in one of her many languages, probably Urdu. Four "big guys" approached her and started saying "blah, blah, blah," in loud voices, "making fun" of her conversation. "When I turned to the cashier and spoke in clear English, they didn't have a word to say," she recalls. "As soon as English came out of my mouth they shut up." Ameera laughs at the story: "You should have said, 'You really ought to try and learn English!'" Khalida: "They anticipated that I couldn't speak. Poor little me. They were just pretty surprised." Ameera had a similar experience in a previous job: "Some people would look at me and wonder, does she speak English or not? Then I would speak English and Spanish and they would think, 'What kind of freak of nature are you?'" In fact, adds Ameera, some people think that a woman wearing a headscarf can't speak at all, let alone in English, that a man "has to speak on her behalf." In this view, adds Khalida, no woman would choose to wear a hijab, so people think, "this man is forcing this woman" to cover her head and be submissive. Ameera: "Cashiers will talk to my husband but not me. They think we're the subdued types of wives and we're not. One of my husband's biggest complaints is that I'm way too independent!" Since Deeba lives in Minnesota, she flies regularly to California and resents the treatment she gets in airports from security personnel: "In all the trips I've made over the last four years, only once have I not been pulled aside." And that treatment reinforces the stereotype that all Muslims are potential threats: "What really bothers me is that all these observers see this woman of color, wearing a hijab, and she's being pulled aside. There goes that stigma, you know."

In some ways, the struggles of the Kemal family have led them to a steadier, more secure place in American life. Haaroon has found an administrative job at an export-import company, run by a fellow immigrant, and they can converse in Urdu, a language he speaks well. Malak still works part-time cleaning buildings and her health is poor, but during the summer months, when Khalida doesn't have to teach, she drives her mother to work, saving her the bus trip. Malak is still very close to her daughters, talking to each of them several times a day and issuing incessant warnings: buckle your seat belt, watch your long skirt on the stairs, call me when you get home safely. And she has accomplished her main goal in life: seeing all three married to Muslim men. "It never occurred to us to marry outside," says Ameera. "Islamic values were so ingrained in us." She actually went first, marrying someone she met through the Muslim Student Union at UCI. "We actually had a friendship; we were working very closely together," says Ameera, but when they realized the relationship was becoming "something more than friends," the young man said, "I'm going to have my parents speak to your parents." Her husband is a software engineer who does not want her to work, but Ameera insists, "I've worked all my life, I can't not work." They dream of moving to Egypt or Jordan, and studying Arabic: "I would learn the language of the Koran, which is very important to me, and learn a lot about my religion. When you translate, you lose a lot."

Deeba married next. Her husband, a relative on her mother's side, grew up in Minnesota but came to California for a family funeral: "There was an attraction and a proposal, and we got married." But it was not that simple. Marrying within the family was a common custom among the Surti back in Burma, but for Deeba, growing up in America, "I really wasn't used to that idea." After several years of courtship that took place mainly through e-mail, she agreed to the match, but moving to Minnesota and leaving her family and the Surti circle behind was the hardest part: "I had a very difficult time with that. I felt really sad when I moved here and there were no parties, no weddings, which happen a lot in California." Her husband, who grew up speaking English and works for a company that makes medical devices, is "more like a pizza guy," but Deeba insists on cooking him traditional Surti dishes: "They really make the house smell good."

Khalida was the least interested in marriage and the last to take the plunge: "I did not want to get married; it took me a long time to warm up to the idea." But two things pushed her into a decision. As Malak's health declined she told her daughters: "You should get married before something happens to me. I don't want to go to my grave knowing that you are not settled." Then a fellow teacher at her school arranged a match with a man who has a degree in computers and a job keeping books for a garment factory. And since the man was not a citizen, Khalida could give him a special wedding gift: "I could sponsor him. I wanted to do something good. I knew the difficulties my parents faced, I could feel the struggle they had gone through, so here was an opportunity to help someone in their struggle."

When Deeba recently applied to a master's program in social work, she was asked how she identified herself. As she described her answer to me, she spoke for all three Kemal sisters: "I am an immigrant, a Muslim, a strong woman of color, and my mother's daughter." Then she paused and added: "And I am a California chick."

Afterword

Immigrants have played a central role in the American experience since our earliest days. With the exception of a few purebred Native Americans, every single family in this country today can trace its origins to somewhere else. My wife Cokie's direct ancestor, William Claiborne, was born in the English county of Kent in 1600 and came to Virginia twenty-one years later as a land surveyor. He became a wealthy planter and trader, led an expedition up the Chesapeake Bay from Jamestown in 1631, and established an outpost on an island he named after his birthplace. Kent Island is the oldest white settlement in Maryland, the state I've called home for thirty-two years, and I have a grandson named Claiborne who was born 370 years after his forebear landed in America. After my own family arrived from Russia in the early twentieth century, they lived in a world populated almost entirely by fellow immigrants. I have the census forms from 1920, showing where my mother's parents and grandparents were living in Bayonne, New Jersey, barely a year after Mom was born. There are a hundred residents listed on the two sheets. About half were born abroad; but when asked where their parents were from, exactly one said America. Most listed Russia, with a sprinkling of Italy, Ireland, Poland, France, Galicia, and Austria. Cokie and I are two ordinary Americans, children of immigrant families, the Claibornes of England

and the Rogowskys of Russia. They just happened to make the journey almost three hundred years apart.

Newcomers have always contributed heavily to the economic prosperity of America. Some, like William Claiborne, were well-connected gentry who traded with their home country. Others, like my people, possessed some skills and education and created small businesses. My great-grandfather owned a dairy farm; one grandfather ran an amusement park, the other built the house I grew up in. Many immigrants were common laborers whose muscle power fueled the rise of an industrial state: Chinese coolies built the western railroads; Irish and German workers dug the Erie Canal in upstate New York; Italian miners quarried slate in eastern Pennsylvania and built the town of Roseto, named for their home village. Of the 146 workers who died in New York's infamous Triangle Shirtwaist Fire of 1911, most were young female immigrants from Italy and Eastern Europe. Today many newcomers still work with their hands, from the Vietnamese harvesting shrimp in Louisiana to the Latinos plucking poultry in North Carolina.

The rise of Hitler in the 1930s, however, sent a new sort of immigrant to these shores: highly educated intellectuals who profoundly influenced the nation's scientific and cultural life. Albert Einstein, born in Germany and raised in Switzerland, is probably the best known. But the United States could not have developed a nuclear weapon without Enrico Fermi from Italy and Niels Bohr from Denmark. Hungary's John von Neumann created the modern computer at Princeton's Institute for Advanced Study, and his countryman Michael Curtiz directed the film *Casablanca* in Hollywood. (My son-in-law's grandfather, Franz Frank, escaped the Nazis and spent his career teaching at the University of Texas.) Their legacy lives on in Jerry Yang, a native of Taiwan who co-founded Yahoo!, and George Soros (Gyorgy Schwartz), the Hungarian-born financier and philanthropist. In 2007, two of the three winners of the Nobel

Prize for Medicine were foreign-born scientists working in the United States: Mario Capecchi from Italy and Oliver Smithies from the United Kingdom. In 2008, three of the four highest-paid corporate executives were immigrants: Sanjay Jha of Motorola (India); Ray Irani of Occidental Petroleum (Lebanon), and Vikram Pandit of Citigroup (India).

American orchestras have often been led by immigrants, from Zubin Mehta (India) to Georg Solti (Hungary) and Daniel Barenboim (Argentina). Some of our finest buildings have been designed by I. M. Pei (China), Eero Saarinen (Finland), and Frank Gehry, born Ephraim Owen Goldberg in Toronto. Foreign-born writers and filmmakers have enriched the country's cultural life, often by using the immigrant experience as their subject. Junot Diaz, from the Dominican Republic, won the Pulitzer Prize in 2008 for his novel *The Brief Wondrous Life of Oscar Wao*, which is largely set in the Dominican community of Paterson, New Jersey. Jhumpa Lahiri, born in London of Indian parents, has written extensively about Bengali families transplanted to America. Her novel *The Namesake* was made into a movie by the Indian-American director Mira Nair. The story was adapted for the screen by Nair's longtime collaborator, Sooni Taraporevala, whose roots are in India's Parsi Zoroastrian community. The women met as undergraduates at Harvard. American athletics, like the arts, would be much poorer without immigrants. Canadians have long dominated the National Hockey League but today's top scorer, Alexander Ovechkin, is Russian. Pro basketball's brightest stars include Dirk Nowitzki (Germany), Tony Parker (France), Manu Ginobili (Argentina), and Yao Ming (China). My favorite baseball team, the Yankees, features pitchers Chien-Ming Wang (Taiwan) and Mariano Rivera (Panama), second baseman Robinson Cano (Dominican Republic), and outfielder Hideki Matsui (Japan).

And yet, throughout American history, immigrants have been demonized for despoiling or diluting the country's ethnic heritage.

In 1753, Ben Franklin called the Germans flocking to Pennsylvania "generally the most stupid sort of their own nation" and warned: "They will soon outnumber us, [and we] will not, in my opinion, be able to preserve our language, and even our government will become precarious." In the mid-nineteenth century, the Irish were widely derided as an ignorant, criminal class. Signs sprouted up announcing, "No Irish Need Apply," and an editorial in the *Chicago Post* said, "Scratch a convict or a pauper and the chances are you tickle the skin of an Irish Catholic." The Know-Nothing Party prospered on an anti-immigrant platform, winning 25 percent of the presidential vote in 1856. Dark-skinned Italians were often considered nonwhite and subject to racial prejudice. In 1891, eleven Italians suspected of killing an Irish police chief were lynched in New Orleans. Cries of "hang the dagos" rumbled through the mob and one newspaper reported: "The little jail was crowded with Sicilians, whose low, receding foreheads, dark skin, repulsive countenances and slovenly attire proclaimed their brutal nature." In the 1920s, the trial and execution of anarchists Nicola Sacco and Bartolomeo Vanzetti, and the rise of Mafia dons like Al Capone, fueled anti-Italian feelings. During World War II, the internment of more than one hundred thousand Japanese-Americans on the West Coast reflected a shameful spasm of racial intolerance. More than half of those interned were American citizens and my friend Norm Mineta, the first Japanese-American congressman, remembers being evacuated in his Cub Scout uniform. I've seldom encountered overt anti-Semitism but I knew certain clubs at Harvard in the 1960s were closed to me. I once dated a girl from a fancy town in Connecticut who took me to a dance at her country club and whispered, "You might be the first Jew who's ever been in here." I live near a neighborhood that was traditionally hostile to Jews and Catholics. But that changed long ago and my friend Bill Safire, the former *New York Times* columnist, lives in the area and hosts an annual party to break the Yom Kippur fast.

This fear of foreigners lurks just below the surface of American life and 9/11 ignited a wave of retaliation against Muslims. In Columbus, Ohio, a mosque was vandalized, and worshippers found water pouring through the ceiling and copies of the Koran ripped and scattered. In Renton, Washington, Karnail Singh, a Sikh from India who wears a turban (and is not a Muslim), was beaten in the lobby of a motel he owns by a man yelling, "Go back to Allah!" A former student of mine, a dark-skinned woman with an Arabic name, says she is stopped for special scrutiny every time she passes through an airport. That stigma was stoked during the 2008 campaign by an underground rumor that Barack Obama was really a Muslim. The falsehood surfaced when a woman named Gayle Quinnell told John McCain at a rally in Minnesota, "I don't trust Obama. I have read about him. He's an Arab." To his credit McCain protested, "No. Nope. No, ma'am. No, ma'am." But then he added, "He's a decent family man," as if no "Arab" could deserve that description. Even after his election, the Pew Research Center reported that only 48 percent of Americans could correctly identify the president as a Christian and 11 percent still thought he was a Muslim.

Latinos and Asians, the two fastest-growing immigrant groups, incite similar antiforeign phobias. One particularly outspoken fulminator, TV commentator Lou Dobbs, said on CNN that it was "crazy stuff" for President Obama to speak before the U.S. Hispanic Chamber of Commerce. That organization, he ranted, favored "Mexico's export of drugs and illegal aliens to the United States." On St. Patrick's Day he made fun of all "ethnic holidays" and said, in a mocking voice, that perhaps there should be an Asian holiday dedicated to "St. Jing-Tao Wow." Some Republicans have mimicked Dobbs and decided that fanning anti-immigrant fears would energize their conservative base, but others, like Bush adviser Karl Rove, call this attitude "suicidal" for their party. McCain won white men in 2008 by 57 to 41 percent, but they only accounted for 36 percent of the electorate. Obama won

2 out of 3 Latinos, and 3 out of 5 Asians, and those groups will continue to grow in both size and influence. "We're fundamentally staring down a demographic shift that we've never seen before in America," says Jon Huntsman Jr., the former Republican governor of Utah.

The thirteen families in this book mirror that shift and make a simple point. The anti-immigrant voices that echo through this country's history, from Ben Franklin to Lou Dobbs, have always been wrong and are wrong today. Barack Obama is absolutely right when he says, "our patchwork heritage is a strength not a weakness." I see this every day at George Washington University, where I meet talented students from immigrant origins who fill my classes and my heart: Reena Ninan from India and Katicia Kiss from Hungary, Claritza Jimenez from the Dominican Republic and Malak Hamwi from Syria, Monica Tavarez from Portugal and Lucy Kafanov from Russia, Charles Vundla from South Africa and Jennifer Tchinnosian from Argentina, Rabitha Aziz from Bangladesh and Sophia Aziz, the daughter of an Egyptian father and Afghan mother who met in Pakistan. When I listen to the voices in this book, and hear the stories of my students, I think of my own grandparents. They had the courage and character to come to a new land, and make a better life for themselves and their grandson. I hope, as you got to know these families, that you thought of your own ancestors, "the risk-takers, the doers, the makers of things." And I hope you will thank them for the gift they have given you and your children.

Acknowledgments

I am deeply grateful to the thirteen families profiled in this book. Each of them gave me many hours of their time, but more than that they contributed their candor and their courage, their humor and their heartache, to this project. I hope in return they will accept this gift from me—their own histories, written down with as much diligence and devotion as I could bring to the task. This book was inspired by my students at George Washington University, who wrote about their own families and showed me what a rich trove of stories were out there to be told. Two of these chapters started life as assignments in that class, and in several other cases students found families for me. This book is dedicated to all of my students, more than six hundred of them over the last eighteen years, but a few deserve special mention for their help: Katie Poole Chastain, Maha El-Sheikh, Mariana Lopes, Reena Ninan, Tony Sayegh, Ted Segal, Thai Phi Stone, Elin Thomasian, and Jessica Wilde (who also served as my translator with the Reyes family).

I owe a huge debt to Stephen Joel Trachtenberg, the former president of GWU, who first recruited me as an adjunct in 1991 and later convinced me to join the full-time faculty by whispering two magic words: "endowed chair." The J. B. and Maurice C. Shapiro Professorship in Media and Public Affairs, which I've been privileged to hold since 1997, was made possible by the extraordinary generosity of Dorothy Shapiro, and I'm grateful every time I see her family's name on my office door. Jean Folkerts, the former director of the School of Media and Public Affairs, first suggested I teach feature writing and was always a strong supporter. The same is true for Jean's successor, Lee Huebner, who also introduced me to the Romero family, and the current director, Frank Sesno. I am often asked how I found the families profiled here, and in addition to my student scouts, I had the help of several friends, colleagues, and family members: my cousin Andrew Mishlove, my sister Laura Roberts, Joe Ryan, Mike Shanahan, John Marks, Moises Naim, Sree Sreenivashan, Mallika Dutt, Yamuna Maynard, Rajeev Sreethran, and Anita Pytlarz Ponchione.

This is my third book edited by Claire Wachtel, and she remains an invaluable source of support and advice. Her assistant, Julia Novitch, and her former assistant, Kevin Callahan, helped make it happen. Several executives at William Morrow and HarperCollins have shown confidence in me over the years and made my writing life more comfortable and productive: Jane Friedman, Lisa Gallagher, Michael Morrison, and Sharyn Rosenblum. Carolyn Hessel and Miri Pomerantz at the Jewish Book Council, Tracy Cook Pannozzo at the National Book Festival, Beth Gargano at the Harry Walker Agency, and Bob Barnett at Williams & Connolly have always appreciated and promoted my work. Many thanks, friends. Julia McCallus and Alan Altman helped us find the dream house on Pawleys Island, South Carolina, where big chunks of this book were written. My previous book, *My Fathers' Houses*, was dedicated to my grandparents and my grandchildren, and they continue to remind me that family stories are still the best stories: Abe and Miriam Rogow; Harry and Sadie Schanbam; Regan, Hale, and Cecilia Roberts; and Jack, Cal and Roland Hartman. My children, Lee and Rebecca, and their wonderful spouses, Liza McDonald Roberts and Dan Hartman, provide insight and affection. My mother, Dorothy Schanbam Roberts, who turned ninety as this book was being finished, inspires me with her strength and her smile. My late father, Will Roberts, was my first and best editor. The ten children's books he wrote himself are displayed behind me as I write this, in case I ever forget his legacy and his lessons. Which I won't. Above all there is Cokie. We've been friends, lovers, and partners for more than four decades. Marrying her is the best thing I've ever done in my life, and every day she makes me a better person. Thank you, angel, for everything.

Insights,
Interviews
& More...

Meet Steven V. Roberts
Professor, columnist, bestselling author

Hilary Schwab

STEVE ROBERTS has been a journalist for more than forty-five years, covering some of the major events of his time, from the antiwar movement and student revolts of the '60s and '70s to President Reagan's historic trip to Moscow in 1988 and eleven presidential election campaigns. After graduating from Harvard *magna cum laude* in 1964, he joined the *New York Times* as research assistant to James "Scotty" Reston, then the paper's Washington bureau chief. Roberts's twenty-five-year career with the *Times* included assignments as bureau chief in Los Angeles and Athens, and as congressional and White House correspondent. He was a senior writer at *U.S. News* for seven years, specializing in national politics and foreign policy. Roberts and his wife, TV journalist Cokie Roberts, write a nationally syndicated newspaper column that was named one of the ten most popular columns in America by Media Matters. In February of 2000, Steve and Cokie published *From This Day Forward*, an account of their marriage as well as other marriages in American history. The *New York Times* called the book "inspiring and instructive," and it spent seven weeks on the *Times* bestseller list. Roberts also writes a bimonthly column, "Hometown," for *Bethesda* magazine, and as a lifelong baseball fan, he reviews sports books for the *Washington Post*. His childhood memoir, *My Fathers' Houses*, was published in the spring of 2005 and was featured at the National Book Festival in Washington. His latest, *From Every End of This Earth*, was published in October 2009. The *Post* called it "compassionate and engaging."

As a broadcaster, Roberts appears regularly as a political analyst on the ABC radio network and is a substitute host on NPR's *Diane Rehm Show*. As a teacher, he lectures widely on American politics and the role of the news media. Since 1997, he has been the Shapiro Professor of Media and Public Affairs at George Washington University, where he has taught for the past nineteen years. His many honors include the Dirksen Award for covering Congress, the Wilbur Award for reporting on religion and politics, the Bender Prize as one of George Washington University's top undergraduate teachers, and four honorary doctorates. Steve and Cokie have two children—Lee, a real estate investor in Raleigh, North Carolina, and Rebecca, a journalist in Washington—and six grandchildren. In his spare time, Roberts is an avid gardener and tennis player, and he coaches third base for his twin grandsons' Little League team. ᘛ

Dreamers and Fighters

THIS BOOK REFLECTS MY DEEP BELIEF in Barack Obama's statement that "our patchwork heritage is a strength, not a weakness." Since its release, my conviction has been reinforced in many ways by many people. I think of the high school teacher in South Carolina who asked after a book talk, "How can I get my American students to work as hard as my immigrant students?" Or the daughter of Vietnamese immigrants who attended a lecture at the Foreign Service Institute and told me she had just returned after representing the U.S. in China for five years. Or a former student of mine, a Pakistani Muslim, who is now in law school and wants to work on human rights issues. On the day this book was published, the Nobel Prize for physics was awarded to three American scientists, two of them immigrants. Willard Boyle, born in Canada, worked at Bell Laboratories in New Jersey to discover the principles that led to digital photography. Charles Kao, a China-born researcher at Stanford, perfected fiber optics. How many Americans today are working in jobs made possible by the insights of these scientists? I recently attended a wedding in Florida between an Irish-American man and the child of Indian immigrants. The church shimmered with rich silk saris of red and pink and purple. Then two flower girls walked down the aisle, young relatives of the couple. The Irish child was tall and pale and timid; the Indian short and dark and peppery. This, I thought, is modern America.

As I was writing this chapter, Ali Farokhmanesh, the son of an Iranian Olympic volleyball player, sank the shot that enabled Northern Iowa to eliminate top-seeded Kansas from the NCAA basketball tournament. José H. Gómez, a native of Mexico, was chosen to head the Roman Catholic Archdiocese of Los Angeles, the nation's largest. Tina Chang, the daughter of Chinese immigrants, was named poet laureate of Brooklyn, an appropriate choice for a place so rich in ethnic tradition. Chang's partner, Claude De Castro, comes from Haiti; her male relatives have married women from Afghanistan, Colombia, and Ecuador. *New York Times* columnist Thomas L. Friedman wrote an article called "America's Real Dream Team" that described all the immigrant children who won top honors in the 2010 Intel Science Talent Search. "If you need any more convincing about the virtues of immigration, just come to the Intel science finals," he wrote. "I am a pro-immigration fanatic. I think keeping a constant flow of *legal* immigrants into our country—whether they wear blue collars or lab coats—is the key to keeping us ahead of China." In fact, he reports, realtors in San José, California, are buying newspaper ads in China and India, urging potential immigrants to buy homes in a school district that recently produced two Intel winners.

The recruitment and retention of top immigrant talent is so vital to American prosperity that two senators, Democrat Charles Schumer and Republican Lindsey Graham, have introduced legislation to reverse a wrongheaded trend that has recently made it harder for job-creating newcomers to obtain permanent residence here. "Ensuring economic prosperity requires attracting the world's best and brightest," the senators wrote. "It makes no sense to educate the world's future inventors and entrepreneurs and then force them to leave when they are able to contribute to our economy." This impulse is also visible on the local level, where aging industrial cities like Philadelphia, Detroit, and St. Louis are making a big push to attract new immigrants. For example, about seventy thousand newcomers from ▶

Bosnia have moved to St. Louis, reports the *Post-Dispatch*: "They have bought homes and started businesses. They stabilized a broad swath of the city and have begun to move to the suburbs. In short, they've done what waves of German, Irish, and Italian immigrants did before them." The *Detroit News* put it this way: "Bring us your fired-up, your hungry-to-succeed, your Ph.D.s. Bring us your entrepreneurial foreign-born, who were 189 percent more likely to start a business in 2008 than those of us born stateside." Richard Herman, coauthor of *Immigrant, Inc.*, a useful book documenting the economic contributions of foreign-born business owners, sent me a graduation speech by Omid Kordestani, an Iranian immigrant who is now a top Google executive. "To keep my edge I must think and act like an immigrant," Kordestani told the graduates of San José State. "There is a special optimism and drive that I have benefited from and continue to rely on that I want all of you to find. Immigrants are inherently dreamers and fighters." With the speech, Herman included a T-shirt decorated with the phrase "Think like an immigrant" in a dozen languages. I wear it proudly.

This is primarily a book of stories, and it prompted many readers to share their own tales of the immigrant experience. I was particularly intrigued by what I call Generation Next, the children of the "sacrifice generation" who were born here or came as young people. Their questions are hard to answer or avoid. How do they reconcile ancient traditions with modern opportunities? How can they become fully American and yet stay true to their family? Their tribe? Their religion? These tensions often crystallize when they get married. Picking a mate defines what they have become and who their parents' grandchildren will be. So I decided to focus on four young women, all in their twenties or early thirties, who are continuing the immigrant journey that never really ends.

*

Lulu Fall: "I want to keep the African values I was taught and explore American values as well. I'm on a quest to find out who I am. I know that's a cliché, but it's truth. It's truth."

Lulu's father is a Muslim from Senegal, her mother a Catholic from Cameroon, so she faces a double bind. First she has to define her African identity and then figure out how that profile merges into her American personality. The elder Falls met in Paris but came to the United States in 1981. In France they faced rising racial intolerance and shrinking economic opportunity, and the United States was a more welcoming place on both fronts. Lulu's dad started as a busboy, became a chef, and today owns his own limousine company in Washington; her mom runs a bank branch in suburban Maryland. Their daughter is a twenty-four-year-old singer-songwriter with "locked" foot-long braids dyed red and pulled back in a ponytail. Large, brushed-gold disks adorn her ears as she describes the cultural conflicts she grew up with: "On the Cameroonian side, Mom's side, everyone drinks. The Senegalese side is much more traditional, much more refined. I love to go out, I'm very social, I love to drink the way Cameroonians do. My dad hates that."

Religion was an even bigger problem. As a child, Lulu attended church with her mother, the family had a Christmas tree, and "religion didn't seem like a big deal" to her father. But once she turned twelve, "things changed dramatically." Her mother bought her a pair of earrings adorned with tiny gold crosses, and when her father saw them lying on a table, he "freaked out" and started screaming, "Whose earrings are these? Why are there crosses in my house?" Then he "confiscated" the jewelry, and today, says Lulu, "I still don't know where my earrings are." The conflict bruised her so badly that, at least for now, she has rejected both Islam and Christianity and instead attends a "nondenominational Japanese prayer center" called a *dojo*: "It's based on spirituality, not religion. It's completely neutral; it's not biased."

Hair has long symbolized Lulu's cultural confusion. In high school she wore it "permed and straightened," a style that "conformed to a Western idea of beauty." And her parents approved: "It was their way of having me blend in." But during her senior year she rebelled, allowing her hair to return to its natural state: "I had a need to be myself. I was born with kinky coiled hair, and I wanted to keep it that way. My parents didn't like it. We were living in America. They wanted me to conform. They told me that people wouldn't take me seriously." But emotions are seldom consistent, and in another sense her rebellion made her more American, not less: "In school I had always been the 'good African girl,' sitting in the front of the room, the teacher's pet. I had so much pressure to be the smartest, the way I was brought up was completely different from the average American girl." But she grew tired of "being goody-two-shoes" and started emulating "the good American girls" who would "sit in the back of the room, wear tight clothes, and amount to nothing. I wanted to see what it was like on the other side, to be the girl who stayed out late and talked back to her parents." Even now she feels pulled in many different directions. "I'm trying to say it's OK to be confused," explained Lulu, who summed up her feelings in a song called "N'Datta," her middle name in Senegalese. The lyrics say in part:

Beautiful little girl has the entire world ahead of her
Smartest girl in class, she gets straight A's but that's just not enough
Her friends don't like her because she's not American ▶

Dreamers and Fighters *(continued)*

Her skin's a little too dark, and she speaks a funny language
Beautiful little girl, she blooms into a teenager
She's got so much poise, don't even pay attention to boys,
    that's not her thing
Starts hanging with the wrong crowd, the walls come tumbling down
    all over
She doesn't wanna be the little girl who follows all the rules anymore
Her parents said she's "too American"
Lost her identity
Smiling yet she's so unhappy

Lulu is particularly unhappy with her father's view of marriage.
He always told her that if she didn't learn to cook she would "never get
married to a nice Muslim guy." But like many immigrant women, she
finds America liberating and rejects traditional restrictions on a woman's
independence. "I can't be subservient" she says. "Dad wants me to get
married like yesterday. My mom will accept any guy, no matter what
color or race or creed, as along as his values are the same. Dad doesn't
believe in interracial relationships; he prefers that I marry a Muslim, but
I tell him that's not going to happen." Her father's prejudices were shaped
by his time in France. He told Lulu's sister: "I got picked on, I had to
prove myself, I had to fight every single day." The lesson he learned
was that white people will "smile and stab you in the back."
So when Lulu went off to college at Michigan State and started dating
a white guy from Wyoming, her father freaked out again. "It was a very
tough pill for him to swallow," she says. "It so happens the person I fell in
love with was white. I told him, 'What's your problem? He treats me well.
Color has nothing to do with anything.'" But of course it did. Eventually
the couple broke up and race was partly responsible: "If we walked down
the street together, we'd get looks and whispers, people would stare at us
funny." And as she launched her singing career, the tension got worse.
"You know what," her boyfriend told her, "I don't think I'm good enough
for you because I'm white." Today Lulu is writing songs, performing
concerts, dating black musicians. But her story is far from finished:
"I want to keep the African values I was taught and explore American
values as well. I'm on a quest to find out who I am. I know that's a cliché
but it's truth. It's truth."

*

Anya Plana: *"In a way it was a reinvention of myself when I came here."*

Anya was twenty-seven and teaching at an all-boys Catholic school in the
Philippines when a recruiter from a Texas school district came to town.

After interviewing her, he said, "Where can I find more like you?" and she replied, "Well, I have a twin sister at home." Leaving that home was a hard decision for the Plana girls, says Anya: "We're really close to our parents, and the custom is you take care of your parents. It's a shame to have your parents taken care of by strangers." But the opprobrium was outweighed by opportunity. As a child, Anya had read about the Smithsonian Institution in Washington and it "represented a whole new world" of cultural and academic achievement. (She now volunteers at the Smithsonian, where she introduced herself after a book talk). She dreamed of writing children's books and "knew it wouldn't happen" if she stayed in the Philippines. But the biggest reason for leaving home was to escape the expectations placed on young women: "If I stayed in the Philippines, I would be questioned incessantly, 'Hey, when are you going to get married?' Getting out, there would be more independence for me as a female. It's easier to date here—the Philippines are so small and America is so big. In a way, it was a reinvention of myself when I came here." Back home the Planas were a prominent family—one uncle was a judge, another an ambassador—and that made it even harder for a high-spirited young woman to define her own destiny. "If I stayed, I would be held to that standard of dishonoring the family name," Anya said. "My identity was tied to my family's name. Here I was free to have my own circle of friends. I could choose to be influenced by people or not. I wanted to be free. I didn't want to think about disappointing people."

The Plana sisters arrived in Pharr, a small Texas town near the Mexican border, in 2003. But after a few years, it started to feel too small ("I wanted to be in a place with more cultural diversity") and they moved to the Washington area, where Anya took a teaching job in the suburbs. Her sister, Regie, who was already married to a Filipino man, started playing in a neighborhood volleyball game. Another regular was David Hutt, a mixture of German, Irish, and French-Canadian stock who had grown up in Syracuse and come to Washington as lawyer with the National Disability Rights Network. "I saw Anya on a bench at the volleyball game and thought, She's cute but she's married," David recalls. But a friend told him, "That's not Regie; that's her twin sister." As David and Anya's romance blossomed, he invited her home to Syracuse for Christmas. She asked him, "Oh my God, do they know I'm Asian?" And he replied: "I told them you're Catholic; that's all they needed to know." Adds Anya: "We both have the same religion, the basic values are the same." But the match was hard on the Plana family. These days American counselor officials worry that travelers will not return home, so they hand out tourist visas sparingly. The Planas showed up at the American embassy with Anya's wedding invitation and a letter from ▶

Dreamers and Fighters *(continued)*

their parish priest, promising they would return to the Philippines to care for Anya's bedridden father, but it was not enough. Their visa application was denied. "My family wanted to make it," Anya recalls. "It was heartbreaking for me." The young couple wants to stay in Washington because it is "neutral ground" and "diverse enough" to embrace a biracial family. But Anya preserves ties with her past. She gives David tapes to learn Tagalog, the Filipino language, and while they remain unopened, she remains undeterred. "I worry about losing my language," she says, "I want to keep my identity and pass it on to my kids."

*

Nancy Trejos: "When I went away to college, I became too American in a way."

Nancy Trejos reviewed this book for the *Washington Post* and understood it well. "The true sacrifice is made for the children," she wrote. "I've learned this from my own experience as the U.S.-born child of a Colombian father and Ecuadorian mother. My parents arrived in New York City with no college degrees and unable to speak English. But they found jobs—my father served food to patients in a Manhattan hospital, my mother cleaned Park Avenue apartments by day and midtown offices by night—and managed to save enough money to buy a house in Queens and send me to Georgetown University." I called Nancy and asked her to expand on her story. Now a travel writer at the *Post*, she described the dignity her parents brought to their menial jobs. Her father, José, always "looked like a gentleman" in a collared shirt, dress pants, and fedora; her mother, Maria, always wore a skirt and blouse before changing into work clothes when she reached Manhattan. "My parents never really saw each other," she recalls. "He'd come home at four; she'd leave soon after for her night job. I'd wait up for her. Sometimes we'd go out to McDonalds at 1 AM—it was our only chance to hang out. That's why I still can't go to sleep at a decent hour." Her parents were frugal, eating rice and fried plantains at many meals, and her mom still owns the same pink sweater she wore throughout Nancy's childhood. Their Queens neighborhood was heavily Hispanic, with salsa music in the air and a local theater playing Spanish-language movies starring the Mexican comedian Cantinflas. "But my parents also grew to love America," Nancy wrote in the *Post* magazine. "They became U.S. citizens. They gave their three children American names: Daniel, Lucy, and Nancy. (In fact, I was named after Nancy Reagan because they liked Ronald Reagan, then a rising star in the Republican Party.)" They also encouraged their children to learn English: "The truth is they didn't want us to be like them. They wanted us to get good educations, to not be teased for mispronouncing words, to not be passed over for jobs because we were not American. They wanted us to be American." But, she adds, "When I went away to college, I became too American in a way."

At Georgetown, Nancy says, "I got caught up in it, I was trying to live a lifestyle I couldn't afford. I became a snob, frankly. I was not the Queens girl any more." She lost her New York accent, spoke Spanish only when she called home, and dated white boys: "I became increasingly detached from my parents, becoming annoyed when they visited me and wanted to sleep on the floor of my group house instead of going to a hotel as most of my classmates' parents did. I rolled my eyes when they couldn't pronounce my roommates' names. Why could they not say 'Kristin'? Why did she always have to be 'Kristina'? Why did they call Mitch 'Meech'?" The most painful incident occurred during graduation weekend: "I insisted on a really expensive restaurant, not the type of place my parents usually go. It was terrible. They felt wildly uncomfortable. My sister had nothing to eat; she asked me, 'What's a Caesar salad?' To this day I feel so guilty about that. It was an awful thing to do to them."

Money became a source of tension. Nancy shed her parents' thriftiness along with their accent and their diet. She plunged deeply into debt and had to ask her parents for a loan. Social life caused more conflict. Her sister had stayed home, married a Latino, and pleased her parents: "Dad loves my brother-in-law; they're very comfortable with him." Nancy found her Anglo boyfriend holed up in a hotel with another woman, and her father ranted, "No more of those pretty white boys." And gradually, Nancy started feeling dissatisfied with her life. The daughter of a cleaning lady had hired another Latina to tidy up her fancy loft apartment. As she rode the bus to work, she felt the eyes of Hispanic immigrants looking at her and wondering, "Is she one of us?" Her answer was "yes—and no," and that ambivalence bothered her: "I'm the only one who left—I've always felt guilty about that. Over the years, I felt I had become less Hispanic. I felt disconnected from where I came from."

When he immigrated to America, Nancy's father had left a young son, Humberto, behind in Colombia. José Trejos had seen his child only once in forty years, but almost on a whim, Nancy decided that visiting her half brother would somehow diminish the detachment she felt from her origins. And in a way it worked. She was surprised to find Humberto's small house filled with pictures of the three Trejos siblings, including one of her graduation from Georgetown. Without telling his other children, José had stayed in touch with Humberto, sending him money and mementos of his American family. During her visit, Nancy ▶

emptied her own wallet and gave everything she had to her Colombian relatives. Today she visits her parents more often. Her father has retired and traded his fedora for "a baseball cap, usually one I bought for him in Washington," she says. "His quick temper has been replaced with an aging man's desire to be loved by his family." When she returns to Queens, her father will "make sure all my favorite foods are in the kitchen, and he'll buy the *New York Times* for me each morning, even though he thinks it's overpriced. If I want to watch TV, he'll give me the remote control, which he would never, ever have done when I was a child." But while she thinks about moving back home, Nancy hasn't done it. She's not the Queens girl anymore. "I think," she says, "I'm a bit of a mystery to my parents sometimes." And perhaps to herself as well.

*

Petra Pryce: "The first time my grandmother met Talan, she smiled, shook his hand, then turned to my mother and loudly whispered, 'Lord have mercy, she's sleeping with the colonizer.' "

"I found out I was pregnant with Tristan my freshman year of college," says Petra Pryce, the daughter of Jamaican immigrants. "I was at NYU and still with my high school boyfriend, Robert. We dated for about two years, and we always messed around behind our parents' backs. His family is Jamaican, too, and strict like mine, and when I found out, at first I hid it. I managed that up until winter break. My mom knew as soon as I got in the door. No freshman fifteen looks like that. She was so angry she walked out of our apartment and didn't even say anything." Her mother had struggled to become a physical therapist and support the family on one income, and she was furious with her daughter for her carelessness. "Why the hell didn't you kill it?" her mother ranted. Says Petra: "I couldn't move. I had no words, and it was like my eyes couldn't even make tears." Robert felt angry as well and soon drifted away. Petra dropped out of school and moved back in with her mother in the Bronx: "We were just like everyone else. He was another deadbeat dad who wasn't around, and I was another teenage 'baby momma.' "

Petra remembers Tristan's first year as a painful blur: "I wanted him to stop crying. I wanted him to go away and be someone else's baby. He was this tiny thing who needed me, and I was a little girl who still needed to grow up." Petra's mother finally saved enough to move the family out of their Bronx apartment and into a house in suburban Connecticut. Everything was strange, another form of immigration to a new country: "The idea of having a backyard and a front lawn was like being in the wilderness." But neighbors started coming over, and one of them, a white woman named Mrs. Porter, brought cupcakes: "We sat them on the kitchen counter and joked around that they might be poisoned. In the Bronx, your neighbors don't just do nice things for the hell of it, so it's best just to mind your business and keep to yourself."

But the Pryces couldn't keep to themselves. The Porters had a son Talan who had moved back home after finishing community college. Tristan was still a toddler and fond of a game he played with his mother: when she called him to come, he would wave bye-bye at her. One day Talan parked in his driveway, saw the game going on, and stopped to laugh. Tristan ran over to him, Petra followed, and a friendship began. As the only young singles in the neighborhood, they were both lonely and happy for the companionship. "It was something to do, shoot the shit," Petra recalls. "It was nothing romantic in the beginning, but it was a regular thing. The first day he had to work late, he looked up our home phone and left a message. I was floored. It was such a small thing, but he didn't have to do it and he did. It was really considerate, and when I called him back, he asked if I'd like to get dinner with him one weekend." Their first date took weeks to arrange; Talan was working late at a local diner, and Petra, who had gone back to school, "was either studying or changing poop." She spent all day curling her hair, and then it rained, ruining all her work, and after two years as a single mom she had "forgotten how to walk in heels." But gradually the relationship deepened. The first time Petra took Tristan to the Porters for dinner she was desperate to make a good impression. She dressed her son in "his Sunday khakis and a sweater vest." She put on her most conservative turtleneck dress with flats: "When we showed up at their door, we looked like Jehovah's Witnesses going caroling."

The dinner was tense and uncomfortable: "Everyone was putting on a show; each of us had something to prove." Petra got up to help with the dishes, and when she returned to the living room, she found her son happily working on a jigsaw puzzle with Talan's dad. "There was nothing forced about it. It had happened while the rest of us weren't looking," she recalls. "But they found something to share. It was just an old man with his gray hair and polo shirt squinting at the tiny pieces and a boy smushing his face together trying to copy him." Still, the ice took a long time to thaw. The Porters returned the visit, and Petra recalls what happened: "The first time my grandmother met Talan, she smiled, shook his hand, then turned to my mother and loudly whispered, 'Lord have mercy, she's sleeping with the colonizer.'" And her grandmother wasn't the only black woman to take offense at her relationship. When she went to church with Talan, Petra heard the whispers, accusing her of "betraying black families" by being with a white man. But her own ▶

Dreamers and Fighters *(continued)*

father had abused her, her son's father had abandoned her, and she was in no mood to listen to the carping: "I used to get so angry when they'd whisper that shit to me because I wanted to yell at them and tell them that my father hit me when my mom couldn't take his slapping her around anymore. Not all black men are like my father or Robert. If I searched, I could find my 'good black man' after all. But I moved here and found someone who I have allowed myself to trust, after two years of putting up all my walls to protect my heart and my son. He happens to be white. That little boy doesn't know Talan is not black, but he knows it's OK to raise up his arms when he needs to be held." Petra and Talan are planning a future together, and she reflects on what she's learned: "Real love is not just a relationship that looks right. Lots of times people look good on paper and don't fit. Talan is a white boy with a Suburu, and I'm a black girl with a car seat. We're a mismatched mess, and we make it work."

This book is dedicated to my students at George Washington University. They continue to supply me with vibrant accounts of contemporary immigration. I am indebted to Leslie Pitterson, a fine young writer from Jamaica, for Petra's story.

Homer's Children

IMMIGRATION IS ONE OF LIFE's most dramatic and compelling experiences, so it has long provided a rich vein of material for poets and novelists, journalists and memoirists. There's no such thing as a dull story about leaving home and journeying to a new land. Homer proved that ten centuries ago, and it's still true. Here are some recent books that enlarged and enhanced my own sense of this experience.

The Girl From Foreign by **Sadia Shepard** (The Penguin Press, 2008). Sadia was living in Massachusetts, the daughter and granddaughter of émigrés from Pakistan. One day she found a small medal engraved to "Rachel Jacobs." "Who is this?" she asked. "Me," said her grandmother. As the tale unfolded, Sadia discovered that her grandmother was born Jewish in India before marrying a Muslim and moving to Pakistan. On her deathbed, Rachel asked Sadia to go back to India and discover her roots. This lovely book describes that journey.

The Long Way Home by **David Laskin** (HarperCollins Publishers, 2010). This book starts from an imaginative premise: profiling men who were born in Europe, came to the United States in the early twentieth century, and then were drafted into the United States Army and sent back to Europe to fight for their new country in World War I. Critics at the time thought these immigrants would fight reluctantly, but the opposite was true. "The most remarkable thing is how well and willingly the foreign element has responded," one government clerk reported. "They seem anxious to serve the country of their adoption."

The Man in the White Sharkskin Suit by **Lucette Lagnado** (HarperCollins Publishers, 2007). Lagnado was born in Cairo into a wealthy Jewish family that originally came ▶

from Aleppo, Syria. Her father, known as "The Captain," was a dashing figure in wartime Cairo, a city that was never overrun by the Nazis and provided a safe haven for refugees from all over Europe and the Middle East. But the wave of Arab nationalism following World War II resulted in the ejection of Jews from Egypt, and the Lagnados settled in Brooklyn, where The Captain never felt happy or at home. Until his death, he kept a suitcase packed, hoping someone would take him home to Cairo, a testament to the truth that not all immigrant stories end well.

Outcasts United by **Warren St. John** (Spiegel & Grau, 2009). One day Luma Mufleh, an immigrant from Jordan, wandered into the Georgia town of Clarkston and saw a ragtag group of boys playing soccer. They were mainly children of political refugees from places such as Liberia and Bosnia who had fled civil strife back home and resettled in this Atlanta suburb. Mufleh kept coming back and eventually formed the boys into a championship soccer team. A moving tale by a writer whose previous work, *Rammer Jammer Yellow Hammer*, is the best book I've ever read on college football.

A Country Called Amreeka by **Alia Malek** (Free Press, 2009). Born in Baltimore to Syrian parents, Malek focuses on her fellow Arabs, a growing segment of America's immigrant population. Americans have always been ambivalent about immigration, extolling its virtues while erupting in spasms of anti-immigrant feeling. Historically, that animosity has been directed at Irish and Italians, Jews and Japanese. Today the victims of anti-immigrant sentiment are often Muslims. The haters were wrong then and they are wrong now, and Malek's portraits of her people show why they, like every immigrant group, make major contributions to our national life.